Faith in the Future

Faith in the Future

Jonathan Sacks

Mercer University Press
Macon, Georgia
1997

To the Members of the Council of
Christians and Jews

ISBN 0-86554-550-2
MUP/ P159

Faith in the Future
by
Jonathan Sacks

© 1997

Mercer University Press
6316 Peake Road
Macon, Georgia 31210-3960
USA

First Published in 1995 by
Darton, Longman and Todd Ltd
1 Spencer Court
140-142 Wandsworth High Street
London SW18 4JJ
(Reprinted Five Times)

Typography by Humphrey Stone
Phototypset by Intype, London

The paper used in this publication meets the minimum requirements
of American National Standard for Information Sciences—
Permanence of Paper for Printed Library Materials, ANSI Z39.48–
1984.

Library of Congress Cataloging-in-Publication Data

CIP, unavailable at press time,
will appear in subsequent editions
and is available from the Library of Congress

Contents

PART III HOLY DAYS

PART IV JEWISH ETHICS AND SPIRITUALITY

Preface

As Chief Rabbi I am usually called on to address Jewish audiences. But there are times when the audience is wider and the message more universal in scope. The chapters gathered here are of the second kind. They form a composite picture of what I have tried to say, these past few years, as a Jew in a society of people of many faiths and some of none.

At first I found this a difficult experience. It is so easy to speak with people who share your faith, and so hard to communicate with those who don't. But slowly I discovered that talking across the fences that divide us is important. Not only because it helps us understand each other and our differences, but also because it helps us understand ourselves. We find out what we share and also what we uniquely own.

I also made a discovery. With the transition of Britain from a strong common culture to a more fragmented, segmented and pluralised one, we suddenly find that we are *all* members of a minority group, practising Christians no less than practising Jews. This is not a bad thing, because it means that paradoxically as we become more diverse we discover more areas of common experience. The problems of Christians, Jews, Muslims, Sikhs, Hindus and others in trying to preserve their values and hand them on to their children become more, not less, alike. In the contemporary situation, to be particular is to be universal and to be a minority is part of the experience of the majority.

Under these circumstances, as we try to renew our own families, communities and faiths, we find that we are not alone. People quite unlike us face the same difficulties and derive strength from sharing experience and reflection. This book, then, is a Jewish contribution to a conversation in which many voices deserve to be heard. Though some of its sections are more specifically Jewish than others, all ultimately turn on the question of whether, in a complex, rapidly changing and ever more interdependent world we can construct a humane social order which honours human dignity and difference, one in which we can be both true to ourselves and a blessing to others. In the confusing state of post-industrial societies in the post-Cold War situation, can we give those who come after us a coherent map of hope?

I have structured this book in four sections. In the first, 'The Moral Covenant', I touch on the broadest issues of morality, the family and the importance of communities in the life of society. In the second, 'Living Together', I ask how we can co-exist while remaining faithful to our distinctive identities and traditions. In the third, 'Holy Days', I describe how one faith, Judaism, lives out its beliefs. In the fourth, 'Jewish Ethics and Spirituality', I sketch some of Judaism's leading themes.

Most chapters had their origins in talks, articles or broadcasts. Often, though, I have redrafted them and in some cases I have written a section especially for this book. With a few indicated exceptions, they have not been published before. No collection of this kind can be seamless, but I hope that it carries a consistency of voice and belief.

In bringing this book to publication I owe many thanks. Mr Colin Shindler, former editor of *The Jewish Quarterly*, first persuaded me that it was worth doing. Working with the publishers, Darton, Longman and Todd, and their editor Morag Reeve, has been a rare and special pleasure. I am particularly honoured that Mr Clifford Longley, one of the country's most distinguished religious voices and a journalist from whose columns I never fail to learn, has written an introduction.

As I prepared the text I was conscious of the thanks I and many others owe to those who sustain the traditions of this country's religious tolerance. As Britons we carry the virtue of self-criticism to a fault, often forgetting the remarkable record of British openness and generosity towards different ethnic and religious groups. Jews know only too well how unusual this is in world history, and how important. I am grateful for the warm relationship I have been privileged to share with the Archbishop of Canterbury, Dr George Carey, the Cardinal Archbishop of Westminster, Basil Hume, and the leaders of many other faith groups. The BBC's Religious Broadcasting department has played a significant role in shaping this climate of tolerance, and I recall with gratitude the times I have spent with Ernest Rea, David Craig, Beverley McAinsh, John Kirby, Norman Ivison and others, coming to understand how communicating faith across boundaries is one of broadcasting's most sacred tasks. Within the Jewish community, the United Synagogue and its President, Mr Seymour Saideman, have shown how tolerance can be combined with firm religious principle. Sir Sigmund Sternberg has set a striking example of leadership in interfaith relationships.

Above all my thanks are due to my wife Elaine and our children,

Joshua, Dina and Gila, whose patience and support have meant everything to me. It is not easy being a religious leader – the great Jewish scholar Jacob Emden used to say in thanksgiving, 'Blessed are You, O Lord . . . who has not made me a rabbi' – and without their faith, mine surely would have had its moments of doubt. The Jewish sages believed that peace in the home brings peace to the world. Certainly it has brought peace and blessing to me.

Jonathan Sacks

Introduction

Western civilisation suffers from a strong sense of moral and spiritual exhaustion. Having constructed a society of unprecedented sophistication, convenience and prosperity, nobody can remember what it was supposed to be for. Just enjoying it does not seem to be enough. Indeed, enjoyment as an end in itself quickly turns to ashes in the mouth. Not only is it boringly bland. It is even more boringly purposeless. There is more to human life than comfort, entertainment, and the avoidance of suffering.

Or there ought to be. Increasingly, people of all sorts and conditions – especially young people – are becoming curious about alternatives, asking questions and seeking answers. Most of them are suspicious of panaceas and simplistic solutions, and reluctant therefore to join organisations, such as cults and fundamentalist churches, that offer short cuts. They are eclectic and even sceptical. But they are becoming open to possibilities that their parents and grandparents would have declined. The difference between the generations might be summed up by saying that the older one mutters to itself, 'There are no easy answers', then shrugs its shoulders and turns away; while the younger generation remarks, 'There are no easy answers so let us consider more difficult ones'.

This is the ideal climate of opinion in which to introduce to a much wider circle of readers the sharp and unusual insights of Jonathan Sacks. Most of those who already know of him, know him as the Chief Rabbi of Great Britain, the head man of the Orthodox Jewish community in Britain. But Orthodox Jews will forgive me for saying, at least in this context, that is by no means the most important thing about him.

Even before his name became prominent in his own community, some of us had picked up rumours that there was a fresh face on the block, a new and exciting talent that had attached itself to one of the more conservative religious institutions in Britain, the United Hebrew Congregations. It was his growing reputation for originality and sheer intelligence that quickly took him to the headship of Jews College in London, which is responsible for training Britain's Orthodox rabbis, and eventually brought him to the attention of the BBC. It was by this means that he first became a national figure, when his series of radio Reith Lectures in 1990 captured widespread attention, if a little puzzlement too, for his lucid and thoughtful warnings about the moral and spiritual state of Western society.

This was a voice we had not heard before. We are used to thinkers of past and present speaking from within a culture formed by Christianity, even if their ideas are not specifically theological or religiously orthodox. We are also used to secularised Jews as philosophers, writers and formers of opinion – one only has to think of Marx and Freud. But what we are not used to is someone speaking to us, and managing to address us where we are, from within the conservative and ancient religious tradition of Orthodox Jewry, and without compromising it in the process. Above all, we are not used to this being done in an utterly English way, with a command of English language and conceptual thought, and with a profound understanding – the sort of understanding that only comes from membership – of modern Western society. Jonathan Sacks is a next-door neighbour, a fellow Englishman, one of us. Even when he is boring, which is not very often, he is boring in an English sort of way.

Yet that is still not quite the essential point about him. He has not invented a new message. What he has done is to understand an old one, but to understand it so well that he can see what it has to say to us, even to non-Jews who inhabit an utterly different world from that in which the message first took shape.

Judaism arose from a very particular experience, the self-reflection and meditation upon God of an ancient Semitic people. Through historical circumstances at the start of the Common Era, most of all because of the way they were deprived of their special homeland for so many centuries, the Jews learnt to detach themselves from one time and place (though they never lost the deep longing for it). Thus they had to learn, as the price of their own survival, how to adapt the principles of their culture and religion to very many different settings, not least to settings which were hostile. Thus did the particular, rooted in one time and place, become the general and transcendent, at home everywhere and nowhere.

The Jews were the first discoverers of a new and radical insight into the nature of reality. They discovered monotheism: that there was but one true God. God was the creator of everything, then and now. God was also personal, able to intervene in human affairs, able even to respond to human pleas for help. Such a God has to be the author of one universal morality, ethical laws which apply everywhere. Monotheism banishes the idea of local moralities, each expressing the will of a domestic deity, where any passing stranger, not a worshipper of that local God, becomes thereby an outlaw and enemy. It is crucial to Jewish mores to acknowledge and welcome the stranger, an ancient way of saluting the fact that strangers are also children of the God of the Jews – for there is only one God.

The notion is so familiar to us we cannot imagine how astonishing it was when first encountered. Even the sophisticated Greeks had to acknowledge that it was a more advanced idea than any they had had. Monotheism is a core idea of Western thought, perhaps even *the* core idea. It makes the world rational, while at the same time enhancing rather than diminishing the importance of mankind in the scheme of things.

Today, Judaism in all its forms is still intensely monotheistic. But the very universality of its creed now commands our attention. Jews do not speak of a Jewish God. He is universal, or else He does not exist. Not the least of the attractions of Orthodox Judaism, many will find, is its extreme disinclination to evangelise. It is not interested in pulling people into its coils. It can be allowed to be an influence, from outside. For the Jews, that is as it ought to be. They are 'to be a light unto the gentiles', not to turn the gentiles into Jews.

This digression should help to explain why I find Jonathan Sacks so significant, and why I think others will do so too. He is not just a leader and spokesman for his own religious community, which now rightly enjoys so much esteem in Britain. He is also a natural and gifted communicator, who is burning with the desire to convey his ideas to others. He is as Jewish as they come, but also as English as they come, and he has a deep regard for his country and his fellow countrymen whatever their race or faith.

Dr Sacks shares the widely accepted view that we are a nation living off our moral capital, having abandoned most of the doctrines of our traditional beliefs; but we have not yet been able to replace it with a moral code which relies on science and rationality alone. Fifty years ago it was widely assumed that that time would come. Now we are not so sure. There is a streak of mischief and wickedness in human nature that defies our modern analysis, and which drives us back to shelter behind the religious and moral codes of our ancestors. Dr Sacks' own analysis is that the very survival of modern civilisation may ultimately depend upon the survival of three things: faith, the family and the community. And of these, faith is fundamental.

Now this is ancient wisdom, some might say inspired by God, some might say the fruit of 4,000 years of deep reflection on the human condition. Nobody who reads, say, the book of Proverbs or Wisdom or the Psalms, or even Job, can fail to be impressed by the humanity and intelligence of their authors, or the extent to which they seem to have shared many of the experiences and anxieties that we also have undergone. Often they seem wiser than we are. And a religious people which is regularly immersed in that literature is likely to become wiser in turn.

Of all the problems facing modern democracies in the future, morality is going to be the most difficult. Democracy may be the most fair and just system of government yet discovered, in the way it treats all its citizens as equal before the law and before the ballot box. Similarly, attempts to improve on a market-based economic system have not so far unearthed an effective alternative. But neither democracy as a political system nor the free market as an economic system can fill a moral vacuum. They are both about method rather than content. They put power in the hands of individuals, so that they can live their lives more nearly as they choose, but they offer no guidance as to the choices themselves: which goods and services to buy, which policies to support. This maximisation of personal autonomy could become very dangerous, once it is perceived as an end in itself. The libertarian dream, as Dr Sacks recognises, could quickly become a nightmare. It is morally bankrupt. Human freedom is only a benefit once we know what freedom is for.

There are moral systems contending to fill this vacuum, of course, and the most useful are likely to be those which rely on ideas of transcendental morality, of universal laws not invented by particular societies – or even worse, by governments – but whose validity is perpetual. Democracy, if it is to have any moral content, will have to learn how to cherish those sources of transcendence in its midst, because in the long term they are its one sure hope.

Democracy will have to outgrow its silly habit of rejecting all that is old and wise simply because it is not new and startling. All those with something to offer to the moral debate will have to be allowed, and if necessary invited, to put their contribution forward. The faith communities in Britain, including the Christian Churches, the Jewish community, and the religions of the Indian sub-continent now amply represented among us, will have to be treated not as anachronisms but as among our most vital national assets. They are our spiritual gold reserves.

But this requires an institutional habit of tolerance that goes beyond peace between factions, and deepens into an ability and willingness to listen and to learn. Faith communities will have their own clear principles, but may find that the uncompromising insistence upon those principles is possible only within their own ranks. They should not for that reason reject the effort to influence the community at large, nor should they give up if they are not totally successful. Faith communities serve the wider needs of society every time they offer moral principles that are out of step with the fashionable morality of the age, even when that offer seems not to have had any effect. In any event, how can they know?

These are among the key principles for the conduct of a plural society, of one that no longer holds strongly to any particular creed. It is difficult to overstate the importance to such a society of the contribution of a man like Dr Jonathan Sacks. It follows that there can be few more important books published this decade than *Faith in the Future*. It is not a religious book in any denominational sense. It is more about us, the majority gentile community, than it is about the Jews. If we neglect it, we shall be passing a vote of no confidence in our own future. For we shall be rejecting the only sort of medicine that can save us. Better by far that we should acquire a taste for it. Thankfully, Dr Sacks makes it so enjoyable to swallow, we are hardly aware it is doing us good.

Clifford Longley

Prologue: Faith in the Future

The thought came, as I knew it would, in Jerusalem. I was sitting one Sabbath afternoon in one of the parks of the rebuilt city, watching children playing. I had come with my family to spend a year in the home of the Jewish soul before taking up office as Chief Rabbi. The responsibility I was about to undertake was heavy, and I knew it. Jews love leadership, but not followership, and as a result we are a fractious people. I felt the need of inspiration to sustain me, and I knew it would come in Jerusalem. Though for centuries it had lain in ruins, Jews never stopped praying towards it. In all that time, wrote Maimonides, the divine presence never left the city. Here, as nowhere else, you are brushed by the wings of eternity.

There is a stillness and peace which exists only in Jerusalem on a Sabbath afternoon. Shops are closed. The streets are free of traffic. The morning prayers are over. The Sabbath meal has been eaten. Rest comes over the city and the setting sun turns the houses red and gold. The only sound came from the children and their games. Then I remembered a moving scene described in the Talmud. It was set in the first century of the Common Era. The Temple had been destroyed by the Romans. Jerusalem lay devastated. It was one of the most tragic episodes of Jewish history, the beginning of an exile and dispersion that were to last almost two thousand years.

The Talmud describes how the great sages, Rabban Gamliel, Rabbi Elazar ben Azariah, Rabbi Joshua and Rabbi Akiva, looked out upon the ruins. Three of them wept. But Rabbi Akiva gave them a message of consolation. The prophets, he said, foresaw this day and it has come to pass. But they also foresaw a later day when the city would be rebuilt. Since one vision has come true, so will the other. The day will come when Zechariah's prophecy will be fulfilled: 'Old men and women will once again sit in the streets of Jerusalem . . . and the streets of the city will be filled with children playing.' Nineteen hundred years later, I had lived to see Rabbi Akiva's hope come true.

I

If only he had known, I thought. If only Rabbi Akiva had known how long it would take, how many exiles, expulsions, persecutions, pogroms, blood libels, Inquisitions and Crusades Jews would first have to endure. If only he had known of the Holocaust and its millions of innocent victims gassed and turned to ashes. Would he not have wept? Would he still have kept his faith? In that moment of truth I knew the answer. Yes, *all the more would he have held to his faith*, knowing that God could not have led this people so long through the valley of the shadow of death without one day bringing them to the city of peace.

Peter Berger once called hope a 'signal of transcendence', an intrusion of God into our lives. For Jews hope was more than that. It was life itself. Without it our ancestors could not have stayed Jews, devoting their best energies to passing on their heritage to successive generations. Much of the time they lived in poverty, but even when they knew better days their lives were etched with insecurity, never sure when their buildings would be burned, their property seized, and they themselves sent into exile or worse. But something of Rabbi Akiva's faith in the future lived on in them. Next year, they said, we will be in Jerusalem; and the next year they said the same.

It sometimes seems as if faith is an empty gesture and prayer a mere striving after wind. It was then in Jerusalem that I knew otherwise. Faith had kept the dream intact across the centuries and had led Jews from seventy countries to come together here in the land of their origins to rebuild themselves as a sovereign State. It had touched the hearts of even assimilated Jews – Moses Hess, Leon Pinsker, Theodor Herzl, Max Nordau, the early protagonists of secular Zionism – as it had touched my great-grandfather, a Lithuanian rabbi, and led him to Jerusalem as one of the early religious advocates of the return to Zion. It had led the Jewish people to begin again after the Holocaust, bringing to pass the most haunting of all biblical prophecies, Ezekiel's vision of the resurrection of a nation, the valley of dry bones which came together and grew flesh and lived. And it had led me here in the still of a Sabbath afternoon to see Zechariah's prophecy and Rabbi Akiva's hope fulfilled: the streets of Jerusalem filled with children playing.

Faith is the space where God and humanity touch. For Jews it has always been symbolised by a journey, the journey begun by Abraham when he left his country and his father's house to travel to an unknown land, the journey taken by the Israelites as they left Egypt for the promised land, the journey each of us could trace if we could follow our grandparents and theirs back through the generations as they wandered from country to country in search of refuge. The way is always further than we thought, the route more complicated and beset with obstacles. But we continue it knowing, sometimes obscurely, sometimes with blazing clarity, that this is what God wants us to do. For we know that so long as the way the world is, is not the way it ought to be, we have not yet reached our destination.

The path we have travelled since the biblical exodus is not just to a land but to a society built on human dignity and compassion and law-governed liberty and justice. The Jewish journey is not just a physical one but a spiritual, moral and political one as well. That is what has long given it a significance beyond itself. It is not just a Jewish journey, but the human journey in a particularly vivid form. It has inspired not only Jews, but all those who, having read the Hebrew Bible, have come to the conclusion that our lives have a moral purpose, that redemption can be sought in this world with all its imperfections, and that by our efforts we can leave society better than we found it. The Mosaic books and those of the prophets have echoed throughout human history, moving men and women to dedicate their lives to the uncertain proposition that by constant struggle we can reduce suffering and enhance dignity not for ourselves alone but for all those amongst whom we live; that we can, in William Blake's phrase, 'build Jerusalem'. Whenever that journey is undertaken it testifies to faith: faith that our hopes are not illusions, that something beyond us answers to our trust, that as we reach out our hand to God, His reaches out to us, giving us the strength to continue though the way is dark. To a Jew in this strange century, surveying the collapse of fascism in Germany and communism in Eastern Europe, the rebirth of Israel as a nation in its own land and its steps towards peace, faith in the future can sometimes seem the strongest thing there is.

ઈટ

We undervalue faith. My grandparents arrived in this country as refugees. On my father's side they came from Poland, part of the vast migration of Jews in flight from the pogroms and anti-semitism of Eastern Europe at the turn of the century. My mother's family came from what was then Palestine. My maternal great-grandfather had gone there in the 1870s and eventually founded an agricultural settlement, *Petach Tikvah*, 'the gate of hope'. After some years he encountered hostility from the local Arabs and was forced to flee, arriving in England in 1894. I was born in the East End of London, the point of arrival for many Anglo-Jews and

3

for other immigrant groups since. By the time I made my appearance most Jews had already left on their slow journey outward toward the suburbs. But there were still enough of them there to give me a sense of what had once been a busy centre of Jewish life.

. Judaism is a future-oriented religion, and Jews are not prone to nostalgia. But I am surely not alone in thinking that our grandparents had something that we have lost. No one who has even the vaguest memories of the East End would wish to return there. Accounts of it in Victorian times portray it as a festering inner-city ghetto rife with poverty, illiteracy and crime. Nonetheless the Jews who arrived there, though they lacked all else, had three extraordinarily powerful assets: a sense of community, of family and of religious tradition. Together, these helped them to preserve their dignity and sense of hope under what might otherwise have been hopeless conditions.

Within the space of a generation, those families had broken free of the chains of deprivation. Their mobility, physical, social and intellectual, was little short of astonishing. Search back into the history of today's Jewish academics, professionals and businesspeople and, as likely as not, you will find a family story not unlike mine, of immigrant grandparents barely able to speak the language or make a living. Their faith, solidarity and pride were all they could confer on their children. But it was enough. It made the difference between hopelessness and hope. And that, in the human situation, is the greatest difference there is.

There is a truth here which touches on the future of Britain and the liberal democracies of the West. The vast increase of wealth in the past century has not made us overwhelmingly happier, nor has it solved society's ills and discontents. Walk through the scarred inner-city areas of Liverpool, Manchester or Newcastle, or return to the East End of London itself, and you will today discover a far more hopeless environment than the one my grandparents inhabited. Poverty, under-education and crime exist now as they did then, but they are set against a background of despair that is both new and chilling. The American writer Charles Murray has introduced into our vocabulary the provocative word 'underclass' to characterise the new groups of urban poor whom every political experiment, from the maximalist to the minimalist state, has failed to help. None of us can be comfortable with such a situation. Whatever our political stance, the sight of today's homeless, and the blighted lives of too many of our children, must move us no less than Dickens' portraits of another age and its heartlessness moved a generation more than a century ago.

I am no less troubled by another kind of poverty which affects even children from relatively affluent homes: a poverty of moral imagination. Many of the young people I meet – advantaged, articulate and well-educated, apparently with everything to look forward to – face the future with surprising apprehension. They are fearful about the erosion of the environment. They are anxious about their careers, knowing how unpredictably markets, technology, industries, exchange-rates and the economy can change, leaving people stranded and their life's work gone. They are uncertain about personal relationships, reluctant to commit themselves to marriage, seeing around them the human wreckage of discord and divorce.

This new fearfulness was brought home to me in an unexpected way. In September 1993, Yitzhak Rabin and Yasser Arafat shook hands on the White House lawn signalling the fateful decision of Israelis and Palestinians to embark on a process of peace. Just before and after that day, I had occasion to visit a number of schools and I was taken aback by the response of the children to the initiative. They were convinced it would not work. They were full of foreboding. Hatred and violence had scarred the relationship between Jews and Arabs for so long that they were convinced that nothing would change. The peace process was doomed to failure.

They may have been right: it is still too early to say. Certainly most of us witnessing the handshake knew the risks both sides were taking. We knew that hostility takes generations to heal, and that there would be attempts by extremists on both sides to sabotage any proposals for co-existence. The schoolchildren were not naive. To the contrary, they were formidably well informed. But they lacked one thing, without which no great initiative can be undertaken. They lacked hope. They were world-weary before their time. They had seen too many political ventures fail, too many expectations dashed. It was as if, to protect themselves against disappointment, they had grown a carapace of pessimism. They had formulated an unspoken rule: Nothing works. They had lost faith in the future.

This loss of faith has been much commented on. One politician recently called it the 'new British disease: the self-destructive sickness of national cynicism'. Merely calling for confidence and a willingness to trust, though, does not bring them about. There is such a thing as an ecology of hope. There are environments in which it flourishes and others in which it dies. Hope is born and has its being in the context of family, community and religious faith.

In stable families, nurtured by those who brought us into existence, we learn to give and receive love. There is no greater crucible of trust than the family bond, for it is here in early infancy that we learn to risk our human vulnerability on the answering affection of others. We find, if we are lucky, that love given is not given in vain, and on this much else in later life depends.

In communities we receive our most practical tuition in the concept of the common good. They are our closest approximation to the extended families of the Bible or the small city-states of ancient Greece, where the concept of virtue was born and our ethical tradition had its origins. Communities are where we acquire a sense of place and belonging. They are usually small enough to allow us to recognise one another, to value the contribution of each to the welfare of all, to bring comfort and support to those who need it, and to extend our horizons from private to collective gain. The local synagogue or church, the parent-teacher association and neighbourhood watch scheme are powerful schools of virtue precisely because they are personal and face-to-face. They are not remote and abstract like the modern state. They are where we speak of duty, not rights; where we focus on what we can give, not claim. As a result they are the best antidote there is to the disillusion that always follows the politics of self-interest.

Families and communities are in turn undergirded by religious faith. In Judaism, at least, the three go hand in hand. Religious faith suggests that our commitments to fidelity and interdependence are not arbitrary, a matter of passing moral fashion. They mirror the deep structure of reality. The bonds between husband and wife, parent and child, and us and our neighbours partake of the covenantal bond between God and humanity. The moral rules and virtues which constrain and enlarge our aspirations are not mere subjective devices and desires. They are 'out there' as well as 'in here'. They represent objective truths about the human situation, refracted through the prisms of revelation and tradition.

Faith, family and community are, I suspect, mutually linked. When one breaks down, the others are weakened. When families disintegrate, so too does the sense of neighbourhood and the continuity of our great religious traditions. When localities become anonymous, families lose the support of neighbours, and congregations are no longer centres of community. When religious belief begins to wane, the moral bonds of marriage and neighbourly duty lose their transcendental base and begin to shift and crumble in the high winds of change. That is precisely what has happened in our time and the loss, though subtle, is immense.

For these are more than just three aspects of our busy and varied lives.

6

They are the matrix of all else. Without them we will find, like the author of Ecclesiastes, that the more we pursue pleasure the less we find happiness. Our relationships will become more fractured. We will retreat into private worlds of solace: the Walkman, the television screen and the computer terminal, the icons of our time. We will build a world of private affluence and public squalor. And we will fail to give our children what they most deserve: a map of meaning by which to chart their way through a confusing and chaotic world.

There is such a thing as an ecology of hope, and it lies in restoring to our culture a sense of family, community and religious faith. The great question facing the liberal democracies of the West is whether it can be done. I believe it can, and that is the theme of many of the chapters in this book. These values never die, though occasionally – as now – they suffer an eclipse. If Judaism and the history of the Jewish people have a message for our time, it is surely this. Faith in the future changes lives and rebuilds the ruins of Jerusalem.

PART I
THE MORAL COVENANT

I

Introduction: Sharing Duties

For Jews, and not only Jews, the religious voice is above all a moral voice. Abraham is chosen so that he will instruct his children 'to do righteousness and justice'. Moses tells the Israelites, 'Justice, justice shall you pursue'. Isaiah begins his prophetic mission with the most powerful speech ever made against the idea that you can serve God in the house of prayer while ignoring Him in the market place. Micah sums up the religious quest in three imperatives: 'To do justly, and to love mercy, and to walk humbly with your God.'

No idea in the Hebrew Bible has been more influential than this, that society is founded on a moral covenant between its members, vested in an authority that transcends all earthly powers, and whose most famous symbol is the Ten Commandments engraved in stone. Underlying it is a proposition which even today has not lost its power to surprise and inspire. *In the beginning God created the world as a home for humanity. Since then He has challenged humanity to create a world that will be a home for Him.* God lives wherever we treat one another as beings in His image.

That vision inspired the great champions of liberal democracy from Locke to Jefferson and beyond. But today, though vestiges remain, it is in eclipse and a quite different set of values prevails. It owes its inspiration morally to Nietzsche and politically to John Stuart Mill. On this view, society is not a collaborative enterprise framed by a shared covenant. Instead it is an aggregate of individuals pursuing private interests, coming together temporarily and contractually, and leaving the State to resolve their conflicts on value-neutral grounds. The key words in this new scheme are not moral rules and duty but *autonomy* and *rights*. The key principle of both morality and politics is that we should be free to act as we please so long as we do not harm others.

On the face of it, nothing could be more desirable. In practice, though, the human cost of this new dispensation has proved very high indeed in terms of fragile relationships, broken marriages, confused and uncared-for children, growing inequalities, rising crime, self-reinforcing circles of deprivation, a decline in civility and a weakening of the civic bond. The strong survive, as they always did. But that was not the prophetic test of a just and compassionate society, nor can it be ours if anything of that older morality persists, if we are moved by the plight of poverty in the midst of affluence, if we see too many wasted lives and wonder what kind of world we are creating for our children.

Worse still, the new individualism narrows the horizons of human happiness. I called one of my 1990 Reith Lectures 'Demoralisation', and I deliberately chose that ambiguous word. There is a deep connection between ethics and the human spirit, between *morality* and *morale*. If we lose the former, the latter begins to fail. It was Emile Durkheim in his classic study of suicide who coined the word *anomie* to describe a situation in which the individual loses his moorings in a shared moral order and becomes prone to a sense of meaninglessness and drift. A straight road leads from individualism to cynicism and despair.

Society *is* a moral enterprise. That crucial insight of the Hebrew Bible remains as powerful now as it ever was. We cannot live alone. But we cannot live together without conflicts. How we resolve those conflicts determines the quality of our lives as members of families and as citizens. It was Judaism's great contribution to see the human arena as something other than a state of ongoing war in which power reigned supreme. A society could be constructed on the rule of law and justice, its rougher edges smoothed by an active sense of kinship and compassion. At the heart of such a society is a concept of the common good, meaning not that there is some ultimate good on which we all agree, but simply that we must learn to live together if we are to pursue any good at all, and that means at least some shared morality.

The following chapters are about family, community and the health, or otherwise, of our moral environment. They begin with a brief article I wrote at the time of the James Bulger case, the tragic murder of a two-year-old child which evoked a rare mood of national introspection. In it I set out what I thought had gone wrong with British society. The subsequent lectures and articles develop the argument in greater depth. In each case I have tried to evoke sentiments that reach beyond the Jewish community or even the community of religious believers, for these are issues which affect us all. The language I use is not theological, but moral. Beneath it, though, is a simple religious conviction, that God is to be found less in the 'I' than in the 'We', in the relationships we make, the institutions we fashion, the duties we share, and the moral lives we lead.

2

Holes in the Moral Fabric

Jamie Bulger is dead, but the debate his murder has provoked refuses to die. No candle we could light to his memory is more important than this.

Moral reflection needs time the way the human body needs oxygen. But time is the one thing of which we starve the great moral issues of our age. When James died the thing I most feared was a surge of attention – massive media coverage – followed by silence as the spotlight shifted and the next crisis filled the front pages. Our ethical seriousness is measured by our attention span, and ours has grown dangerously short.

Blessedly, this has not happened. That is perhaps the best news to have emerged from this bleak and hellish tragedy. We rightly sensed that something more was at stake than the murder of a two-year-old child by ten-year-old children, a freak outbreak of unrestrained evil. There were larger issues, and we who had no part in the act nonetheless felt implicated.

That is not moral panic but an honest recognition of the threads of collective responsibility that make society more than an aggregate of individuals. Together we form a moral entity. 'Any man's death diminishes me', wrote John Donne. The fact that we felt personally diminished by James's death tells us that we are still morally alive.

Morality begins with law, and law is predicated on individual responsibility. But morality does not end there. Nor does James's death end with the trial and sentencing of his murderers. Though the murder itself was a cruel aberration, it had a social context. It was this. The moral fabric with which we clothe our children has grown threadbare. The holes have begun to show.

We have bestowed on our children a culture of violence, ritually celebrated at football grounds and on films and videos. Our children experience violence as street culture, as male initiation, even as quasi-religious

The Times, 3 December 1993

catharsis. No society can allow this and survive. Violence has victims, and they are usually the most vulnerable and innocent.

We have systematically dismantled our structures of authority. Who, today, has survived our relentless iconoclasm? Politicians, religious leaders, the royal family, have been mercilessly savaged until there is no one left whose word carries moral force. We recognise public faces by their caricatures on *Spitting Image*. They have become figures of fun. In the process, we have robbed our children of any credible model of who we would wish them to be.

We have tolerated the collapse of the family. We have done so in the name of personal fulfilment, sexual liberty and the inalienable right to follow our desires. No abdication has had more fateful consequences. We have allowed the social stigma attaching to absconding fathers to disappear, assuming that their place could be taken by the State. But the State is not a person, and it is from persons – especially parents – that we learn what it is to be moral. The result is lawless children who have to be restrained because they have not learned restraint.

We have dissolved the bonds of community. The most piercing fact about James's death was the number of people who saw him being abducted and did not come to his rescue. We cannot blame them. The privatisation of morality has taught us not to interfere. This too cannot continue. We need the support of neighbours, friends and an active community, none more so than mothers struggling to bring up children alone.

In teaching our children moral relativism we have placed them in the world without a moral compass, even hinting that there is no such thing. In the name of tolerance we have taught that every alternative lifestyle is legitimate and that moral judgement is taboo, even 'judgemental'. What is right becomes what does not harm others, and in time degenerates to what I feel like doing and can get away with.

We have given children no framework within which to learn civic virtue and responsibility. We must devise ways by which service to the community becomes part of every child's experience of the growth to adulthood. Morality is taught by being lived. It is learned by doing. Community service is more powerful than any formal moral instruction, even supposing an agreed curriculum could be devised. Nothing would more dramatically change our children's world. It will cost much to do it. But *not* to do it will ultimately cost more.

These are starting points for a debate that must continue until it reaches practical conclusions. The most important thing the government can now do is to establish a formal framework to take the argument further before interest dies. It should be non-political, and should acknowledge frankly that *governments alone cannot change people*. There are other agents of change in society. They include religious leaders and educators. If they are denigrated, moral renewal will fail. If they are enlisted, it may succeed.

We have reached a critical juncture in our social evolution. A political order based on liberty and tolerance has yielded a Britain significantly less tolerant and more violent, harsh and abrasive than the one my grandparents knew. A single, unspeakable tragedy has made us look at ourselves in the moral mirror, and what we have seen looks dishevelled and tired. A child has died. Our national soul must not die with him.

3
Why Morality Matters

The contemporary world has given morality a rough ride. The word itself evokes all we distrust most: the intrusion of impersonal standards into our private lives, the presence of judgement where judgement does not belong, the substitution of authority for choice. When a politician moralises we suspect that he or she is searching for an excuse not to pay for something. When a religious leader moralises we fear the imposition of certainties we no longer share, and we suspect that fundamentalism is not far behind. When a particularly newsworthy crime or social trend provokes ethical debate, it will not be long before voices are heard dismissing the conversation as 'moral panic'. We have come to share George Bernard Shaw's conviction that morality is one person's way of disrupting someone else's innocent enjoyment, or as H G Wells called it, 'jealousy with a halo'.

But this cannot be the whole picture. We do still care, and care passionately, about concerns that are essentially moral. We are disturbed by legal injustice and extreme economic inequality. We care about war and famine and their toll of innocent lives. We are distressed by our destruction of the environment in pursuit of economic growth. We are not indifferent to the suffering of others or to the harm we may be laying in store for future generations. We are as moral as any other generation. Perhaps more so, for television has exposed us in the most vividly immediate ways to sufferings that in a previous age we would hardly have known about, let alone seen. And our greater affluence and technological prowess have given us the resources to address ills – physical and economic – that an earlier generation might have seen as something about which nothing could be done, part of the sad but natural order of things. We are certainly not amoral. We remain sharply aware of the difference between what is and what ought to be. Morality matters to us now no less than it did to our grandparents. But undeniably its *agenda* has changed. That is what deserves reflection.

Many reasons have been advanced as to why the concept of morality as a set of rules beyond the self has suffered an eclipse. We have become less religious, and religion was the classic source of our belief in a revealed morality, commandments engraved on tablets of stone. We have become more culturally diverse, and we now know that what seems wrong to one group may be permissible in a second and even admirable in a third. We have inherited, however indirectly, a set of ideas from Marx and Nietzsche, that what passes for morality may be the mask over a hierarchy of power, a way of keeping people in their place. From psychoanalysis we have developed a suspicion that morality is a way of suppressing natural instinct, and as such is an enemy of self-expression. Perhaps, after the horror of two world wars, we simply reached the conclusion that previous generations had led us into the wilderness instead of the promised land, and the time had come to try another way. Each of these analyses has truth to it, and there may be many more.

But there is, I suspect, a political dimension too. The twentieth century has witnessed a vast expansion of the power and presence of the State. Things that were once the province of families, communities, religious congregations, voluntary organisations and co-operative groups have been appropriated by governments; among them education, health care, and welfare. In part this was motivated by economic and political necessity. The modern nation-state needed a mobile population, one whose members shared a common culture and education. As women joined the workforce, care facilities had to be provided by the State. The standardisation required by industry and war spelled the break-up of more local traditions and associations. But there was also a profound moral dimension to the growth of the State, namely a terminal dissatisfaction with the inequalities of privilege. Why should some people but not others have access to the best schools and doctors? Could a decent society allow families to languish because of poverty and unemployment? These were, I believe, the right questions at a certain period in the development of western democracies, and they led to the caring State.

But even the right decisions have long-term consequences, not all of which are benign. The growth of the State meant the atrophy of many of those local institutions, from the family outwards, where people learned the give-and-take of human relationships and the subtle codes of civility without which it is difficult for people to live closely together for very long. More importantly it broke the connection between what we do and what happens to us, which is of the essence of moral responsibility. A child 'going wrong' in the past would be supported by family and friends, but they would deliver an unmistakable moral rebuke. Continued support came with conditions. The caring State can deliver no such message because a State is neither family nor friend. It is of its essence impersonal. It is there to help with few strings attached. It cannot, may not, make moral judgements. It is beyond its competence and remit to make distinctions between the sufferings that befall us and those we bring upon ourselves. No one sought to have the State undermine moral responsibility. But inevitably that has been its effect. It left it redundant and unemployed.

The story of the late twentieth century is one of the displacement of the community by the State and hence of the replacement of morality by politics. That is why our moral agenda has changed. Our concerns – with inequality and injustice, war and famine and ecology – go deep. But these are issues to be addressed to governments. We are willing to make sacrifices on their behalf. We join protests, sign petitions, send donations. But these are large-scale and for the most part impersonal problems. They have relatively little to do with what morality was traditionally largely about: the day-to-day conduct between neighbours and strangers, what Martin Buber called the 'I-and-Thou' dimension of our lives. Instead, in our personal relationships we believe in autonomy, the right to live our lives as we choose.

A profound political change took place in the 1980s. It surfaced as Thatcherism in Britain, Reaganomics in the United States, and most significantly in the collapse of communism in Eastern Europe. It was as if the realisation had dawned in many countries simultaneously that what had once been a solution – the hyperactive State – had now become a problem. The pursuit of equality interfered with liberty. State intervention inhibited economic growth. High taxation thwarted enterprise. Collective spending was less satisfactory all round than individual spending. The government should do and take less, the individual should do and keep more. It was one of those swings of the pendulum that occurs periodically in human affairs, from centralism to localism or vice versa. But what has become increasingly clear in the 1990s is that *the 'State' and the 'individual' are not two opposed forces*. They belong to one another. They are twins. Without the modern State the modern individual could not have come into being. They have grown together like ivy against a tree.

The modern individual is defined by his or her independence from long-term commitments to the past or the future. Authority is not vested in the past, in the form of parents or traditions or communities of belonging. Even Philip Larkin's wonderfully embarrassed description of mid-twentieth-century religious awe – 'Hatless, I take off my cycle-clips in awkward reverence' – is too pious for us now. Nor are we comfortable with the idea of personal responsibility towards an open-ended future. Marriage and parenthood have become contractual and conditional rather than 'till death do us part'. Individualism of this order could not have existed without a powerful and all-present State. Collectivism and individualism, though they seem opposed, are two sides of the same coin. The responsibilities shouldered by the one give the other the freedom to be what it is.

The eclipse of collectivism and the retreating tide of the State form our foreseeable political future. On this, parties on both the left and right of the political spectrum currently agree. And just as people of moral conviction welcomed the advancing State as an answer to deep social injustices, so they can see in its subsequent retreat other moral gains. The Judaeo-Christian tradition places great weight on individual responsibility and liberty. Government is necessary, but the less the better. That is the consistent message from Samuel to the last of the prophets. The more responsibility we delegate away, the less we are called on to act as the image of God, shaping our world individually by His will. Virtue is greater for being uncoerced. Better the good deeds that grow from below than those which are imposed from above.

What, though, has now become clear is that political change has moved far in advance of moral change. The tree has been removed, leaving the ivy unsupported. We have abandoned collectivism but not yet the individualism which was its symbiotic partner. As the State withdraws part of its protective shelter, many people find themselves suddenly exposed. Single-parent families, the unemployed, inhabitants of inner-city ghettoes and others become the casualties. It is, and will continue to be, a traumatic experience whose pain only the most heartless can ignore.

A world in which, in many areas where we had grown used to seeing it, the State is not there will be one in which we will have to re-learn many of the moral habits which came so naturally to our ancestors but have come to seem strange to us. We will have to rebuild families and communities and voluntary organisations. We will come to depend more on networks of kinship and friendship. And we will rapidly discover that their very existence depends on what we give as well as what we take, on our willingness to shoulder duties, responsibilities and commitments as well as claiming freedoms and rights. The 'I-It' relationship of taxation and benefit will increasingly be replaced by the 'I-Thou' of fellowship and community. And we may well come to see that the eclipse of personal morality, which dominated the consciousness of a generation, was a strange and passing phase in human affairs, and not the permanent revolution many thought it to be.

If so, I welcome the future. For it promises to restore to human relationships the compassion and grace, the mutuality and faithfulness, which the Hebrew Bible saw as a lasting ideal – more than that, as the way we bring the divine presence into our lives. The unattached society of the past thirty years has been one of unparalleled personal freedoms. But it has also been one of growing incivility and aggression, of exploitation and manipulation, of temporary alliances rather than enduring loyalties, of quick pleasures over lasting happiness. It has been, quite simply, immature. So long as someone was there – the omnipresent State – to pick us up when we fell, it was overwhelmingly seductive. But it has become dysfunctional and cannot be sustained.

Morality matters. Not because we seek to be judgemental or self-righteous or pious. Not because we fondly recall a golden age that never was, the world of Jane Austen perhaps, when men were chivalrous, women decorous, sin discreet and all ranks of society knew their place. It matters not because we are fundamentalists, convinced that we alone possess the moral certainties which form the architecture of virtue. Nor is it because we wish to relieve ourselves of responsibility for the pain, suffering and injustices of the world by blaming them on the victims who made the wrong choices. It matters not because we wish to impose a tidy-minded order on the chaos of human imagination and experiment, nor because we are ignorant of *autre temps, autre meures* and of the fact that ours is not the only way people have chosen to live.

Morality matters because we cherish relationships and believe that love, friendship, work and even the casual encounter of strangers are less fragile and abrasive when conducted against a shared code of civility and mutuality. It matters because we care for liberty and have come to understand that human dignity is better served by the restraints we impose on ourselves than those forced upon us by external laws and punishment and police. It matters because we fear the impoverishment of significant groups within society when the only sources of value are material: success and wealth and physical attractiveness. In most societies – certainly ours – these are too unevenly distributed to be an adequate basis of self-worth.

Morality matters because we believe that there are other and more human ways of living than instinctual gratification tempered by regret. It matters because we believe that some projects – love, marriage, parenthood – are so central to our being that we seek to endow them with as much permanence as is given to us in this unpredictable and transitory life. It matters because we may not abdicate our responsibility for those we brought into being, by failing to provide them with a stable, caring environment within which to grow to maturity. It matters because we believe there are other routes out of the Hobbesian state of nature – the war of all against all – than by creating a Leviathan of a State. It matters because as long as humanity has thought about such things, we have recognised that there are achievements we cannot reach without the collaborative bonds of civil society and the virtues which alone make such a society possible.

Morality matters, finally, because despite all fashionable opinion to the contrary, we remain moved by altruism. We are touched by other people's pain. We feel enlarged by doing good, more so perhaps than by doing *well*, by material success. Decency, charity, compassion, integrity, faithfulness, courage, just being there for other people, matter to us. They matter to us despite the fact that we may now find it hard to say *why* they matter to us. They matter to us because we are human and because, in the words of Sir Moses Montefiore, we are worth what we are willing to share with others. These truths, undervalued for a generation, are about to become vital again; and not a moment too soon.

4

The Future of the Family

A friend told me the following story. He and his wife had had an argument. They were happily married – in fact their marriage is one of the strongest I know – and the difference was soon resolved. But that night his nine-year-old son sought him out on his own. He asked: 'Does this mean that you and mummy are getting a divorce?'

It shook me as it shook him. They were, as I say, a strong family. They were deeply religious Jews. Their son went to a religious school. Until recently this was a world in which divorce was relatively unknown. But it had now begun to strike even here. There were children in his son's class who had experienced family break-up. It had left them, as it always does, traumatised and disturbed. The other children in the class, strongly bonded by their shared faith, had tried to help and had taken on some of their pain. They too now knew that divorce was not just a theoretical possibility, something that happens to other people far away. It had entered their world, and destabilised it.

They had discovered that in this new world parents were not people who were always there. Sometimes they split apart, emotionally splitting apart their children with them. Suddenly, even for the children from stable families, a disturbing reality had dawned. Arguments of the kind all families have took on a new significance. Was a quarrel what divorce is, or at least how it begins? Instead of learning what they might have learned – that marital happiness consists in negotiating conflicts, in being able to have an argument and yet resolve it, love intact – they now felt fear. The marital bond was no longer like the familiar mug that you use cheerfully, knowing that when you accidentally drop it, it will not crack. It had become a cup of the finest china that you are reluctant to drink from for fear of breaking it. Divorce, my friend concluded, now affected everyone, not just those who were divorced.

Beginning with my 1990 Reith Lectures, I have written and spoken much about the family. It has seemed to me to be the arena of the central moral crisis of our time. The family is not one social institution among others, nor is it simply one lifestyle choice among many. It is the best means we have yet discovered for nurturing future generations, and for enabling children to grow in a matrix of stability and love. It is where we acquire the skills and language of relationship. It is where we learn to handle the inevitable conflicts within any human group. It is where we first take the risk of giving and receiving love. Of all the influences upon us, the family is by far the most powerful. Its effects stay with us for a lifetime. It is where one generation passes on its values to the next and ensures the continuity of a civilisation. Nothing else – not teachers or schools, not politicians or the media – so shapes us and what we have a chance of becoming as our experience of early childhood. For any society, the family is the crucible of its future.

In ours, it is beginning to crack. In Britain, and throughout the liberal democracies of the West, family norms have disintegrated with astonishing speed. Today, three of every ten children are born outside of marriage. One in five is brought up in a one-parent family. Almost four in ten marriages end in divorce. There are inner-city areas in Britain and the United States where the stable nuclear family is almost unknown. A few years ago a vicar in Newcastle told me that throughout his working life he had gone into schools, teaching children about religious faith, and about 'God our father'. Now, at the end of his career, he discovered that he could no longer do so. The children did not know what he was talking about. The word they did not understand was not 'God', but 'father'.

Nothing so contradicts our new secular mythology – that life is made of unfettered individual choices through which we negotiate our private paths to happiness – than this. In his *The Wealth of Nations* Adam Smith forged an image which has dominated our age. It was the image of the free market which, as if by an 'invisible hand', turned the myriad self-interested decisions of the economy into the collective good. Each sought his or her own gain but somehow, through the positive energies released, everyone benefited. Since the 1960s we have acted as if that metaphor were valid for personal relationships as well. We forgot what Adam Smith so convincingly remembered, that alongside *The Wealth of Nations* lies *The Theory of the Moral Sentiments*. Smith believed that the market was sustained by institutions whose inner logic was the reverse of the market, above all else the family. It was here that we learned sympathy and fellow feeling, sociability and altruistic love. The family is the oil in the engine, the fluid which saves the system from frictions which would destroy it otherwise.

For a time it could be believed that the 'invisible hand' operated in relationships too. The values invoked by those who criticised the family and its conventions were positive enough. They spoke of personal freedom, experimentation, liberation. They touched a chord. Who would not be attracted by the prospect of pleasure without responsibility, relationships sustained by personal attraction with no attached bill of lasting commitment? One of the early advertisements for credit cards exactly caught the new moral mood. The card – it said – 'takes the waiting out of wanting'. The long-standing basis of morality, the capacity to delay instinctual gratification, seemed no longer necessary. This was a new world of instant consumption, governed by a law of inexorable growth. Economies grow. Incomes grow. Happiness grows. They grow by getting, using and expending, and then making more. The more you discard, the more you produce and therefore the more there is.

The turning point came when we discovered that, even for the economy, Adam Smith's metaphor had limits. Economic growth is not open-ended, nor does it operate in a self-contained system. It too rapidly consumes finite natural resources. It puts at risk the delicate ecological balance. It is subject to uncertainties, inflations and recessions. Unexpected changes in trade and technology can leave whole groups of people devastated and unemployed. If that is true for the economy, it is even more so for relationships. A generation after the planting of the new morality we are left with a harvest of new pain. Men have suffered. Jack Dominian's researches have shown the brute physical effects of divorce, more marked for the husband than the wife. They show in the doubling of heart attacks and strokes and other symptoms of depression such as alcohol and cigarette consumption. Women have suffered more. Overwhelmingly they remain the carers, and in single-parent families they are left to carry a double burden, of economic and emotional support, that is hard enough for two. Too often they live in poverty, struggling to make do on an inadequate income and trying constantly to control children who, in the absence of a father, have grown unsocialised and wild.

Unquestionably, though, the greatest victims have been children themselves. Professor A H Halsey, summarising the research on children from broken or one-parent families, came to the following conclusion: 'On the evidence available, such children tend to die earlier, to have more illness, to do less well at school, to exist at a lower level of nutrition, comfort and conviviality, to suffer more unemployment, to be more prone to deviance and crime, and finally to repeat the cycle of unstable parenting from which they themselves have suffered.' Halsey, himself a sociologist and 'ethical socialist' of immense distinction, once said to me, 'Our age is often referred to as the Century of the Child. I do not believe it is. I think it has been the Century of Child Neglect.'

If there is a fracture at the heart of our collective conscience, it is this. There have been protests in full measure against economic inequalities. But there have been far too few against the greatest inequality of all, that which condemns a significant and ever-growing proportion of our children to lasting disadvantage in almost all spheres of life. In *The Times* in 1993, in a piece subsequently taken up by politicians, I wrote: 'Nothing more threatens to return Britain to Disraeli's "two nations" than a division of the population into those who have known a stable caring childhood and those who have not.' The controversial American thinker, Charles Murray, later wrote a long analysis in the *Sunday Times*. He spoke of a deepening rift in the social fabric of modern societies. The more educated and affluent classes were beginning to realise the mistake of the 1960s and were returning to conventional marriages. The less well-off, particularly those trapped in inner-city ghettoes, were not. The pattern of single-parenthood was replicating itself and extending its hold into a new generation. He spoke of a schism between the 'new Victorians' and the 'new rabble'. It was, like so much of his writing, a brutal and unlovely analysis. But it rang true. For years his has been a lonely voice warning of the centres of self-sustaining disadvantage at the heart of our cities, which have grown worse not better through the interventions of the State. He, like a growing number of others, has seen family breakdown at its core.

There have been protests, too, against the erosion of the natural environment, and they have been loud and long. But there has been no equivalent protest at the erosion of our human environment, the world of relationships into which we bring our children. How, I have often asked, can we devote our energies to saving planet earth for the sake of future generations while neglecting our own children who *are* our future generations? The ethical issue of the environment is a genuine one. But it is also a relatively abstract one. It is about long and unexpected sequences of cause and effect. The connection between using an aerosol spray and global warming is distant in both space and time. Yet it has caught the moral imagination in a way that the disintegration of marriage has not. None the less, if anything is a moral issue, this is. We did not bring the planet into being, but we bring children into being. As John Stuart Mill rightly said, 'The fact itself, of causing the existence of a human being, is one of the most responsible actions in the range of human life.' And if the *ought* of responsibility is there, so too is the *can*. Our individual acts have little effect on the environment. Only in the aggregate do they make a difference. But our individual acts as parents have a decisive influence on our children. In fact, they make almost all the difference there is.

Our conscience has been extraordinarily selective. Nothing so character-ises the contemporary moral landscape as Dickens' portrait of Mrs Jellyby in *Bleak House*, a lady of 'rapacious benevolence' who spends her life in good works for the natives of Africa while utterly neglecting her own children. She could almost be us. Our moral sentiments have been inverted. Adam Smith used to say that the closer a disaster was to us, the more our sympathies were enlisted. Today the opposite seems to apply. Our moral antennae are attuned to distant famines and wars, remote rainforests and threatened species. To the things closest to us, our children and their appeals to us for attention and stability, we seem curiously ambivalent and defensive.

Our attitudes are inverted in another way as well. The things we are *least* able to affect – global phenomena like the economy and unemploy-ment – we are most vociferous in wanting to change. In the thing we are *most* able to affect – our way of life – we are most insistent in rejecting calls to change. Whenever the call is heard summoning us back to the traditional family, a host of columnists and commentators is readily to hand, arguing that it is gone, never to be recovered. The genie is out of the bottle, the toothpaste has left the tube. Those who argue for the return of the stable nuclear family, they say, are like Canute trying to turn back the waves. It is crucial to understand that this is self-evidently false. If there is one thing we *can* change by our own decisions it is the way we act as spouses and parents. The argument of the commentators is a moral one masquerading as a fact. It is a claim to the right to leave all living arrangements uncriticised, however harmful their consequences for others. What is, is what ought to be. There is no right and wrong, only alterna-tives. What needs to be said about this never fully articulated line of thought is that if it is true, there is no morality of personal relationships. And if there is no morality of personal relationships it is hard to see how there can be morality of any kind. It is untrue. But it is significant that it is said, and said so often as to have become a cliché.

Melanie Phillips, a journalist who has stood out against the trend and has shown great courage in doing so, related a telling personal incident in an article she wrote in *The Tablet*. She had been to a seminar at which Professors Halsey and Norman Dennis surveyed some of the research data on the harm caused by family breakdown. She was impressed by the strength of the case, and wondered why the material was not better known. She telephoned another social scientist to ask him about his hostility to the claims advanced by the two men. The following then ensued:

> He released a stream of emotional invective, calling into question the mental faculties of those distinguished academics and asking excitedly, 'What do these people want? Do they want unhappy parents to stay together?' After being pressed repeatedly to identify the research which repudiated the Halsey-Dennis thesis, he said, in summary, this: of course it was correct as far as the research was concerned, but where did that get anyone? Nowhere! Was it possible to turn back the clock? Of course not! And why were they so concerned above all else for the rights of the child? What about the rights of the parents, which were just as important?

This surely is the heart of the matter. In the field of personal relationships two systems of thought, two ways of life, have collided, one which speaks of interdependence, the other of independence. The battle against the family has been conducted in terms of rights, the rights of men to have relationships unencumbered by lasting duties, the rights of women to be free of men, the rights of each of us to plot our private paths to happiness undistracted by the claims of others, willing to pay our taxes in order to be able to delegate our responsibilities to the State and otherwise to be left alone.

But something happens in this scenario to make it unsustainable. Assisted by birth control, abortion, new work patterns and the liberalisation of all laws and constraints touching on relationships, we have divorced sex from love, love from commitment, marriage from having children, and having children from responsibility for their care. That extraordinary institution, marriage, which brought together sexuality, emotional kinship and the creation of new life and wove them into a moral partnership suffused by love, has been exploded as effectively as if someone had planted a bomb in the centre of our moral life. What remains are fragments, chance encounters, temporary attachments, terminable and contractual arrangements, unpredictable sequences in which our lives are thrown together without expectation, hope or emotional investment. Above it all hangs the smoke of war, conflicts of gender and liberation, turning our most intimate relationships into the potential battlefields of date rape, sexual harassment and divorce.

John Stuart Mill defended liberalism on the grounds that there were things – above all personal relationships – that were inherently private. Since his claims have been put into practice all that was once private has become massively public: in films, pop concerts, law cases, newspaper reporting, explicit speech and graphic portrayal. On university campuses the most casual relationships have become subject to codes of political correctness as casuistic, intrusive and relentless as any Victorian manual of propriety; worse, since the censoriousness of public opinion has been supplanted by litigation and the courts. The I-and-Thou of male-female relationship has been turned into a confrontation of Us and Them.

Mill himself spoke of the need to conduct 'experiments of living'. His concept of liberty was related to his understanding of science. But science, as Sir Karl Popper has taught us, is a matter of conjectures and refutations. An experiment has been tried, and has failed. The family turns out to be not one stage in the evolution of mankind but the permanent condition of its happiness. It is, as Winston Churchill said about democracy, the worst system we have, apart from all the others. Ways of life are susceptible to refutation. The clearest sign that one has failed is that it cannot reproduce itself; it cannot sustain its own continuity. No society can survive the breakdown of half its families, the vehicles of its own journey across the generations. No society *ought* to survive, which provides its children with so little stability, security, attention or love. The family is the refutation of individualism.

Fortunately, it can be recovered. One of the most striking findings revealed by research is how firmly the family remains at the apex of our aspirations. What we do turns out not to be the measure of what we want. Overwhelmingly we still value the concept of a stable, lasting relationship. Most single parents do not choose to be single parents. Many divorcees marry again. This may be, as Samuel Johnson called it, the 'triumph of hope over experience' but it is significant that we continue to hope. Making a documentary on the family recently for the BBC, I visited Sherborne House, the centre for young offenders described by Roger Graeffin in his book, *Living Dangerously*. I was struck as he was by the fact that these young men, most of whom came from broken homes, were fiercely attached to the ideal of family and wanted desperately to be good parents. It is not that we no longer value the family. It is that we have forgotten the disciplines that make it work.

The family can be recovered because it is, first and foremost, a moral institution. It is made or unmade by our choices. It is built on bonds of commitment, fidelity and self-restraint. In it a couple pledge themselves to one another, and through love bring new life into the world. Prosaic though its daily reality may be, it is vast in its moral power, weaving together the physical, moral and spiritual aspects of our being into a sense of the unity and continuity of life. It is more than a moral institution. It is the birthplace of the moral sense. It is where, as children, we discover who we are and develop a sense of personal worth. It is where, as parents, we encounter the most inalienable of responsibilities, for those who without us would not exist.

It is within the family that the three great ethical concerns arise: *welfare*, or the care of dependents; *education*, or the handing on of accumulated wisdom to the next generation; and *ecology*, or concern with the fate of the world after our own lifetime. As James Q Wilson has pointed out, the family is our best guarantor of moral courage: studies of those who risked their lives in Nazi Germany to rescue Jews showed them to be people who had been particularly close to their parents and had learned from them the importance of dependability, self-reliance and caring for others. Nothing could be less just than Edmund Leach's famous verdict, in his 1967 Reith Lectures: 'the family, with its narrow privacy and tawdry secrets, is the source of all discontents.' To the contrary, it is the most reliable training ground of sympathy we know.

The family is ultimately a religious institution. It is born of, and gives birth to, faith. It is hard to imagine a world of sexual chaos and random family structures responding to the idea of a morally ordered universe created in love. The biblical word *emunah*, usually translated as faith, means among other things 'faithfulness' as in a marriage, and 'nurturing' as in bringing up a child. God, for the Hebrew Bible, is one who brings us into being as Creator, who betroths us as covenantal partner, and having done so does not walk away. Religious and marital fidelity are almost inextricable in the biblical vision of the world. Only through the experience of secure childhood can we grow to see the universe as a place which answers to our trust.

The congruence between family feeling and religious experience is close. Seeing something of ourselves live on in our children is the nearest we come in this life to immortality. Seeing our children develop in unexpected ways is the nearest we will come to the pure mystery of creativity. Stephen Hawking was wrong in his *A Brief History of Time*. It is not through theoretical physics that we will approach an understanding of the 'mind of God'. It is through the feelings we have when we watch our children playing and they are unaware that we are watching them.

Wittgenstein once said that the task of philosophy was to show the fly the way out of the fly-bottle. The way back to the family is not closed. We have simply become trapped in a set of habits of short-term self-gratification that cause us and others great unhappiness in the long run. I have faith in the future of marriage precisely because mankind is a learning animal. We have survived by recognising and rectifying our mistakes. Moral habits may suffer a temporary eclipse, but we would not have come this far without an inner gyroscope that kept us from tilting into the abyss. Natural ecology has taught us to place limits on our patterns of consumption. Human ecology will teach us, no less surely, to set limits on our patterns of relationship and live within them.

Marriage and the family will matter more in the future, not less. For our children are now born into a world of unprecedentedly rapid change, economic, political and technological. They do not have what most people at most times have had: a set of stable expectations about what they will do and experience and become. Chaos theory is the most characteristic discovery of our age. More than any previous generation, our children need what Alvin Toffler calls 'personal stability zones' that will sustain them in the midst of flux. Of these none is more powerful than the family. Far from being over, its greatest time is yet to come.

5
The Moral Context of Crime

Some time ago my wife and I were walking down a busy shopping street in London in the middle of the day and the middle of the week. The pavements were crowded. The streets were full of shoppers. Behind us was a group of six children of school age, between twelve and sixteen years old. Gradually I became aware that something was wrong. They were walking a little too close, a little too purposefully. One of the group had gone on ahead of us. The rest were in tight formation behind.

It dawned on me that they were about to make a raid on my wife's handbag. We crossed the road and began walking rapidly in the opposite direction. The children followed. We felt a slight push, then nothing. When we reached the next corner, we turned around. The children were gone. I asked my wife to look in her handbag. Her wallet had gone. We phoned the police. They took the details. But they were not seriously interested. They didn't even ask for a description. We understood. Things like this happen. Children miss school and go out for a day's shoplifting or casual theft. There is not a lot we can do about it except take precautions and get insured.

Crime, and certainly juvenile crime, has multiplied to the point where it has become part of our normal expectation. If you have a car, it gets stolen. If you have a house, it gets broken into. If you walk alone down certain streets at certain times, you count yourself lucky if you are not attacked. This represents a significant erosion of our human environment, of our sense of security and trust.

At moments like this, our thinking about crime should shift into a more fundamental mode. A certain level of law-breaking occurs at all times in all non-totalitarian societies. But for the most part it is exceptional, a deviant phenomenon. In these circumstances we relate to crime in terms of the institutions of society which are directly involved: police, the courts,

---

Address to the Institute of American Studies, London University, 9 May 1994

judges, the law, and the sanctions applied for breaches of the law – punishments and penalties.

We may ask questions about the effectiveness of these various elements. Do we have enough police? Do we apprehend a high enough proportion of offenders? Are the courts successful in identifying and convicting the guilty? Do judges apply appropriate sentences, and do those sentences succeed in their several aims of retribution, deterrence and reform?

But there are moments in the history of a society when we are bound to ask larger questions. The Bible provides several eloquent examples: in the days before the Flood, for example, when the 'earth was corrupt in God's sight and the land was full of violence' or at the end of the book of Judges when 'everyone did what was right in his or her own eyes'.

So it is in any society when crime figures escalate rapidly without any obvious explanation. We have now reached that point in both Britain and America. In Britain the crime rate has risen more than tenfold since the mid-1950s, and despite the scholarly debates as to whether this represents actual, perceived or reported crimes, the escalation, especially since the late 1970s, is undeniable.

The figures for juvenile crime in the United States are particularly alarming. Though they are not fully mirrored in the British statistics, none the less there is enough evidence of dysfunctional behaviour amongst the young, from alcohol and drugs to petty crime and violence, to give people in Britain pause for thought too.

It may be that we will decide that we simply have to adjust to higher levels of crime in the world of the future, just as we may have to adjust to different patterns of work and employment. But the cost, surely, will be very high indeed in three directions: for the victims, for the perpetrators, and for all of us and the climate in which we live. A society of more, and more armed police, of video surveillance and alarms on every car and house, of barricaded shops and locked churches and synagogues, a society in which neither the young nor the old feel free to go out at night, in which the rich build protected enclaves while the vulnerable become the victims, is not one to which any of us can look forward with any promise of collective trust or grace.

Precisely because we do not wish for such a world, we have been engaged in deeper thinking for some time. What, we ask, are the roots of crime, its fundamental causes, the fissures and fractures in our social system? But this deeper thinking has so far failed to yield significant results. There may be a relationship between crime and unemployment. But we know that the crime rates rose, in the late 1950s and early 1960s, at a time of low unemployment and high economic growth. There may be a relationship between poverty and crime. But poorer countries than Britain have lower crime rates. There may, quite simply, be more things to steal: videos, computers, audio systems and cars. But that leaves open the question of why in some countries cars can be left unlocked, and in others even the most sophisticated security systems fail to deter. In short, the research thus far has failed to provide simple answers, perhaps rightly so since crime itself is a complex human phenomenon.

Rather than yield to despair, however, let us turn the problem on its head and ask the fundamental question: not why do some people commit crimes, but why do some people *not* commit crimes? Not why do people break the law, but why do people *keep* the law?

Framed this way, the question takes us to the very roots of our civilisation, and to its twin foundations in the Greek and biblical traditions, for it is just this issue which lies on or near the surface of much of the Hebrew Bible. It was most famously asked within Greek philosophy by Plato, in the form of the story of Gyges' ring. Suppose, he said, you had a ring which made you invisible. You could commit a crime and no one would know it was you. What would stop you? Today that remains a highly relevant question because for every hundred crimes committed, only fifty are reported, thirty recorded, seven solved and only two result in a conviction.

Plato's own answer was notoriously unsatisfactory, the response of the intellectual throughout the ages. It lay simply in knowledge. We are rational creatures and if we know that something is wrong, we will not do it. The Bible was more realistic. It knew that we are perfectly capable of doing things we know to be wrong, because we have an almost infinite capacity for convincing ourselves that they are right. The Hebrew Bible's own answer is that crimes are never undetected. They are witnessed by God before whom we will one day come for judgement.

Even the Bible, though, had to confront what the book of Psalms calls 'the fool who says in his heart there is no God', just as Aristotle had to face the problem of the weakness of the human will. Knowledge of God or the good were not in themselves sufficient. A more encompassing account had to be given of human action. What emerged from both traditions was a response so simple and profound that at most stages of our history we have simply taken it for granted. It was this.

We are, by our nature, social animals. We need societies, and therefore we need laws. The laws that govern human behaviour are unlike the laws that characterise natural phenomena. They are prescriptive rather than descriptive. They do not just happen. They need to be enforced. *How*, then, are they to be enforced?

At the core of both traditions is the fundamental principle that it is better for laws to be self-imposed than imposed by external agencies. They are transmitted from one generation to the next by habit and example. They are acquired pre-reflectively before they become the subject of reflection. They are learned in early childhood through the family and reinforced in later life through education, the community and social sanction. The rules are objective, known and shared by everyone, and a central task of society is to ensure that they are internalised by the young and thus perpetuated and adhered to over time. The entire mechanism of law-enforcement occupies only a subsidiary place in this scheme. It is what happens when the mechanism breaks down. The main burden of the system is internal, not external, restraint. Law enforcement begins in the mind, not on the street. Better to control oneself than to have to be controlled by others.

At stake in this conception is a fundamental idea about human dignity, namely that we reach our full dignity as human beings when our behaviour flows from our own decisions rather than from threats of external force. That is the difference between what Locke used to call liberty and licence. It is what Burke had in mind when he said, 'Men are qualified for civil liberty in exact proportion to their disposition to put moral chains upon their own appetites.'

Because not all of us would arrive at these laws by our own reflection, and because they must be handed on to the young before they reach the age of reflection, society depends on its mechanisms of moral transmission being in good order. That involves general consent to certain laws as expressions of the collective good. It involves the family as what sociologists call the agent of primary socialisation. And it involves a supportive role for schools, voluntary associations and local communities. Without these, the process of moral transmission will fail, and many things besides law and order will begin to disintegrate.

What has happened – and it is the single most important thing about our social environment – is that these structures have very largely broken down. The story of that breakdown has been told many times, and there is no need to rehearse it here other than to say that it is a story in two chapters. The first belongs to the history of ideas, from Kant to Nietzsche and John Stuart Mill. The second belongs to sociology and to that period in the 1960s and 1970s when ideas that had been circulating among an élite for over a century became lived reality for a whole generation. Today we live with the consequences, some good, others little short of disastrous.

We no longer believe in an objective moral order. Instead we think of the good as something to be pursued individually rather than sought collectively. Education is no longer seen as the induction of the young into the rules and virtues of society. Rather, it has become a way of helping children make private choices as individuals. Above all, we are in danger of witnessing the end of the family as a stable and persisting unit through which future generations are nurtured and internalise the rules we have so painfully arrived at on our collective journey through history. If one of the consequences has been a rise in crime among the young, *how could it be otherwise*, since we send them so few clear moral signals and are dismantling the one structure – the family – within which we can effectively do so?

Let me be clear. I am not laying the blame for the rise in crime on the breakdown of the family, still less on one-parent families. Instead I am suggesting that a complex set of interlocking processes has taken place in which the breakdown of the family has been both a consequence and an accelerating cause. In such circumstances I am reminded of the question which, according to the Talmud (*Berakhot* 32a), Moses asked God: given such a background, what should Your children have done *not* to sin?

When one in four children is born outside marriage, when one child in three grows up without a father, when four marriages in ten end in divorce, when the very concept of parental responsibility is seen as an affront to women's right to pursue careers and men's right to pursue their inclinations, when the responsibility for socialising and controlling children has been abdicated in favour of the state in the form of schools, councils, and the police, what shall some children do not to turn to crime?

Let us not underestimate the momentous significance of this change. We have deconstructed the mechanism of primary socialisation. We have abandoned the task of teaching our children a clear sense of right and wrong, perhaps because we are no longer sure that there is such a thing. When our children need us, we are not there. We have given them videos, but not our time, computer games, but not our guidance, condoms, but not an ethic of self-restraint. Who can blame them if they translate our relativist ethics into the proposition that what is right is what I feel like doing and can get away with. We have placed the full burden of the maintenance of social order on external agencies. We have moved the enforcement of law from 'in here' to 'out there'. In the name of liberating our children we have done what a future age will surely see as abandoning our children. In so doing, we have effectively turned our backs on the biblical tradition on which our conception of a free society was built.

I believe that no civilisation can go far down this road and yet survive. This is not a matter of party-political controversy, but a matter of social ecology, of the conservation of our environment of law-governed liberty.

Far more interesting than the questions a society asks about itself are the questions it pointedly does *not* ask about itself. Whereas we have had vigorous debates in Britain about the relationship between crime and the economy on the one hand, crime and law enforcement on the other, the debate we have *not* had is about the relationship between crime and the devastated moral landscape we have created for our children. Whenever it seemed to be about to begin it was shot down with Macaulay's famous remark that 'nothing is so ridiculous as the British public in one of its periodical fits of morality'.

If we cannot have this debate, then we will indeed have arrived at the stage about which Livy said, contemplating ancient Rome, 'We have reached the point where we cannot bear either our vices or their cure.' At such a point a religious voice becomes invaluable because it brings to the relativities of our time the perspective of a long ethical tradition. From that perspective, I sense the need for a prolonged and rigorous conversation between educators, judges, the police, politicians of all shades, religious leaders and parents about what we need to do to repair the broken cross-generational transmitters of moral rules and virtues.

If that conversation is to begin, one proposition must be ruled out at the outset, the proposition that has been used to silence debate thus far: namely that the stable family, and with it an objective moral order, have died like the dinosaur, never to return. This fallacy deserves to be challenged. It is not so. There are certain things that, as private individuals, we cannot change. We cannot single-handedly end unemployment, or bring world peace, or save the whale. But we *can* affect our children. Over them we have an influence greater than any pop star or politician. And a greater responsibility, because it was we who brought them into being. We severally took the family to pieces, and severally we can put it back together again.

A society in which the whole burden of law and order is placed on the police, the law courts and parliament is unsustainable. It cannot be done, nor should we wish it to be done. If we believe in personal moral responsibility, then we believe that a law-abiding society is created by the habits of self-restraint, cultivated in early childhood and reinforced thereafter by the moral signals we send. To put it simply: every law enforced in the heart means one less policeman on the street.

6

In Defence of Judgement

King Solomon, acceding to the throne, is said by the Bible to have been granted one wish. He asked not for wealth or long life or the defeat of his enemies but simply this: 'Grant Your servant a discerning heart to govern Your people and to distinguish between right and wrong.' Such has been at most times in most civilisations, not perhaps what people sought, but what they believed they *ought* to seek: discernment, wisdom, insight, understanding, judgement. In the Jewish prayer book these are the things we pray for before all else. Plato, believing that wisdom comes from reason not revelation, sought to have it enthroned in the form of philosopher-kings. Most cultures have had their wisdom literature, the sifted cumulative experience of those who had lived long, seen much, and learned to tell the difference between the desirable and the merely desired. King Solomon was not alone in knowing that even in a society with as clear a moral code as ancient Israel, there are times when it needs discernment to distinguish between right and wrong. It would be hard to find a society without its sages, and one which did not place judgement at the summit of the virtues.

Ours is one, and that is what makes it unusual, possibly unprecedented. Future historians will find one of the most remarkable features of our culture the use of the word 'judgemental' to rule out in advance the offering of moral judgement. This is not a superficial feature of our language but part of the deep structure of modern morality. Today almost any public pronouncement on personal morality will be greeted by a chorus of disapproval. When a Church leader recently criticised adultery on the part of figures in public life, he was subject to a torrent of abuse, in some cases by other religious leaders. Adultery was acceptable; judgement was not. The stand taken by politicians and academics of different shades in defence of the family has been routinely greeted as a group libel against single mothers and working wives. When the age of homosexual consent was recently lowered, a journalist on *The Times* – himself a homosexual – lamented that the victory had been won without a fight.

Where, he asked, was the voice of reasoned opposition? The answer is obvious: it had been intimidated into silence. Nietzsche, the anti-moralist, has won and we have undergone what he called the 'transvaluation of values'. What other ages saw as the supreme virtue, we see as a vice. Judgement has become taboo, and to believe otherwise is, as Michael Novak puts it, to 'risk excommunication from the mainstream'.

This attitude is based on a fallacy, and one which is in need of exposure. The word 'judgement' has two distinct, if related, meanings. The first is what we are looking for when we seek advice. We seek wisdom, experience, sagacity. Whether the counsel we wish for is moral or practical, we turn to those who have had long and successful encounters with the problem at hand. Whether we go to a tennis coach or a master craftsman or a lawyer, the very act of taking advice presupposes that there is excellence within an activity and that it is learned rather than immediately acquired. If this applies to specialised compartments of human behaviour, how much more so does it apply to life itself taken as a whole. There may not be – indeed there is not – a single model of the good life. Even in a world as cohesive and structured as eighteenth-century East European Jewry, you went to Vilna for scholarship, to Mezerich for mysticism, and to Lubavitch for piety. But within each form of life there are exemplars and sages, and consensus tells us who they are. When we seek judgement in this sense, what we want is something forward looking, the bringing to bear of considered experience on decisions we have to make. It responds to the request, 'Tell me what to do', or 'Show me how to do it'.

But there is judgement in a second sense, a metaphorical extension of what judges do in court. They pass a verdict. They acquit or condemn. Moral judgement in this second sense is, as it were, passing a sentence on what we or other people have done. It is backward looking, after the event. It is about *this* that we have hesitations. Who are we to pass a verdict on other people's lives, and who are they to pass sentence on ours? This reservation is well-founded. Judgement assumes authority, and the sources of moral authority have become unclear in our time. It assumes a shared set of standards, and perhaps in a diverse society there is no such thing. Besides which, moral judgement seems to presuppose knowledge that none of us has. How are we to administer blame until we know the motives and intentions of the agent, things of which he himself may not be fully aware? Judges and juries *have* to come to a decision about such things on the basis of the available evidence. But that is what makes legal and moral judgement different. Law is a practical compromise, the best we can do given that we have to do something. But morality seems to admit of no such compromise. When it comes to moral rather than legal guilt, only God can be the judge.

So we are reluctant to be judgemental in this second sense. But *so we always were*, or were taught to be. The Judaeo-Christian tradition is full of admonitions against it. 'Do not judge your fellow human being until you have been in his place', said the rabbis. 'Judge all people in the scale of merit', and 'One who calls for judgement against his neighbour is punished first.' The Christian tradition warned, 'Judge not that ye be not judged', and 'Let him who is without sin cast the first stone.' Both traditions spoke against hypocrisy and self-righteousness. Both valued generosity and forgiveness in human relationships. When the sons of Jacob feared that their brother Joseph, whom they sought to kill and eventually sold into slavery, would take revenge, he replied, 'Am I in the place of God? You intended to harm me, but God intended it for good.' That sublime note, on which the book of Genesis ends, is the common ideal of both faiths. So reticence in passing judgement is not new. It is one of our oldest moral traditions.

What is new is the confusion of one kind of judgement with the other. Most of those who speak in defence of moral principle are seeking not to condemn but to guide. That has always been the responsibility of one generation to the next, to set out the map of human relationships and point out the places of danger, the glaciers and quicksands and marshes, as well as the points where the view is worth the climb. To fail to do this – to send off children or pupils on a journey without a map on the grounds that this will inhibit their choice – would in any other civilisation be seen as a dereliction of duty of the worst kind. I believe it is in our case as well. Why has it happened?

In large measure it has been the combined impact of two fateful modern ideas: the relativity of morality and the quasi-scientific explanation of human behaviour. We know more clearly than our ancestors that other people do things differently. Thirty years ago you could walk along the sea front in Southend and see one café after another offering the same fish and chips. Today the average supermarket offers a choice of cuisine from West India to China. And what applies to food applies to moralities. Instead of a single tradition we are faced with lifestyle options. So morality becomes a matter of taste and choice, and *de gustibus non est disputandum*: there is no point in asking an expert which to prefer.

If the significance of choice has been expanded in one direction, it has been contracted in another. A whole range of human sciences – biological, sociological, physiological and psychological – has been constructed on the idea that what we do is caused rather than chosen. It has its origins in external forces, not the human will. So our behaviour is not the proper subject of praise or blame, and the concept of moral responsibility has been placed in doubt. We are what our genes or early childhood or human instinct or social class have made us, and if we are to change what people do, we must change those external forces rather than address the responsible self, for there is no such thing. The dual impact of moral relativism and scientific determinism has been to weaken the metaphor of the journey and the map. For on this interpretation of the human condition there is no map and no considered journey, only our unchosen desires and the techniques of satisfying them.

I believe this to be a disastrously diminished view of human life, and moreover, few of us believe it. Which of us, faced with a plumber who does not show up, or a lawyer who gives us the wrong advice, seriously believes that no one is to blame; that it is genetic determinism or maternal deprivation? Which of us would defend wife-battering on the grounds that there are cultures in which it is a male prerogative, even a legitimate assertion of patriarchal authority? Blessedly, we are neither determinists nor relativists. We know that people can be disadvantaged in different ways, and we work to minimise them. But we also know that human will triumphs over circumstance. We know that different civilisations have their own moral conventions. But we know brutality and injustice when we see them, and we do not defend them because they have their own cultural integrity. The illusion of relativity may be fostered by television programmes on ethical dilemmas to which ten experts give ten different answers. But we know that the existence of hard cases does not prove that all cases are hard, any more than the existence of grey refutes black and white.

What has added to our confusion, however, has been a blurring of the boundaries between politics and morality, most notably in the failure to keep apart the quite different concepts of 'right' and 'rights'. Not everything that we *have* a right to do *are* we right to do. The first is a matter of politics, the second, of morality. We have a legal right to be rude but it remains morally wrong. We have a right to do what the law of the land does not forbid. But within the range of legally permitted acts are some which are morally right, some wrong and others neutral. How could we confuse the two? Yet confusion there is.

Much of it is the legacy of John Stuart Mill. More than most, Mill found Victorian society deeply oppressive. He wrote a famous tract, *On Liberty*, in which he argued against what he called, following de Tocqueville, the 'tyranny of the majority'. Liberty, he argued, depends not only on the form of government but on its limits. Democracy could threaten freedom if it meant that the majority passed laws which excessively intruded into private life. The principle he advocated was that 'The only purpose for which power can be rightfully exercised over any member of a civilised community, against his will, is to prevent harm to others.' A century after he wrote it, that argument was victorious throughout the democracies of the West, as one country after another liberalised laws relating to divorce, abortion and homosexuality. The result was – or should have been – to open a gap between law and morality. Acts might be wrong, but it was against the principle of a free society to punish them with the force of law. Legal right and moral right became two quite separate things.

However, Mill went significantly further. He argued that not only laws could be oppressive; so could public opinion. We can be as inhibited by censure as by a court of law:

Protection, therefore, against the tyranny of the magistrate is not enough: there needs protection also against the tyranny of the prevailing opinion and feeling; against the tendency of society to impose, by means other than civil penalties, its own ideas and practices as rules of conduct on those who dissent from them.

Society should refrain from judgement. In this further step, Mill was wrong, even incoherent. For if a society has any moral principles at all, it will seek to inculcate them. And it cannot do so without holding up some conduct for approval and some for disapproval. To call this a form of tyranny is stretching language beyond the bounds of sense. It is one thing to sentence a writer to death for blasphemy, quite another to express moral outrage and censure. The one is a clear limitation on freedom. The other is one of its inevitable conditions. There can be no experiment without risk, nor can we eliminate from the moral life the occasional need for courage. It was not tyranny that Stravinsky experienced when his audience booed the first performance of 'The Rite of Spring'. It is not tyranny when we express our disapproval of a way of life. Without disapproval there can be no approval, and hence no moral teaching, and hence no moral community.

The greatest of modern libertarians, Friedrich Hayek, said that for Mill, 'freedom means chaos'. He added:

Whether or not we wish to call coercion those milder forms of pressure that society applies to nonconformists, there can be little question that these moral rules and conventions that possess less binding power than the law have an important and even indispensable role to perform and probably do as much to facilitate life in society as do the strict rules of law.

Despite this, Mill's second argument today holds sway, in the form of violent antipathy to public expressions of traditional moral judgement. Had Mill foreseen how his essay had given rise to the concept of 'political correctness' he would have been appalled, for what he saw as the tyranny of the majority has been replaced by the tyranny of an influential intellectual minority. The political battle for legal rights has been succeeded by the moral battle to render 'lifestyle choices' immune to criticism: to turn what I *have* a right to do into what I *am* right to do. This is intolerance in the name of tolerance, and will indeed lead, unchecked, to chaos.

'Civilisation', Jacob Neusner has written, 'hangs suspended, from generation to generation, by the gossamer strand of memory. If only one cohort of mothers and fathers fails to convey to its children what it has learned from its parents, then the great chain of learning and wisdom snaps.' We owe it to our children, as parents, to our pupils, as teachers, and to our fellow citizens, as heirs to a civilisation, to hand on what we have learned. Just as we fight for the conservation of ancient buildings so we must fight for the conservation of moral traditions. Just as we protest the destruction of rain-forests, so we must protest the destruction of the institutions which sustain our moral environment. That is the imperative of moral judgement: not to blame but to build, not to condemn but to guide. And if it now needs courage, we owe it no less.

7
Law, Morality and the Common Good

The Hebrew Bible paints a strange picture of the people of the covenant. The Israelites emerge from its pages as a stiff-necked and backsliding
people, often lapsing into idolatry and dissent. A detached reader of the
Bible must find himself asking: why did God choose this people from
among all others to be His special witnesses? The book of Genesis answers
this question at only one point, and the answer is striking. Genesis 18:19
tells us that God said of Abraham: 'I have chosen him so that he will
instruct his children and his household after him to keep the way of the
Lord by doing what is right [*tzedek*] and just [*mishpat*].' *Tzedek* and
mishpat are both legal virtues. We might best translate them, respectively,
as distributive and procedural justice.

The verse suggests that whatever else Abraham's children might do or
not do, they would respect the ideals of justice and the rule of law. This,
the Bible implies, is a transcending virtue, one that may compensate for
many shortcomings. And this is surely a cardinal feature of the Hebrew
Bible and of the Jewish contribution to civilisation ever since: the belief
that a people, a nation and a society are judged by the extent to which
justice and the rule of law prevail. Few religions have placed law and its
just administration so close to the heart of its concerns.

Throughout the Pentateuch we find repeated injunctions to this end.
'Judges and officers shalt thou make thee in all thy gates . . . and they
shall judge the people with righteous judgement . . . Justice, justice shalt
thou pursue that thou mayest live' (Deuteronomy 16:18–20). Moses, in
appointing judges, tells them to 'Hear the causes between your brethren,
and judge righteously between a man and his brother, and the stranger
that is with him. You shall not respect persons in judgement. You shall
hear the small and the great alike. You shall not be afraid of the face of
any man, for judgement belongs to God' (Deuteronomy 1:16–17).

At the core of the covenant is a magnificent legal code which reaches

---

The 1993 Warburton Lecture, Lincoln's Inn, London, 16 June 1993

its most exalted expression in the Ten Commandments communicated by God Himself to the assembled Israelites at Mount Sinai. In the prophetic books the rule of law becomes a momentous and moving vision: 'Let justice roll down like a river, and righteousness as a never-ending stream' (Amos 5:24).

Never has this idea lost its power or relevance. For such seems to be the unalterable or at least not yet altered constitution of human nature – that we are prone to conflict. And unless regulated by law, conflict finds its resolution in violence, war, tyranny, inequity, the defence of privilege, the oppression of the powerless, and the substitution of might – economic, political or military – for right. Against all these, the Hebrew Bible offers the alternative of law, a law that treats great and small alike, that owes its ultimate authority to a power beyond all earthly rulers, a law that bears the signature of transcendence.

Although this noble proposition has since become the shared property of human civilisation, Paul Johnson rightly reminds us of its origin:

Certainly the world without the Jews would have been a radically different place. Humanity might eventually have stumbled upon all the Jewish insights. But we cannot be sure. All the great conceptual discoveries of the intellect seem obvious and inescapable once they have been revealed, but it requires a special genius to formulate them for the first time. The Jews had this gift. To them we owe the idea of equality before the law, both divine and human; of the sanctity of life and the dignity of the human person; of the individual conscience and so of personal redemption; of the collective conscience and so of social responsibility; of peace as an abstract ideal and love as the foundation of justice, and many other items which constitute the basic moral furniture of the human mind. Without the Jews it might have been a much emptier place.

The Minimalist Conception of Law

Having paid this tribute to law and the Hebrew Bible and the relationship between them, I want to focus on a subject which has been the cause of much debate, not only in our time, but at many other critical junctures in civilisation. I refer to the *scope* of law and its role in society, to law's place in the ultimate scheme of things.

I want to contrast two conceptions of law, one exemplified by the Jewish tradition, the other known to it and indeed accepted by it, but not as an ideal. I call them, respectively, the *maximalist* and *minimalist* interpretations, and these terms will become clearer as we proceed. Doubtless, no actual legal system conforms to either of these two idealised types, but I present them as contrasts for the sake of clarity. I begin with the

44

system Jews did *not* adopt for themselves, although they recognised its validity and at times its necessity, namely the minimalist conception of law.

My starting point is the Mishnaic tractate of *Avot*, known as the 'Ethics of the Fathers', an anthology compiled in the first half of the third century of the Common Era, though its component texts have an earlier origin. The rabbis quoted in *Avot* took a sceptical view of public life. 'Be careful in your dealings with the ruling powers', said the sages, 'for they only befriend a man when it serves their purposes, but they do not stand by him in his hour of need' (*Avot* 2:5). None the less they recognised the need for government and the rule of law, and they did so in the form of a famous statement. 'Rabbi Hanina the deputy High Priest used to say: Pray for the welfare of the government, for were it not that people stood in fear of it, they would swallow one another alive' (*Avot* 3:2).

On the face of it this is an early anticipation of Thomas Hobbes' description of society in a state of nature: a war of all against all in which life would be, in his phrase, 'nasty, brutish and short'. However, a close examination of the text reveals a peculiar poignancy to Rabbi Hanina's remarks. A manuscript reading of the Mishnah yields a text in which Rabbi Hanina's statement appears not in the third but in the first person: not 'they' but '*we* would have swallowed up each other alive'.

To understand the significance of this detail we must recall Rabbi Hanina's formal office: deputy High Priest. This allows us to date his remark with some precision. Rabbi Hanina lived during the last days of the second Temple, in the second half of the first century CE. He officiated there. He was a senior member of the priesthood. We can now sense the full pathos of his dictum.

Rabbi Hanina lived through the destruction of the second Temple by the Romans, one of the greatest catastrophes to have befallen the Jewish people. It led to nearly nineteen centuries of dispersion, powerlessness and persecution. We know from Josephus, however, that while the Romans were at the gates, within the walls of the besieged Jerusalem a divided Jewish people was engaged in bitter and self-destructive civil war.

The government of which Rabbi Hanina spoke was not a Jewish government but none other than the Roman power which had desecrated Judaism's Holy of Holies and destroyed its central religious institutions. None the less, he prayed for its welfare and urged others to do so. For he had seen, within Jerusalem besieged, the terrifying spectacle of life without law, the war of all against all. Any law is better than no law. Hence the minimalist definition of law as the instrument which prevents us from swallowing each other alive, or as John Stuart Mill was to put it eighteen centuries later: 'The only purpose for which power can rightfully be exercised over any member of a civilised community against his will is to prevent harm to others.'

Mill arrived at this conclusion in a book entitled *On Liberty*. He believed that the cause of liberty was best served by having as little law as possible, or at least by marking out certain territories as being – as the Wolfenden Committee on Homosexuality put it – 'crudely and simply not the law's business'. But this is not the only or even the most helpful way of reaching the conclusion. Jews, for example, have always cherished liberty since the exodus from slavery in Egypt. None the less, for Judaism freedom is not achieved by restricting the scope of law. It is precisely a life lived *within* the law, a law that covers all aspects of life.

A more helpful way of understanding the minimalist conception is that it arises in a society in which the concept of a common good, promulgated by the central institutions and educational structures of its culture, has eroded or is beginning to erode. We have seen one way in which this can happen. There were few values held in common by the deputy High Priest Hanina and the Roman government which had destroyed his people's Temple. There is another way in which it can happen. A society can move to a less collective, more individualistic sense of morality. Such was beginning to be the case in 1859 when Mill wrote his treatise on liberty, and the process has continued unabated to this day.

Under either circumstance, an extensive system of laws can come to seem an unwarrantable intrusion into the lives of individuals, minority groups or subject populations. Law is necessary, but it should be kept to a minimum, defined as the prevention of harm to others. It is an infringement on liberty. Therefore, though there must be law, there should be as little as possible, at any rate in matters where we regard liberty as of the essence, especially those involving moral judgement.

A Maximalist Conception of Law

Against this I want to contrast the Judaic view of Jewish law, one that I will call a maximalist conception. I refer here to a set of beliefs with a long and continuous history, originating in the Pentateuch, echoed in other books of the Bible and given consistent expression in the rabbinic literature from the first centuries of the Common Era to today.

This view can be characterised in three propositions. The first is this. Not only does the religion of the Hebrew Bible contain laws which carry the legislative authority of God himself, but it is *through law* that God chooses to reveal Himself to mankind. When God speaks to the assembled Israelites at Mount Sinai and to Moses at other times, what He communicates is not oracles about the future nor metaphysical truths about the nature of reality but *Torah*, law, and *mitzvot*, commandments.

To be sure, God in the Hebrew Bible is a God of miracles, redemption and grace. He intervenes in history, rescues His people and offers them – if they will live by His law – protection and prosperity. But this is, as it were, secondary to the essence of the covenant, about which Moses reminds the people in these words:

See, I have taught you decrees and laws as the Lord my God commanded me, so that you may follow them in the land you are entering . . . Observe them carefully, for this will show your wisdom and understanding to the nations who will hear about all these decrees and say, 'Surely this great nation is a wise and understanding people' . . . What other nation is so great as to have such righteous decrees and laws as this body of laws I am setting before you this day? (Deuteronomy 4:5–8).

Psalm 199 presents this same proposition from the perspective of personal spirituality:

I will always obey your law, for ever and ever. I will walk about in freedom, for I have sought out Your precepts. I will speak of Your statutes before kings and will not be put to shame, for I delight in your commandments because I love them (Psalm 119:44–7).

Two striking expressions of this view are to be found in statements of the early rabbinic sages in the Babylonian and Jerusalem Talmuds. One declares: 'From the day the Temple was destroyed, the Holy One, blessed be he, has nothing in this world except the four cubits of law.' The other attributes to God the statement: 'Would that My children forsake Me and yet occupy themselves in the study of My law, for the light it contains would bring them back to Me.' In short: *if we seek God we will find Him in law*. Admittedly, God reveals himself in nature and history as well. But neither nature nor history point as unambiguously to the existence of God as does law.

The second proposition, and perhaps the single greatest contribution of Israel to the religious heritage of mankind, is what is often called ethical monotheism: the idea that God is not merely the author of the moral law but is Himself bound by it. It is this that gives rise to some of the most awe-inspiring passages in the Bible in which Moses, Jeremiah, Job and others argue with God on the basis of the shared code of justice and mercy which binds both creature and Creator, reaching a climax in the question of Abraham: 'Shall the Judge of all the earth not do justice?'

For Judaism, the connection between religion, law and morality is this. God and man come together to form a covenant which binds both to a morality which each recognises as righteous and just, much as two partners come together to form a marriage which both recognise as imposing obligations. Neither God nor man arbitrarily invent morality, just as neither husband nor wife invent marriage. By entering into a covenant, both agree to bind themselves to one another within its terms. Thus love is translated into a moral relationship whose terms are law.

So there is a substantive relationship between God and law, and between law and morality. Admittedly, it is loose rather than precise. There is much law in the Bible whose content we could call ritual, not moral. And there is much morality in the Bible – such as Leviticus' command to love one's neighbour as oneself – which is not articulated in the form of a detailed code of law. But the connection is of the essence of religious life.

The picture set forth in the Bible is not one of *legal positivism*, in which, to quote Austin, 'The existence of the law is one thing; its merit or demerit is another.' Nor is it one of *natural law*, in which obligation flows from human nature. Law, as portrayed in the Bible, is *covenantal*. It is born in the mutual agreement of God and humanity to engage in constructing a society on the foundations of compassion, righteousness and justice.

The third and most distinctive feature of Judaism is the connection between law and *education*. It can best be expressed in the proposition that Judaism expects its adherents not merely to obey the law, but to be lawyers: *students* of the law. Indeed this is one of the meanings of the phrase in which God, in giving the Ten Commandments to Israel, calls on them to become a 'kingdom of priests'. For the priest in biblical times was not only one who served in the Temple but also one who acted as a judge and instructed the people in the law.

In a biblical passage which Jews recite several times daily, we are told: 'You shall teach these [laws] diligently to your children, speaking of them when you sit at home and when you travel on a journey, when you lie down and when you rise up.' On the brink of exodus from Egypt, Moses instructs the Israelites not merely in a variety of laws, but also in how to teach and explain these laws to their children in generations to come. From the days of Ezra, if not before, the heroes of Israel have been its teachers. And by the first century of the Common Era, Jews had established the first system of free, compulsory and universal education known to history – an education first and foremost in the law.

The question is why. Here we can only speculate, but the reason seems straightforward. Inescapably there is a conflict between the rule of law and individual freedom. A civilisation can resolve this conflict in a variety of ways. It can place a low value on the rule of law, and thus favour anarchy. It can place a low value on individual liberty, and thus favour tyranny. It can make a third choice, the one favoured by John Stuart Mill, H L A Hart, Ronald Dworkin and other liberal thinkers, which is to say that liberty is a supreme if not always overriding value, and that therefore the domain of law should be restricted in areas where personal choice is particularly important. As Dworkin puts it in his recent book, *Life's Dominion*: 'Whatever view we take about abortion and euthanasia, we want the right to decide for ourselves, and we should therefore be ready to insist that any honourable constitution, any genuine constitution of principle, will guarantee that right for everyone.'

Dworkin presents this as a conclusion to which any reasonable individual would be forced. But in one respect I believe he is wrong. The Hebrew Bible places a high, even a supreme, value on the individual and on freedom. The individual is, as the first chapter of Genesis states, made in the image of God. As the Mishnah puts it: 'One who saves a single life is as if he saved an entire universe.' Freedom, too, is of the essence of serving God. Israel's history begins with an act of liberation, and the laws of the Sabbath, the Sabbatical and Jubilee years and the many laws providing aid to the poor are all practical expressions of a social order designed to minimise the varieties of enslavement. So the Bible sets a high value on the individual and on freedom, but *it sets an equally high value on law*. How then does it reconcile the apparent conflict between these principles?

The answer lies in a particular concept of education, one sharply at odds with prevailing moral fashion but which can be found in Aristotle and until relatively recently might even have been described as self-evident. On this view education is not simply a matter of imparting information, inculcating skills and training the individual to make autonomous choices. Instead, it is a matter of *inducting successive generations into the society in which they will become participants*. It involves transmitting a particular society's history, norms and 'habits of the heart'. Education is an *apprenticeship in being a citizen*. It is a process of learning certain rules and then internalising them so that the law is no longer an external constraint but becomes, in Jeremiah's phrase, a law 'written in our inmost being and

49

inscribed upon our hearts' (Jeremiah 31:33). Law then represents not a set of regulations but that configuration of character that the Aristotelian and Maimonidean traditions call virtue.

The Judaic connection between law and education is this: that only when our sensibilities are educated by the law can we associate the law with freedom rather than with constraint, and say with the Psalmist, 'I will walk about in freedom, for I have sought out Your precepts.' Teaching, instruction or education – understood as the transmission of a moral tradition across the generations – resolves the conflict between liberty and law without forcing us to choose between anarchy and tyranny. Law is seen as part of a moral order which, to the extent that it is internalised as self-restraint, does not need to be enforced by external agencies such as police, courts and punishment. Education becomes the guardian of liberty, because it maximises the degree to which civil society is sustained by self-imposed restraints and minimises the degree to which we depend on the intervention of outside force. The more law is inscribed upon our hearts, the less it needs to be policed in the streets.

This, then, is the portrait of law we find in the Bible. To this I add one final observation. For there is an obvious question to be raised. Why does the Hebrew Bible emphasise law more than (though it does not neglect) individual salvation and private faith? Surely law is a highly secular phenomenon. It deals in matters of this world, the original meaning of the Latin *saecularis*. Religion, surely, is a private transaction within the soul and bears only tangentially on legislation, crime, punishment and the social order?

The answer, I believe, is this. The Hebrew Bible portrays God as One concerned above all with how we behave towards others. God is to be found in relationships, and relationships take place within the framework of society and its institutions and rules. Faith is thus linked with morality, and morality is an essentially shared, collaborative endeavour. Its smallest unit is the family, its largest unit is humanity, and between them lies a variety of communities from the neighbourhood to the nation state. What morality is not and cannot be is a private enterprise, a form of self-expression. What liberal individualism takes as the highest virtue – each person doing that which is right in his own eyes – is for the Bible (Deuteronomy 12:8, Judges 17:6; 21:25) the absence or abdication of virtue, and indeed a way of describing the disintegration of society.

Morality and Law

This takes us directly to the present. In 1959, Lord Devlin delivered a lecture which subsequently became the basis of much discussion, entitled 'Morals and the Criminal Law'. In it he said this:

Societies disintegrate from within more frequently than they are broken up by external pressures. There is disintegration when no common morality is observed and history shows that the loosening of moral bonds is often the first stage of disintegration, so that society is justified in taking the same steps to preserve its moral code as it does to preserve its government and other essential institutions.

That argument was rejected, and since then many laws thought to have a moral or religious basis have been repealed or liberalised. But something else has happened, almost without comment. What provoked Lord Devlin's response was a sentence in the report of the Wolfenden Committee (1957) which said this: 'Unless a deliberate attempt is to be made by society, acting through the agency of the law, to equate the sphere of crime with that of sin, there must remain a realm of private morality and immorality which is, in brief and crude terms, not the law's business.' The report then added, by way of postscript, 'To say this is not to condone or encourage private immorality.'

Let me say, lest I be misunderstood, that on the substantive point I agree with Wolfenden. Jewish law itself draws a clear distinction between matters to be adjudicated by a human court and those where judgement is the exclusive prerogative of God. However, subsequent experience has shown one thing to be false, namely the assumption that you can change the law while leaving morality untouched. The authors of the Report evidently believed that homosexuality could cease to be a crime while remaining in the public mind a sin. It would no longer be punished; it would merely be denounced. Morality would not be enforced by law. It would instead be reinforced by teaching and preaching.

That attractive prospect has proved to be unfounded. The extent to which changes in the law set in motion a wholly unforeseen series of developments can best be measured by this fact: that were the authors of the Wolfenden Report to repeat today that certain sexual behaviours whilst not criminal are nonetheless sinful, they would find themselves banned from most British classrooms and American universities on the grounds of 'homophobia'. The liberalisation of the law has led to an astonishingly rapid eclipse of the very idea that there are shared moral norms. What a single generation ago was the avant garde of radical liberalism would today be seen as the politically incorrect face of moral fundamentalism.

We are all too familiar with the consequences. An environment in which moral judgement is condemned as being judgemental, in which the one concept to have universal currency is that of rights but in which there are no agreed criteria by which to adjudicate between conflicting rights, in which the idea has become an orthodoxy that there is no sexual ethic beyond the consistent application of personal choice, has caused the disintegration of one after another of the bases of our shared moral universe. In such an environment there can be no moral authority beyond the self or the sect of the like-minded. There can be no moral institutions, such as that of the family, in which obligations self-evidently override personal preference. There can be no moral role-models who epitomise our collective values and virtues, because we are too divided to reach a consensus on whether to prefer Mother Teresa to Madonna. There can, in short, be nothing beyond the random aggregation of individuals and groups living in accidental proximity, each with its own lifestyle, each claiming our attention for the duration of a sound-bite. The moral voice has been replaced by noise, coherence by confusion, and society itself by a series of discreet particles called individuals.

It is as if, in the 1950s and 1960s, without intending to, we had set a time-bomb ticking which would eventually explode the moral framework into fragments. The human cost has been colossal, most visibly in terms of marriage and the family. There has been a proliferation of one-parent families, deserted wives and neglected and abused children. But the cost has been far wider in terms of the loss of authority, institutions in crisis, and what Durkheim called *anomie*, the loss of a public sense of moral order.

It is precisely at such times that an immense burden is placed upon the law, law specifically in the minimalist sense I described above. Law at such points in the history of civilisation is seen not as the expression of something wider and deeper, what Leslie Stephen described as 'the seal on the wax of moral sentiment'. Rather it is seen as an external constraint, limited to the prevention of harm to others. But because our internal constraints have been eroded, the police, the courts and Parliament are hard pressed to contain the tide of crime. And because we no longer have a shared moral code, the law is called on to decide what has become effectively undecidable, namely what *constitutes* harm to others. Does abortion? Does the withdrawal of a life-support machine? Does the destruction of an embryo created by *in vitro* fertilisation?

We turn to the law to answer such questions for us, as Americans have recently turned to the law to tell them what constitutes sexual harassment or adequate fatherhood. But the law no longer reflects moral consensus because there is no consensus for it to reflect. The law is placed in an increasingly invidious situation as we expect more from it and as society's moral code and institutions give it less and less support. The law becomes our only authority in an age which is hostile to authority as such. The result is the situation described in the opening words of the book of Ruth, conventionally translated as 'In the days when the judges judged', but which rabbinic tradition translated as 'In the days when society judged its judges'.

We are, I believe, at a difficult time for religion, morality and the law. There is only a fine line dividing liberalism from individualism, and freedom from the disintegration of the concept of the common good. My own view is this. Though I value the contribution of liberalism to the opening up of society to a multitude of voices, we are in danger of finding ourselves having gone too far in abandoning the idea of society as a shared moral project, and this will have tragic consequences for both our public and our private lives. There are things we cannot achieve without collaborative effort framed by shared rules, roles and virtues. Among them are peace, compassion, justice, and the resolution of conflict in a way that both sides can see as fair. These are the very things by which, according to the Hebrew Bible, God judges that most risky of His undertakings: the creation of mankind.

We cannot undo what we have done. Having de-legislated large sectors of morality we cannot re-legislate them. The necessary consent has gone and there is no point in moral nostalgia, fondly remembering the days when you could go out leaving your front door unlocked. But we can summon the courage to rebuild a moral consensus, beginning with that most fundamental of questions: what sort of world would we wish to bequeath to our children and grandchildren?

I believe that the law needs and deserves this from all who have moral influence in our society, not least from religious leaders. We must have the courage to make judgements, to commend some ways of life and point to the shortcomings of others, however much this offends against the canons of our non-judgemental culture. We must lead by moral vision and example, and be prepared to challenge the icons of individualism, the idolatry of our age.

My argument, then, is this. At a certain point in the history of civilisations, a moral consensus breaks down. The connection between law and morality becomes problematic, and an attempt is made to solve the problem by conceiving law in minimalist terms. It is there to do no more than to prevent harm to others, to prevent us, in Rabbi Hanina's words, from swallowing one another alive. The passage of time, however, invariably exposes the contradiction at the heart of this idea. Law is left to solve problems which it cannot solve alone. We then painfully rediscover the ancient truth of the Hebrew Bible, that the rule of law is compatible with a sense of personal liberty only when supported by at least some collective moral code and by an educational system which allows successive generations to internalise it. Society cannot live by law alone. It needs our common commitment to the common good.

8

Faith in the Community

The question that haunted the 1993 party conference season was the one no one asked. Do we have faith in the political system any more? Do we believe that a government – *any* government – can solve the problems by which it is beset?

In my lifetime political authority has rarely seemed more tenuous than it does now. The leaders of the major parties face internal divisions. Survey after survey reveals disenchantment with politicians of all shades. Newspaper columns are filled with meditations on the nature of the elusive quality called leadership. And if one message has sounded more loudly than any other, it is the call for a political vision, domestic or international, that would lend coherence to what otherwise seems destined to be a troubled and confusing decade.

I sense among the young people I meet in schools and youth groups something I have not met with before: cynicism and an absence of hope, as if, every political alternative having been tried and failed, an expectation of things getting better is bound to be disappointed.

Beneath this disillusionment is a specific and seemingly unanswerable dilemma. The 1980s were the decade in which we lost faith in the State as the vehicle of salvation. Neither socialism nor communism delivered what they had promised. Collectivist economies inhibited growth, which alone could pay for the services provided by the State.

There was an alternative, and it captured imaginations not only in Britain and America but even, dramatically, in the erstwhile Soviet Union precipitating its collapse. What we could not achieve collectively as states we could achieve privately as individuals. The State would withdraw, leaving private initiative and the free market to produce and distribute goods. Most people would benefit from greater wealth and the freedom

---

The Daily Telegraph, 2 October 1993

55

to spend it as they chose. The minimalist State would limit itself to providing a safety net for those in dire need.

For a time this was a compelling vision. But the 1990s have been marked by a growing sense of its shortcomings. Major social ills continue unabated. Unemployment is high. Crime figures still rise. Our expectations of health and welfare services outgrow our ability to fund them. The inner cities still fester. There are persistent, even growing sectors of under-privilege and disadvantage. And despite the best efforts of race relations policies, ethnic tensions remain.

Not only this, but the institutions which framed our public life and gave us a sense of national belonging have come under massive assault. None has been spared: the monarchy, the government, the Church, the courts. A decade of individualism has taken a heavy toll of the traditions by which our collective identity was given shape. It would be hard, today, to describe what being British is, in any terms other than nostalgia for a long-vanished past.

From where, then, is a new vision of Britain in the 1990s to emerge? Neither collectivism nor individualism seems to have worked. We are caught between the interventionist and the minimalist State, knowing the failings of both, and without a third alternative. The major parties battle, internally and against one another, over the precise balance to be struck between the two. But this is not a debate from which we can expect a new language of politics equal to the challenges of the 1990s.

In 1990 I argued, in my Reith Lectures, for the third and missing term in our political vocabulary. I called it *community*, by which I mean any voluntary association of people larger than the individual and smaller than the State. The smallest unit of community is the family, and it extends to cover such diverse phenomena as charitable organisations, religious congregations, neighbourhood watch schemes, local race relations groups and parent-teacher associations.

The community is as potent a factor in the life of society as either the individual or the State. But it has been given short shrift in our political discourse. Unjustly so, because it is in these associations that we acquire the virtues that sustain our common life: duty, honesty, service, self-sacrifice, integrity, neighbourliness, fortitude and civility. Without these, the workings of the market are too impersonal and arbitrary to sustain a sense of shared belonging.

Society as the arena of private choice is a very harsh place for those who make the wrong choices. The shift from State to individual at a time when communities are being eroded has carried a high price in poverty, homelessness, broken families and the drug abuse, vandalism and violence that accompany the loss of meaning. The political domain becomes a place where there are winners and losers, and where there is nothing to give the losers hope.

The Thatcherite vision which so dominated the 1980s had power because it spoke lucidly to one source of human motivation: economic self-advancement. The drive to work, create and retain the fruits of one's activity are immensely energising. The prospect of lower taxation, and more widely distributed home and share ownership spoke to the real concerns of an entire generation.

But Thatcherism was vague, even self-contradictory, at a critical point. Margaret Thatcher herself knew, along with democratic capitalists since de Tocqueville, that liberty, democracy and the workings of the free market are built on moral foundations larger than self-interest. They are sustained by the family and other institutions and traditions which human-ise the effects of competitive striving and provide a critical counterbalance to its unequal rewards.

Margaret Thatcher herself placed immense weight on the family as the matrix of social as well as individual responsibility. In this, I believe she was right. But at the very time she was doing so, the family itself was disintegrating at unprecedented speed, with cohabitation, divorce and single-parenthood rapidly becoming not the exception but the norm. Nor was this accidental, for it was a direct consequence of the individualism that so marked the Thatcher years.

The time has come to re-explore the moral basis of society as a com-munity of communities. Such an exploration would focus less on the two terms that have dominated modern political debate – liberty as against equality – than on the neglected word fraternity. It would speak less of rights than of duties, and less of justice than of citizenship. It would see the political order as founded on something stronger than a social con-tract, namely a *covenant*, a commitment to the common good. It would see *homo politicus* as something other than an economic animal, driven by production and consumption.

What those involved in communities know is that there are other sources of human motivation no less powerful than self-interest. I am regularly amazed at the sheer motive force of the human desire to help others and to be involved in projects for the common good.

I have seen a secondary school of streetwise teenagers transformed by a challenge to provide help for a mother in need of assistance for an operation for her child. I have seen senior, hard-pressed businessmen devote large sections of their time to welfare, educational and medical causes. I have seen congregations turn themselves into support groups for the unemployed, giving them hope and practical expertise. These are sources of energy which Britain badly needs if it is to remain a society in which we feel proud to live.

For the foreseeable future, we will be beset by social problems which will yield neither to State intervention nor to private initiative. The missing third alternative is the new partnership waiting to be forged between politicians, religious bodies and voluntary organisations to empower local associations where the civic virtues are practised and learned. Underlying it would be a concept of society as the place where, in local contexts, we bring our diverse talents and traditions as gifts to the collective good.

There are problems that neither the State nor the individual can solve. Our political vocabulary must now widen to encompass a vision of Britain as a community of communities.

9

Putting Duties to Rights

For some time now, there has been a perceptible change in the language of British politics. A new agenda for the Nineties is beginning to form, and its protagonists can be found on both sides of the political divide. Its themes are the family, community and the renewal of the bonds of interconnectedness that make up civil society. Increasingly, politicians have felt the need to enter territory that was traditionally the preserve of moralists and religious leaders.

The debate is bound to be sharpened by David Selbourne's new book, *The Principle of Duty*. Selbourne argues that what has destroyed our political culture has been an over-insistence on rights at the expense of responsibilities. What is now needed is a politics of duty enforced if need be by new 'courts of obligation'. Citizenship is no longer to be seen as a set of automatic entitlements. In the future it will have to be earned, and those who abuse it will risk having their civic entitlements withdrawn.

It is a timely analysis. The concept of rights has played a vital role in modern politics, securing a domain of individual liberty against the tyrannical or over-intrusive power of the State. But rights are only one element in the life of society. When they dominate at the expense of all else, they distort and undermine the political process.

One reason is that rights conflict, leaving us with no criterion for preferring one to the other. Does a foetus have a right to life, or does a woman have the right to choose to abort it? Does an author have the right to freedom of expression, or do religious groups have the right to protection against blasphemy? Do parents have the right to go their separate ways, or do children have the right to paternal support? These questions generate fierce, even violent, controversy. But they cannot be answered in the terms in which they are asked. If we want to settle a conflict of rights we must find some larger principle than rights.

The Times, 31 May 1994

The other reason is that rights are like cheques. They have value only if there is money in the bank. They presuppose a society in which we are collectively willing to pay the price of the many claims made upon us. As advocates of liberty have long recognised, without duties there can be no rights. John Locke, the great philosopher of rights, none the less wrote of 'every man's indispensable duty to do all the service he can to his country'. Friedrich Hayek, the hero of today's libertarians, spoke of obedience to moral rules as part of the 'apprenticeship of liberty'.

When rights are claimed in isolation from the rest of moral and political life they devastate public debate. Rights-talk leads to a politics of single-interest lobbies, pressure groups and competing claims which cannot all be satisfied. The result is disillusionment and cynicism, the most notable feature of societies in which rights-talk has prevailed.

Selbourne is right to insist on recapturing the sense of duty. Where he is less helpful is in suggesting how this might happen. His primary answer is law: Draconian sanctions against those who fail to make their contribution to the common good. But law is the crudest of all instruments of moral education. Laws can prevent us from doing evil, but they cannot make us good. Nor in a free society can laws do more than enforce the morality we have. They cannot recreate a morality we have lost.

Far more compelling is the view of American social theorists like Amitai Etzioni and Robert Bellah who have focused our attention on the real birthplace of responsibility: families and communities. It is in these intimate associations that we learn and practise responsibility, understand the mutuality of the social bond and discover the power of the good we seek in common.

It is no accident that rights, not responsibilities, have come to the fore in political debate. The modern State, having lost the underpinning of a shared morality, is too abstract to enlist our loyalties. It is not something in which we feel involved. Instead it is something against which we make claims. In the meantime, family and community have eroded as institutions, leaving us to form more temporary and conditional alliances. Our range of commitments has narrowed and our historical horizon foreshortened. The sense of belonging to a long-term project, society, of which we are the collective guardians for the sake of our children, has suffered an eclipse.

But it need not be permanent. Among the young people I meet I see no lack of a desire to serve. What they lack is a framework in which to do so. If community work were to be part of the national curriculum and if religious groups, voluntary organisations and local associations were enlisted in training for citizenship, a new and practical expression could be given to civic duty. It is a supreme irony that we treat community service as a punishment instead of a universal and challenging part of education.

'Duty,' said Lord Acton, 'is not taught by the State.' But the State can empower other groups to do so. The transition from rights to duties is possible. It is urgently necessary if we are to preserve our law-governed liberty. But it will happen through the agents of moral change in our society, not through the brute force of law.

10

Renewing the Covenant

In 1981 the philosopher Alasdair MacIntyre published a book entitled *After Virtue*. It was a startling work. As its subtitle stated, it was 'a study in moral theory'. But it was quite unlike other studies in moral theory produced in the preceding decades. At Cambridge I had studied philosophy, or as it was then called 'Moral Sciences'. What I learned there was that it was not the task of the philosopher to advocate any particular morality. Instead it was the philosopher's role to analyse the *language* of morality, and the first thing we discovered was that moral language was misleading. Words like 'good', 'right', 'duty' and 'obligation' seemed to point to some objective reality. But in fact, it transpired, there were no objective moral truths. Morality was a matter of subjective choice, personal decision or private will. One Oxford philosopher, J L Mackie, wrote a book called *Ethics* and subtitled it 'Inventing Right and Wrong'.

Moral philosophy in those days was breathtaking in its iconoclasm. The twin sources of our moral tradition – the Bible and ancient Greece – were summarily dismissed. The Bible rested on the supposedly erroneous notion that morality could be commanded by God. Plato's *Republic* and Aristotle's *Nicomachean Ethics* depended on the unsustainable idea that human life had a purpose. Indeed all substantive moralities rested on the 'naturalistic fallacy' of confusing 'is' with 'ought', descriptions with prescriptions, or facts with values. In a mere twenty pages of his *Language, Truth and Logic*, A J Ayer dismissed the whole of ethics, aesthetics, metaphysics and religious belief as neither true nor false but meaningless. We were left wandering amid the ruins of the systems of the past, convinced that never again could we build ethical structures in the public domain. And over this ravaged scene hovered the ghost of Nietzsche who had warned: 'How greatly we would like to exchange these [ancient religious] ideas for truths which would be just as healing, pacifying and beneficial . . . But there are no such truths.'

The resigned agnosticism of linguistic analysis was suddenly disturbed by the appearance of MacIntyre's work. Modern moral philosophy, he argued, was not a timeless set of propositions about the nature of moral language. It was instead a symptom of the *breakdown* of moral language at a particular time and place in the history of Western civilisation. What had happened in the vast economic and intellectual changes of the past two centuries was the collapse of a stable social order in which the individual found meaning in the context of a community and its traditions. Society had fragmented, and with it any coherent idea of morality. Moral judgements could no longer be justified – as they had been, for example, in the Greek city states – by reference to agreed standards which made sense in terms of the shared life of the *polis*. All that was left was private emotion masquerading as morality. But this was no mere fact about our situation. It was little short of catastrophic for the prospect of constructing any vision of a society built around virtue. 'Modern politics', wrote MacIntyre, 'is civil war carried out by other means.'

After Virtue ended on an apocalyptic note unprecedented in the sober literature of British philosophy. Drawing a comparison between our age and the era in which the Roman empire declined into the Dark Ages, MacIntyre wrote:

A crucial turning point in that earlier history occurred when men and women of good will turned aside from the task of shoring up the Roman *imperium* and ceased to identify the continuation of civility and moral community with the maintenance of that *imperium*. What they set themselves to achieve instead – often not recognising fully what they were doing – was the construction of new forms of community within which the moral life could be sustained so that both morality and civility might survive the coming ages of barbarism and darkness. If my account of our moral condition is correct, we ought also to conclude that for some time now we too have reached that turning point. What matters at this stage is the construction of local forms of community within which civility and the intellectual and moral life can be sustained through the new dark ages which are already upon us. And if the tradition of the virtues was able to survive the horrors of the last dark ages, we are not entirely without grounds for hope. This time however the barbarians are not waiting beyond the frontiers; they have already been governing us for quite some time.

This diagnosis by one of the foremost historians of ethics was alarming enough. But as the 1980s progressed, other voices from different disciplines shared in the general sense of foreboding. In 1985 Robert Bellah, one of the United States' leading social theorists, co-authored an influential study, *Habits of the Heart: Middle America Observed*. He concluded that contemporary Americans, confined to the language of individualism, had lost the ability to make moral sense of their lives. He too was of the view that this had dangerous implications for the future of society. Our social ecology, he wrote, 'is damaged not only by war, genocide, and political repression. It is also damaged by the destruction of the subtle ties that bind human beings to one another, leaving them frightened and alone. It has been evident for some time that unless we begin to repair the damage to our social ecology, we will destroy ourselves long before natural ecological disaster has time to be realised.'

Nor were these isolated voices. In one discipline after another, leading academics began to question the fragmentation of culture, the collapse of the family, the ghettoisation of cities and the loss of a sense of continuity with the past. Taken together, these amounted to nothing less than a seismic shift in intellectual life. For what was being systematically called into question was a profound set of assumptions, usually associated with the Enlightenment, which had dominated academic orthodoxy for more than a century.

At the core of those assumptions was a lonely figure called the individual, disconnected from all binding ties of kinship, tradition or authority. There were no limits to what the individual could pass judgement on, nor constraints on what he or she could be. Guided only by abstract reason and personal subjective choice, the individual was free to chart any course he chose through a neutral world of facts that laid no claim upon him. Neither civic society nor the State was the embodiment of any particular collective aspiration. Instead the State was confined to arbitrating neutrally between competing claims. The individual had no larger loyalties beyond personal choice and provisional contracts. About this complex of suppositions, leading thinkers now raised a revolutionary possibility. Might this be a vision not of heaven but of hell?

As I read these and other works in the same vein I began to realise that I was hearing an altogether new configuration of attitudes, as important as those which two centuries ago laid the intellectual foundations of modernity. MacIntyre and those who followed him were not simply figures, to be found at most times, who lament change and look back with nostalgia at a golden age that never was. They were not suggesting that the Enlightenment, with its scepticism, individualism and traditionless rationality, was a mistake that should never have happened. Instead, they were arguing that it had run its course. It had freed energies which had produced the Industrial Revolution and the modern democratic state. But it had also set in motion processes which had eroded the beliefs, communities and institutions within which we found meaning and common purpose. We were richer and freer than our ancestors, but we were beginning to lose the framework in which wealth brought happiness, and freedom a promise of personal enlargement.

What I was beginning to hear was nothing less than a new voice of prophecy. Here was Jeremiah foretelling the destruction of Jerusalem or Ezekiel, the watchman, seeing the sword come against the city. Today's prophets, I realised with some sadness, are often not religious leaders but a small group of academics, who, breaking free of disciplinary specialis-ation, have surveyed our age from the broadest of perspectives and brought back a report of imminent danger.

The hope of the Enlightenment was of open-ended progress. Its central metaphor was science. Through freedom, experimentation, reason and enquiry, we could achieve mastery not only over the natural world but also over humanity and our multiple strivings. However, as the twentieth century nears its close, we have discovered that science has brought as many problems as solutions. Used industrially it has eroded our environ-ment. Used militarily it has given us an unprecedented capacity for destruction. Used politically it has created totalitarianisms. Allied to ancient hatreds it produced the Holocaust, the most controlled and sys-tematic attempt at genocide ever undertaken. We have come to realise the presence of limits: to the indefinite expansion of economies, to the power of reason to control human passion and prejudice, and to the ability of governments and markets to solve social problems.

More importantly we have begun to recognise the importance of human relationships and the environment in which they take place. Enlightenment thought paid scant attention to the framework of personal relationships: to families and communities and to the rules, rituals and traditions that sustained them. These things were, after all, *unscientific*. Our communities and traditions are inescapably local and idiosyncratic. They are where we become people in particular, not humanity in the abstract. As a result they simply failed to register on the Enlightenment map, with its obsessive focus on what was universal and therefore rational. Whatever failed this test was dismissed as myth and prejudice, the subjective imposition of individual will. Thus began the disintegration of those institutions within which human beings have, since the birth of history, found meaning and identity through their relationships with others and membership in a community with its memories and hopes. Humanity in the abstract has proved to be too abstract to be human.

MacIntyre, Bellah and others have been signalling for some time that this process cannot continue without severe damage to society. What should be our response? First should be a *principled rejection of despair*.

65

Just as the optimism of the Enlightenment proved to be exaggerated, so too will the pessimism of those who speak today of the 'new dark ages'. At the heart of biblical faith is a series of images – Noah after the Flood, Job after his trials, Isaiah contemplating the destruction of Jerusalem – which testify to the unbroken human capacity to rebuild life after disaster. Our moral and religious beliefs *have* been damaged by two centuries of assault, but they are not beyond repair. They are never beyond repair. What made the prophets of the Bible eternal spokesmen of the human condition is that beyond every warning of catastrophe they discerned a distant horizon of hope. Jeremiah, in the midst of prophesying the defeat of Jerusalem, bought a field there as a gesture of his conviction that Jews would one day return; and they did return. In those who undertake to guide us through the wilderness, pessimism is an abdication of responsibility and we must reject it.

No less importantly, we must reject the absurd test the Enlightenment imposed on religious and moral beliefs, namely that only if they were *universal* could they be *true*. As anthropologists began to uncover the full diversity of human behaviour, philosophers drew the conclusion that since many of our deepest convictions about humanity were not universal, they must be false. This is a fallacy and deserves to be challenged.

Moralities are like languages. We are born into them and we must learn them if we are to communicate and have relationships with others. Like languages, moralities embody ancient and living social processes. We do not invent them by our individual choices. Instead, by learning them we take our part in a particular tradition which long preceded us and which will continue long after we are no longer here. Like language, morality testifies to the paradox that only by yielding to something which is *not* individual can we become individuals. There is nothing unique about a baby's cry. There is something unique about Shakespeare's sonnets. It takes a long apprenticeship in the rules of grammar and semantics before we express what we alone wish to say. Only by a similar apprenticeship in the rules and virtues of a moral tradition can we shape the life that we alone are called on to live. Like languages, moralities are not universal. But neither are they the product of private and personal choice. We can no more sustain relationships without shared rules of fidelity and trust than we can sustain communication without shared rules of grammar. And without a stable framework of relationships we are left confused, vulnerable and alone.

Ultimately, of course, moralities are more than languages. They make claims upon us. The key word in biblical ethics is *brit*, or 'covenant'. In a covenant, parties come together to pledge themselves to a code of mutual loyalty and protection. Like a contract, a covenant is born in the recognition that no individual can achieve his or her ends in isolation. Because we are different, we each have strengths that others need, and weaknesses that others can remedy. Unlike a contract, however, a covenant is more than a narrow legal agreement bound by mutual interest. It involves a commitment to go beyond the letter of the law, and to sustain the relationship even at times when it seems to go against the interests of one of the parties. As Daniel Elazar puts it, 'In its heart of hearts, a covenant is an agreement in which a higher moral force, traditionally God, is either a direct party to or guarantor of a particular relationship.'

The concept of covenant and the analogy with languages help us rescue morality from the false dichotomy between the universal and the individual. Enlightenment thought, caught in this contrast, could find little that was universal in morality and relegated the rest to individual choice. The result has been to rob of their legitimacy the great but particular traditions through which human beings came together to form enduring relationships. Lacking these bonds we have become isolated particles in independent orbit, and the central terms of modern moral discourse – autonomy and rights – have merely emphasised that isolation, seeing the individual rather than the collective enterprise as sacrosanct. The analogy with language reminds us that communication depends on rules that are *not* individually chosen. The idea of covenant reminds us that there are some rules whose claim upon us is stronger than short-term self-interest and involves a commitment to the institutions into which we were born and from which our identity derives.

The breakdown of morality – for it has been a breakdown, not simply a change – can be seen in retrospect as a natural response to the massive social, economic and political changes that have marked the past two centuries, leaving the human landscape transformed. For a time it seemed as if the most important thing was to liberate our energies from all but the most minimal constraints, and progress would ensue. Economic freedom would deliver economic growth. Intellectual freedom would produce scientific discovery. Moral freedom would permit what John Stuart Mill called 'experiments of living', from which would flow the same kind of advance so evident in industry and science.

But morality has turned out to be different. It is not one human enterprise among others. Instead it is the base which makes other enterprises possible and the vantage point from which they are judged. Without it all our other strivings are blind. Unless we are capable of making moral judgements, we have no way of deciding whether to pursue economic growth at the cost of unemployment, or industrial development at the price of harming our environment. So long as our dominant assumption was one of open-ended progress, these issues did not need to be faced in their full pathos. But we have now run up against limits of progress.

In retrospect the most important change to have happened in recent years has been the displacement of science by ecology as the central metaphor of our condition. We now know that the unfettered choices of individuals can have harmful as well as beneficial consequences, and that the uncontrolled pursuit of economic growth can damage the natural and social environment in which we live and move and have our being. We need morality as well as markets if private gain is not to turn into public loss.

Without shared codes of conduct there can be no stable human institutions. Without a willingness to forego personal advantage for the sake of larger ends, there can be no collaborative endeavour: no academic fellowship, no business partnership, no lasting families, no civic society. Morality is the institution which defines and makes sense of the limits by which our behaviour is bound. The more we become aware of the dangers of limitless freedom, the more we will search for moral rather than mere technical guidance. Moral codes, for so long seen as repressive barriers to individual fulfilment, will come to be recognised for what they always were: the language of relationship and the precondition of trust. When that happens we will begin to renew the covenant which turns competing strangers into the shared enterprise that we call society.

PART II
LIVING TOGETHER

I I

Introduction: Sharing a World

A N Wilson begins his tract *Against Religion* with the following words:

> It is said in the Bible that the love of money is the root of all evil. It might be truer to say that the love of God is the root of all evil. Religion is the tragedy of mankind. It appeals to all that is noblest, purest, loftiest in the human spirit, and yet there scarcely exists a religion which has not been responsible for wars, tyrannies and the suppression of the truth.

As a religious leader I do not take that proposition lightly. I spent the whole of the Gulf War in Israel with my family, watching our children put on their gas-masks as, thirty-nine times, Scud missiles rained down on civilian targets in a country not at war with Iraq. None of us knew until the war was over whether the next would contain chemical weapons. As I write these words, our house is under twenty-four-hour guard following two terrorist bombs on Israeli and Jewish targets in London. I know that religion kills.

But so does the absence of religion. People have killed in the name of God. But their crimes do not rival the crimes of those who have killed believing that they were gods. The greatest crimes of this century, those of Nazi Germany and Stalinist Russia, were committed by secular regimes, and they remind us of the force of the words of Abraham, 'I said to myself, "There is no fear of God in this place, and they will kill me" ' (Genesis 20:11). Christian theologians have written about Christian guilt for the Holocaust, and there can be no denying that racial anti-semitism had its roots in religious anti-Judaism. None the less, the distinguished Jewish historian Yosef Hayim Yerushalmi has argued that Christianity, so long as it was the dominant belief, actually *prevented* a Holocaust. Christians had every interest in preserving Jews, albeit as pariahs, as evidence of the truth of Christianity. The Holocaust, he says, was possible only when religious prejudice was freed from religious restraints. George Steiner traces a direct line in German thought from Nietzsche's declaration of the 'death of God' to the attempted murder, sixty years later, of the people of God.

Wilson's critique is too easy. Religion is not the source of evil. Humanity is, and religion is sometimes powerless to prevent it. But a question remains. How is it that a religion based on love can have a history of hate, and one which values peace can engage in holy war?

It was Reinhold Niebuhr, in his *Moral Man and Immoral Society*, who pointed out the difference between the behaviour of individuals and groups. Individuals 'are endowed by nature with a measure of sympathy and consideration for their kind'. They can behave with great altruism. Once organised into groups, however, 'there is less reason to guide and to check impulse, less capacity for self-transcendence, less ability to comprehend the needs of others and therefore more unrestrained egoism'. That difference is magnified when applied to religion.

Traditions of faith bind us together as communities. Through our several religious heritages we arrive at a special sense of kinship and compassion towards those who share our belief and way of life. But the very walls we build around ourselves for mutual protection serve to divide us from those who do not belong to the group. Forming an 'Us' also creates a 'Them'. There is a difference between insiders and outsiders. 'We have truth, they do not. We have the salvation that they are denied.' It is relatively easy to love our neighbour as ourself. It is considerably more difficult to love the stranger, the outsider, the one whose way of life is so unlike our own. The stronger are the bonds of fellowship within a community, the more likely is there to be suspicion and fear of those outside. That is why a religion, even as it promotes peace within its own borders, can inspire war across the frontiers of faith.

This fact is always disturbing, but there are times when it is simply intolerable. In the aftermath of the Holocaust, those who had seen into the abyss came to a conclusion: Never again. Never again should hostility be allowed to fester between peoples, races and religions, for the road that begins with hatred in the heart can end in attempted genocide. Thus began the great conversation across faiths, most notably between Judaism and Christianity, in an effort to find another way. Dialogue has been one of the great religious achievements of the past half-century, and it has promoted a new mood of mutual understanding and respect. But its work has hardly begun. There are too many parts of the world and too many faith communities it has not yet touched. Religion is still used to defend ethnic or national rivalries, and it still claims human sacrifices.

In Northern Ireland, the Middle East, Bosnia and elsewhere, religion fuels the flames of conflict, justifying the unjustifiable and allowing people to believe that by aggression, terrorism and murder they contribute to the greater glory of God. At such times the voice of religious leadership must be heard, loud and unequivocally, saying: This is not the way. God is found in life, not death; in reconciliation, not hate; in justice, not vengeance; in peace, not war. As a religious leader I have always tried as forcibly as possible to urge co-existence and oppose ethnic conflict and war. The chapters in this section include my responses, at the time, to the war in Bosnia, the peace process in Israel and the massacre at Hebron. Often I discovered that mine was a lonely voice, and perhaps that is a measure of the task that still lies ahead.

The rabbis of the first centuries of the Common Era communicated profound truths in a deceptively simple way. Commenting on the phrase 'the God of faith' (Deuteronomy 32:4) they said, 'This means the God who had *faith in the world He was about to create.*' In that sentence lies an extraordinary suggestion of the *risk* God took when He made mankind.

Biblical faith, with its emphasis on free will and responsibility, constantly holds before us the paradox of human history. There are times when we scale the heights of goodness. But there are others when we descend to the depths of evil. Modern thought has focused on the wrong question. It has asked how God could have created nature. The rabbis posed a question altogether more profound. *How could God have created man?* It is one thing to believe that God in His goodness made the universe. It is another to believe that God in His goodness made a form of life, *homo sapiens*, capable of inflicting untold cruelty and suffering on its own members. The Torah says that before the Flood, contemplating the violence that filled the world, God 'regretted that He had made man on earth and His heart was filled with pain' (Genesis 6:6). After Auschwitz, that verse echoes with almost unbearable pathos.

The rabbis gave a remarkable answer. Creation testifies not merely to God's power but also, as it were, to His belief in mankind. At the heart of religion is not just the faith we have in God. No less significant is *the faith God has in us.* That faith is surely often tested. It is tested when we turn our back on God. It is tested no less when we commit evil in His name. Yet He does not lose faith that one day we will learn this: that God has given us many universes of faith but only one world in which to live together.

12

The Interfaith Imperative

Many years ago I had the privilege of meeting one of the great religious leaders of the Jewish world. He was a Hassidic Rebbe, head of a large group of Jewish mystics. I was inspired by his teachings and impressed by the spirituality of his followers. But I had a question about the way of life he advocated. It seemed exclusive. In its intense and segregated piety it shut out the rest of the world. Was there not – I asked him – beauty and value outside the narrow walls in which he lived? He answered me with a parable.

Imagine, he said, two people who spend their lives transporting stones. One carries bags of diamonds. The other hauls sacks of rocks. Each is now asked to take a consignment of rubies. Which of the two understands what he is now to carry? The man who is used to diamonds knows that stones can be precious, even those that are not diamonds. But the man who has carried only rocks thinks of stones as a mere burden. They have weight but not worth. Rubies are beyond his comprehension.

So it is, he said, with faith. If we cherish our own, then we know the value of others. We may regard ours as a diamond and another faith as a ruby, but we know that both are precious stones. But if faith is a mere burden, not only will we not value ours. Neither will we value the faith of someone else. We will see both as equally useless. True tolerance, he implied, comes not from the absence of faith but from its living presence. His words rang true. My own experience had taught me likewise.

I grew up in Finchley, and my parents sent their children to the schools closest to hand. Both were Christian establishments, and I have often reflected on how my brothers and I, members of an Orthodox Jewish family, reacted to a religious environment so different from what we knew from the synagogue and home. The answer is simple. We encountered

---

Lecture to the Annual General Meeting of the Council of Christians and Jews, 1989

teachers who valued their religion, and as a result we learned to value our own. We were conscious of our difference, but the difference was respected. Interacting with our teachers and friends we learned that those who are at home in their own faith, who are confident in their beliefs and assured of their own religious heritage, are not threatened by another faith. On the contrary, they are capable of valuing and being enlarged by it.

So, at an early age, I learned how the encounter between Christians and Jews can benefit both traditions by teaching us pride in our own heritage, and humility in the face of another. That is the great truth on which the Council of Christians and Jews is predicated. But – and this is the crucial question – how many people still share that vision?

Twenty or thirty years ago, the answer would have been: a great many. There was a time – it reached its high point in the 1960s – when the word 'interfaith' was on many people's lips. It seemed then as if dialogue would bring about a momentous transformation in the relationship between the great world religions. It was as if we were about to enter a new era in inter-religious understanding. There was a widespread sense that we had been estranged for too long.

For centuries, even millennia, religions had seen themselves as possessors of exclusive truths and of unique paths to salvation. Each in affirming its own faith, denied the integrity of others. Above all, the relationship between Judaism and Christianity had been fraught with tragedy. As centuries of suspicion, even hostility, reached their shattering climax in the Holocaust, men and women of faith knew in their hearts that some other understanding had now to emerge. So, in a historic gesture of reconciliation, Christians and Jews alike began to reach out to one another, determined to turn a history of alienation into a legacy of love.

It was, and in retrospect will be seen to be, a heroic undertaking. But the world has moved on, and in some respects not for the better. Today we stand between the beginning of two new decades, the 5750s in the Jewish calendar, the 1990s in the Christian calendar. And from both perspectives, the future seems more sombre than it did twenty or thirty years ago. In Judaism, Christianity, Islam and other world faiths the voice of tolerance and moderation has become muted, even unsure of itself. Those who claim to represent religious authenticity have been those who, by and large, reject dialogue, accommodation and pluralism, and speak instead of authority, exclusivity and the uncompromising fundamentals of faith. As a result, religion in the contemporary world has become again a scene of conflict rather than reconciliation.

Specifically in terms of the Jewish-Christian encounter there have been tensions on both sides. For Jews there has been a sense of unease. They ask the following questions. Have the Churches fully come to terms with the centrality of the State of Israel in Jewish consciousness? Have they understood what its security means to a people who came face to face with the angel of death at Auschwitz, and had no inch of the planet Earth that was their refuge and their home? Have they reflected fully on the pain caused by the convent at Auschwitz, a pain whose dimensions are too deep for me to analyse here? Do the Churches understand the particular assault on Jewish sensibilities caused by missionary activities targeted on lonely or vulnerable Jews? More deeply: Has Christian theology yet fully come to terms with the contemporary vitality of Jewish existence, with the miracle of Jewish religious and national rebirth after the Holocaust, with the fact that *Am Yisrael Chai*, the people of the covenant lives?

I speak as a Jew. But a Christian would surely set forth another perspective and testify to pain on the other side of the relationship as well. In Christian eyes it must at times seem that the State of Israel is a dilemma, not just an achievement. How can Jewish and Palestinian claims co-exist and be resolved? How, in Israel, can military and religious values live alongside one another? Can there be a religious ethic, not of powerlessness, but of power? Must our hearts not go out to the Palestinians as they once went out to the Jews? And as for the Holocaust, have we not moved beyond the time of remembering to a time of forgiving? Is there not a certain unforgiving relentlessness about bringing aged war criminals to trial forty years after the event? As a Jew, I must hear that voice and that pain and know that they express sincere Christian concerns.

These tensions do not exist in isolation. They are part of a much deeper shift in religious consciousness. One image brings this vividly to mind. Two years ago a great hurricane swept across southern England. As Jews, we remember the date because it took place on the night of one of the great festivals of the Jewish year, *Simhat Torah*, the day of 'Rejoicing in the Law'. Our family was in the West End of London at the time, because my synagogue is next to Hyde Park. Just before dawn broke I went out to see what had happened. I came upon a scene of devastation. There was silence. No one else was yet about, and the wind had died. But everywhere, great trees had been uprooted and branches hurled across roads. The order of the park had been reduced to chaos. As the sun rose over that ravaged landscape it seemed for a moment like the end of the world.

A fearful thought then occurred to me. It was in just such moments that our ancestors saw God. Didn't the Psalm – the very Psalm which rabbinic tradition associated with the giving of the Torah – declare: 'The voice of the Lord breaks the cedars, the Lord breaks in pieces the cedars of Lebanon . . . The voice of the Lord twists the oaks and strips the forests bare' (Psalm 29:5, 9)? God was not only in the still small voice that spoke to Elijah. He was also in the mighty east wind that divided the Red Sea. He was in the earthquake that swallowed Korach. He was in the volcanic upheaval that swept away Sodom and the cities of the plain. He was in the tempest that threatened to sweep away Jonah's ship.

That moment came back to me when the Salman Rushdie affair first began. I spoke about it on the radio. I said that for the past two centuries in the West we had seen God in the order of the garden and not in the mighty wind that wrecks the garden. We had seen Him in quiet faith, not in the fire and the thunder and the hurricane. The Rushdie affair took us by surprise because we had edited out of our image of religion a whole range of passion that submits to neither moderation nor tolerance. We remembered that God spoke to Elijah in a still small voice. We forgot that He spoke to Job out of the heart of the whirlwind.

And there lies the problem. The great conversation between faiths, which reached its heights in the 1960s, was predicated on a series of assumptions that had their roots in the Enlightenment. We were gradually moving from a world of tradition to a society built on rationality. We were passing, slowly but inexorably, from the particular identities of particular faiths to a more universal conception of humanity. Society was becoming, as the sociologists said, secularised. Religious belief was still strong, but it was becoming marginal to our public decisions. Passion and prejudice were gradually dying, and in their place reason and moderation would hold sway. On that scenario, the bitter religious conflicts of the past looked very much like things of the past. It was a time for reconciliation.

But it didn't happen that way. Almost immediately, a new kind of religiosity began to emerge, or re-emerge, in Christianity, Judaism, Islam and other world faiths. It transpired that secularisation had failed to provide us with our most basic human needs: the need for meaning and personal identity. And the way to meaning and identity lay in highly particular religious traditions. So we began to see, and have become increasingly aware of, religious revivals built on intense hostility to the assumptions of the modern world. Critics call it Fundamentalism, a word I do not like because it groups together many different phenomena under a single name. But several things followed, and have become more and more noticeable over the passing years.

Firstly, religion, far from being a force for reconciliation, has become the battleground of some of the fiercest and most intractable conflicts in the contemporary world, from Northern Ireland to Lebanon and beyond. Secondly, the kind of religion that has real power over the lives of its followers is increasingly exclusive and confrontational. Thirdly, the theology that speaks of tolerance and openness and dialogue with the modern world is seen, by many believers in search of the truth, as a compromise that lacks content and authenticity. The result is that the most passionate religious believers today, in many faiths, are more concerned with their own destiny than with our collective destiny in this tense and troubled world.

Restating the Interfaith Imperative

So, as we face a new decade, we must begin to restate the inter-religious imperative in more forceful terms. We must see it not simply as a gesture of goodwill undertaken by men and women of exceptional liberalism and vision, but as a set of religious axioms that must be confronted by all believers, even those who do not as yet see the need for meeting and reconciliation. We must focus our search not on the modern world and its values, for these are precisely what many religious believers reject. Instead we must take our stand on the classic texts and principles of our great religious traditions. What, as a Jew, impels me to enter into conversation with men and women of other faiths?

The Hebrew Bible contains the great command, 'You shall love your neighbour as yourself' (Leviticus 19:18), and this has often been taken as the basis of biblical morality. But it is not: it is only part of it. The Jewish sages noted that on only one occasion does the Hebrew Bible command us to love our neighbour, but in thirty-seven places it commands us to love the stranger. Our neighbour is one we love because he is like ourselves. The stranger is one we are taught to love precisely because he is *not* like ourselves.

Time and again the Hebrew Bible emphasises that we are judged by how we act to those who are unlike us, and who may even call into question everything we stand for. Rabbinic tradition held that Abraham was a greater man than Noah. Why so? Noah, the Torah says, was 'a righteous man, blameless among the people of his time' (Genesis 6:9). None the less, said the rabbis, when the world was drowning, Noah saved only his own family, whereas Abraham fought a war and later prayed for the inhabitants of Sodom and the cities of the plain. The Jewish mystics once asked: Why is the *hassidah*, the stork, an unclean animal? Its name means 'the compassionate one'. How can a bird called 'compassion' be unclean? They answered: the *hassidah* has compassion only for its own kind. Compassion only for your own is not compassion.

Just before the story of Abraham and the covenantal people begins, the Bible relates the episode of the tower of Babel. In broad outlines, the moral of the story is clear. People gathered together to build a tower that would reach to heaven, but the proper place of man is on earth. They were guilty of hubris and they were punished by nemesis. The story is a satire of the pretensions of Babylonian civilisation and of the thought that because man has technological mastery, he can become like God. But this does not explain the story's central message, that after Babel the world is split into many languages, and that until the end of days there is no single universal language.

Babel is the essential preface to the history of Abraham. Without it, we might have thought that the covenant with Abraham was universal like the covenant with Noah, that it applied to all humanity and that it expressed a universal religious truth. It did not. Just as after Babel there is no single universal language, so there is no single universal culture and no single universal faith. The faith of Abraham left room for other ways of serving God, just as the English language leaves room for French and Spanish and Italian.

Faiths are like languages. There are many of them, and they are not reducible to one another. In order to express myself at all, I must acquire a mastery of my own language. If I have no language, I will still have feelings but I will be utterly inarticulate in communicating them. The language into which I am born, which I learn from my parents and my immediate environment, is where I learn self-expression. It is a crucial, perhaps even an essential, part of who I am. But as I venture out into the world I discover that there are other people who have different languages which I must learn if we are to communicate across borders.

A faith is like a language. I am at home in my own language as I am at home in my own faith. True conversions are rare. But I am not compromised by the existence of other languages. To the contrary, the more languages I can speak, the more I can communicate with others and the more I am enriched by their experience. To believe that our faith is the only religious reality there is, is rather like the old-fashioned British tourist who believed that you could communicate with the Spanish by speaking English very slowly and very loudly. After Babel, the religious reality, like the linguistic reality, is inescapably plural.

In recent years we have become conscious of global ecology. Environmental thinking has made us aware of the inter-connectedness of our actions. The destruction of a rain-forest in one part of the world can affect the climate in another. So it is with our social ecology. Once, religions and cultures could live for the most part at a safe remove from one another, as if each was an island entire of itself. Today there is no safe remove. Walk down a modern city street, and you will pass people of a dozen different cultures and languages. Our economy and politics are affected by the actions of a hundred different countries. Our very survival depends on the decisions of several powers not to use nuclear or chemical weapons. International terrorism may suddenly involve us in someone else's argument thousands of miles away. Our inter-connectedness has become tangible. Modernity has cast the wholly other directly into our lives.

Judaism long ago recognised the significance of social ecology. It formulated the idea of *darkhei shalom*, 'the ways of peace'. It took this not as a pious sentiment, but as a significant factor in Jewish law. *Darkhei shalom* asserts that the basic duties that I owe to the members of my faith community, I owe to those outside it as well – not because we share a faith but because we share an environment, a society, and we must be able to live together if we are to be able to live at all. Faith sometimes demands radical and uncompromising action. But *darkhei shalom* tells me that I must exercise restraint and moderation if I am not to destroy the social environment in which I live along with those who have a different faith. *Darkhei shalom* is an ecological principle that tells us that we live in a world of complex interdependencies, and we must exercise self-restraint in order to preserve that world.

These ideas are undergirded by the most fundamental proposition of all. Before there were religions, even before there were human beings, God pronounced the still awesome truth of the human situation: 'Let us make man in our own image, after our likeness' (Genesis 1:26). On this, the sages of the Mishnah delivered the following commentary: When human beings make things in a single image, they are all alike. God makes humanity in a single image, yet each of us is unique.

A faith built on the Hebrew Bible must come to terms with the stunning implications of that remark. We have great difficulty in recognising the integrity – indeed the sanctity – of those who are not in our image, whose faith and traditions and culture and language are not like ours. None the less we are told, and must struggle to see, that the wholly other, he or she who is not in our image, is yet in God's image.

I have tried to show in this chapter how a Jew, through his or her commitment to Judaism, is led outward to the realities of a multifaith world. My argument rests on no hidden liberal or modernist premises that could be rejected by a religious extremist. Christian theology will find its own way at arriving at these conclusions. But arrive at them we must. For if we are to co-exist in a world of rising religious intolerance, we shall have to find an interfaith imperative that speaks not only with a still small voice, but also out of the heart of the whirlwind.

13

Religious Responsibility at a Time of Ethnic Conflict

The conflict in Bosnia sent shockwaves through many Jewish minds. Here in the heart of Europe, less than half a century after the second World War, bitter civil war was once again raising the spectre of violence in the name of race and killing in the cause of ethnic purity. Despite the political and strategic difficulties of military intervention, this was not a cause about which I felt religious leaders could be silent. I wrote and spoke about it in the national press and on television and radio, and the following was a speech I gave on the subject (26 January 1993) at a dinner in honour of the Centre for the Study of Jewish-Christian Relations, Selly Oak Colleges, Birmingham.

There are times when good relations between religions are no more than a matter of decency, politeness and good citizenship. We learn each other's customs. We share each other's celebrations. These are no small things.

In Golders Green, where we used to live, our next door neighbour was a Christian. One day she knocked on our door carrying a cardboard model that her son had made at school. It was a model of a *sukkah*, the hut that Jews live in on the festival of Tabernacles. She said: 'I tried the Muslims next door and it wasn't theirs, and I knew it wasn't ours. So I came to the conclusion that if it wasn't a Muslim hut or a Christian hut it must be a Jewish hut.' It was. And a few weeks later we were able to take them into our garden to see the real thing. That is the easy but vitally important part of interfaith relations. We learn about each other and begin to banish the myths, the prejudices and the stereotypes.

There are other times when interfaith relations become part of our own self-knowledge. Jews, Christians and Muslims meet and face the humbling fact that ours is not the only faith, the only gate through which men and women have come to God. But there are rare times when our ability to speak across the boundaries of faith is nothing less than a matter of life and death. Now is such a time.

Think back to our mood barely three-and-a-half years ago, to the glorious false dawn of 1989. The Berlin Wall came down. Communism was being dismantled in Eastern Europe. The cold war was at an end. Francis Fukuyama, an American historian, announced the 'End of History'. His thesis was that people were now more interested in living standards than ideals. Ideology was dead, and all the wars and conflicts once driven by ideology would be a thing of the past. Life would be dull but peaceful. We were in for a quiet time.

I knew then that he was wrong, and I said so in my Reith Lectures. Hatred, rivalry and animosity were no more likely to be buried by the collapse of the Soviet Union than they were two hundred years earlier by the French Revolution. I argued then that the greatest danger facing humanity after the collapse of secular ideologies was religiously-fuelled nationalism: the cloak of sanctity over the politics of hate.

Since then we have seen the Gulf War and its still unfinished aftermath. We have seen the rise of racism, xenophobia and right-wing nationalism throughout Europe. We have seen neo-Nazism resurgent in a united Germany. And we have seen bloody ethnic war ravaging what was once Yugoslavia. The mood in world politics is dark, darker than I have known it in my lifetime. What makes it worse is that in many cases what has risen to the surface are not new grievances but old, and we had thought long-buried, animosities: ethnic rivalries that had been dormant for decades. Ogden Nash once said: 'No man ever forgets where he buried the hatchet.' He was right. Prejudice is like a virus that can be frozen into suspended animation, but once unfrozen it remains as virulent as ever.

So today we are faced with a question that only rarely surfaces in human affairs, but once it does, it demands an answer for the sake of humanity itself. Does nothing change? Are we destined to repeat history as if all the tragedies of this terrible century had taught us nothing? Have the millions of pages written on racism and prejudice since the Second World War proved powerless to prevent their recurrence? Can we stand a bare half-century after the Holocaust in a Europe that today witnesses neo-Nazi rallies, immigrants burned to death in Germany, a Europe which once again houses concentration camps, and which has replaced the word *Judenrein* with the equally repellent phrase 'ethnic cleansing', and not ask the most fearful question of all? *Were we wrong to say: never again?*

In the 1870s anti-semitism entered the vocabulary of German politics. In the 1880s there were pogroms in Russia, turning millions of people into refugees. In the 1890s there was the Dreyfus affair in France, which convinced even the assimilated Theodor Herzl that the writing was on the wall for the Jews of Europe. We are not today plunged back into the

1940s. The concentration camps of Bosnia are not Auschwitz or Bergen-Belsen, nor are the neo-Nazi rallies in Hungary what they were in Nuremberg. But we are unmistakably at the beginning of a process that is all too familiar, in which instability turns to anxiety which becomes hostility to the outsider, and thus is born xenophobia, ethnic conflict and the politics of race.

And we, the onlookers, find ourselves paralysed by a sense of *déjà vu*. Events unfold before our television screens like a horror film we have seen somewhere before, many years ago. We know that something dreadful is going to happen in the next scene, and we long to be able to warn the hero to look out and save himself. And we can't.

But we can. Because if we believe anything on the basis of the Bible we believe this: that history is not a film endlessly replaying itself. It has not been pre-scripted. The ending has not been written. 'Behold I set before you today the blessing and the curse, life and death. Therefore choose life.' History is made by our choices. Nothing that has happened in the past forces us to let it happen again.

Far from being called into question by recent events, the importance of interfaith and inter-racial understanding can hardly be overstated. To put it bluntly, if religion is part of the problem then religion must be part of the solution. If conflicts between Jews, Christians and Muslims have been fuelled by the clash of faiths, then it must be the leaders of those faiths who rise above the conflict and say: in the name of God, stop. Let me, in the name of religion, say how.

First, the Bible – the common core of the three great monotheisms – issues a remarkable command. It is contained in one word: *zakhor*, 'remember'. The verb 'to remember' occurs no less than 169 times in the Hebrew Bible. The great historian Yosef Hayim Yerushalmi writes that 'Only in Israel and nowhere else is the injunction to remember felt as a religious imperative to an entire people.'

Why? The Bible tells us with absolute clarity. 'You shall not oppress the stranger because you know the heart of the stranger, because you were once strangers in the land of Egypt.' We are commanded to remember so as not to let history repeat itself. If we were once oppressed, we cannot become oppressors. And if we once cried for help and no one came, we cannot stand idly by when others cry for help. Memory is the driving force of morality.

Today we are faced with an almost monstrous desire to forget. There are countries which even today have not yet come to terms with what happened during the Holocaust. There are revisionist historians who try to deny Holocaust history itself. We have recently had a revisionist reading of Churchill which suggests that if only Churchill had made peace with Hitler, Britain might have saved its empire. Almost at the same time we discovered in the case of Guernsey what might have been the price of that peace. Britain might have saved its empire, but it would have lost its soul.

Someone once said that the only lesson that history has taught us is that we have not yet learned anything from history. If so, we must go back and learn again. Memory is a religious imperative, and we now know why. There are people who will try to make us forget in order that the same crimes can be committed again in temporary blindness to their consequences. There are too many parallels between the mood of Europe now and that of a hundred years ago, and we have too much knowledge to ignore the line that leads from hatred to holocaust. The first thing we must do is to remember.

The second thing is to be prepared if necessary to intervene. We have heard, and surely we respect, the case against military intervention in Bosnia. There is the pragmatic danger of being caught up in a long, bloody and indecisive conflict. There is the political case which rightly urges caution before an outside party involves itself in the affairs of another country, even, or perhaps especially, in the case of civil war.

But my thoughts go back to a passage we read in synagogue a few weeks ago. I refer to the passage describing Moses before he became leader of the children of Israel. The Bible tells us little about the character of the young Moses. It does not say that he was righteous or pious or exceptionally spiritual. It merely relates three episodes in his life before the revelation in the burning bush. He saw an Egyptian attacking an Israelite, and he intervened. He saw an Israelite attacking an Israelite, and he intervened. He saw Midianite shepherds preventing Jethro's daughters from watering their flocks, and he intervened. Here were three conflicts: non-Jew against Jew, Jew against Jew, and non-Jew against non-Jew. In each case, Moses intervened. We need no further commentary. After reading these passages, we understand why it was Moses whom God chose to lead His people from slavery to freedom.

The Bible commands us not to stand idly by the blood of our neighbour. It was Cain who uttered the terrible words, 'Am I my brother's keeper?' There are some evils which, because they are crimes against humanity, implicate us all. We are sometimes morally responsible for what we fail to prevent, as well as for what we do. I am persuaded by the statement in *The Times* which said that 'The moral case for intervention in Bosnia has been clear for many months. Mass rape, medieval siege warfare, starvation and disease disfigure Europe's claims to civilisation.' The international community must act if it is to stop the slide towards catastrophe, and religious leaders must say so.

Finally there is a dimension in the politics of Europe and the Middle East for which a special responsibility lies specifically with religious leadership. Here I want to point out one salient fact. The Hebrew Bible tells the story of one people, the people of Israel. However, for the first eleven chapters of the book of Genesis there is no mention of the people of Israel. There is only humanity. There are the archetypal figures of Adam and Eve, Cain and Abel, Noah and the builders of the tower of Babel. And at the beginning of the beginning there is the declaration that in the entire created universe there is only one thing of absolute value, only one thing in which God has chosen to set His image: the human individual. *Any* human individual.

For too long the great monotheisms – Judaism, Christianity and Islam – have sanctioned suspicion and hostility to the outsider, the one who is not of our people or our faith. That hostility costs lives even today between Catholics and Protestants in Northern Ireland, between Christians and Muslims in Bosnia, and between Muslims and Jews in the Middle East. Even today, theology drives anti-semitism in Poland and fuels the politics of fundamentalism.

But the Bible teaches today, as it has always taught, that our common humanity precedes our particular faiths, and that the ethnic outsider is in God's image even if he or she is not in our image. To put it simply: crimes against humanity are not crimes against humanity alone. They are crimes against God, even when – *especially* when – they are committed in the name of God.

The time has come for religious leaders of all faiths and denominations to alert the world to what is at stake in the ethnic war in Bosnia and the rise of racism throughout Europe. Who in future generations could forgive us if we, who have lived through the century of the Holocaust, did not rise up and prevent the beginnings of a second Holocaust, whoever are its victims and whoever its perpetrators? Let us invoke the moral imperative of memory. Let us support international intervention. Let us teach that there is no religious justification for xenophobia or ethnic cleansing or holy war. And let our 'Never again' *mean* 'Never again.'

14
Taking Risks for Peace

I

On 13 September 1993, three days before the Jewish New Year, Yitzhak Rabin and Yasser Arafat shook hands on the White House lawn in a momentous gesture for peace.

It was a moment fraught with emotion for Jews throughout the world. But unlike an earlier gesture, the visit of the late Anwar Sadat to Jerusalem, the occasion provoked violently mixed reactions. On the one hand, among Jews in Israel and elsewhere, there was a powerful longing for an end to the constant fear of terrorism and war which has marked the State of Israel since its birth. Having been in Israel throughout the Gulf War, I knew how weary the majority of Israelis were at having to live in daily insecurity. A perpetual state of military alertness is no way for Israel to fulfil the dreams of those who see it as the renaissance of the Jewish people in our time.

Set against that, though, there were many anxieties. Were the Palestinians ready for peace? Would the agreement raise expectations that could not be delivered? Would it be sabotaged by those on both sides who saw any negotiation as compromise? At the most visceral level, the sight of an Israeli Prime Minister shaking hands with the leader of the Palestinian Liberation Organisation, which had been responsible directly or indirectly for so many brutal terrorist attacks on innocent civilians, was disturbing for many Jews. Was this an act of statesmanship or simply of betrayal?

As a religious leader, my duty is not to offer political or military judgement, but spiritual and pastoral guidance. The government of Israel was taking a risk for peace. The road to peace is invariably tortuous, full of setbacks and bestrewn with obstacles. But it is the road we are called on to take. My task was to set that route and the emotional difficulties it involves in a spiritual context, and to help Anglo-Jewry frame their perceptions of what was happening. The conflicts Jews felt were genuine, and they had their precedents in our religious literature. But that did not mean that there was no clear counsel. In Judaism, peace is a supreme value, and one must sometimes take risks to secure it.

The following text was sent to rabbis before the White House ceremony, and many of them read it as a sermon on the preceding Shabbat.

These are critical days for Israel. They are days of hope, but they are also days of anxiety and fear. They have taken place between the week in which we read the Torah portion of *Ki Tetse* (Deuteronomy 21:10) which describes the Israel of war, and the week in which we read the passage of *Ki Tavo* (Deuteronomy 26:1), which describes the Israel of peace.

But is there peace? Israel is divided, as we are divided, between those who are moved by the imperative, 'Seek peace and pursue it', and those who warn, like the prophet Jeremiah, against saying 'Peace, peace when there is no peace'. Even the great Jewish sages of our time have been divided between those who say that Israel must make concessions for the sake of peace, and those who say that every concession only increases the likelihood of war and terrorism and bloodshed. How then shall we respond?

We are an ancient people, and one of our great strengths is that for us what is old is also new, and what is as new as today's newspapers is as timeless as the Torah. We face the prospect of the government of Israel recognising the head of what has been seen until now as a terrorist organisation committed to the destruction of Israel. But we know that our forefather Jacob, after whom the State of Israel is named, once faced the same prospect. The Torah tells of how Jacob prepared to meet his brother Esau who had earlier sworn to kill him (Genesis 32:4–33). Like Israel today he was prepared for three things, 'for diplomacy, for prayer and for war'. And like Israel today, preparing for that encounter involved Jacob in an intense inner struggle. 'A man wrestled with him until the break of dawn.' Jacob had to wrestle, as Israel has to wrestle, between contending forces and conflicting inclinations. It is from that struggle that, as a people, we get our name.

What is even more striking is that when Jacob and Esau met, they kissed one another. If you examine a Torah scroll, you will see that at the word *vayishakehu*, 'he kissed him', there are dots over the letters. Tradition tells us that in the rare cases where there are dots over a word in the scroll, this indicates that there is a doubt about its meaning. In this case, the doubt was about the kiss itself. Was the gesture genuine? Was Esau sincere in his act of reconciliation? Rabbi Shimon bar Yochai said he was: 'It is well known that Esau hated Jacob. But at that moment he had a change of heart and he kissed him with true friendship.' Rabbi Yannai disagreed. 'Esau did not come to kiss Jacob but to bite him.' When the leader of the PLO shakes hands with the Prime Minister of Israel, will we not have exactly the same doubt?

Not only does this division apply to our understanding of Esau and Jacob. It applies to the Jewish law of war and peace. The relevant biblical verse states, 'When you come near to a city to make war against it, you must first offer it peace' (Deuteronomy 20:10). Peace takes precedence over war. The question is, to whom does this apply? On this, the two greatest rabbis of the Middle Ages, Rashi in the eleventh century and Maimonides in the twelfth, disagreed.

Rashi says that it applies only to 'cities that are far away'. It refers to towns and populations that lie outside the boundaries of Israel. But according to Maimonides, it applies even to nations living *within* Israel's borders. He rules: 'One may never wage war with anyone until one has first made an offer of peace.' Peace *always* takes priority over war, regardless of who and where are our adversaries.

This disagreement led Rashi and Maimonides to differing interpretations of the wars described in the book of Joshua. According to Rashi, Joshua fought in order to conquer the land. But according to Maimonides, Joshua only fought because the nations then living in the land declined his offer of peace. Had they accepted, they and the Israelites would have lived together in the same territory.

In the days of Joshua, one group *did* establish a peace treaty with Israel: the Gibeonites. They did so on the basis of an elaborate deception. They pretended to have come from outside the land. They put on worn-out clothes and took with them old and mouldy bread and pretended to have travelled a great distance. According to Rashi this was because they knew that Joshua intended to conquer the whole land including the territory in which they lived. According to Maimonides it was because they knew that their neighbours had rejected peace with the Israelites, and they did not realise that Joshua would have been prepared to sign a separate peace treaty with them.

As soon as the deception was discovered, the Israelites complained and wanted to have the agreement declared null and void. But the leaders of Israel insisted that since a settlement had been reached, Israel was bound to keep to its terms. The treaty was honoured. Shortly afterwards, Israel had to come to the defence of the Gibeonites when they were attacked by those among the Canaanites who objected to them making peace with Israel. Centuries later, King David punished the descendants of Saul who had unjustly attacked the Gibeonites.

Once again, we find our concerns today anticipated in the Bible. The

Gibeonites were capable of saying one thing and meaning another. There was a conflict between the people and the leadership of Israel. The people said that the Gibeonites could not be trusted. The leadership said: We have given our word. There was even civil war among the non-Israelites between moderates like the Gibeonites who were prepared to recognise Israel, and militant Canaanites who were not; and Israel had to intervene. None the less, the peace treaty held, as it did between Jacob and Esau throughout their lifetimes.

How then, in the light of our history and faith, shall we respond to the perplexity of this time? First, we must recognise that there can be legitimate disagreement in Israel and outside as to whether to make concessions to the Palestinians for the sake of peace. There was a disagreement amongst the sages as to whether Esau was genuine in his desire for peace. There was a disagreement between Rashi and Maimonides as to whether Israel may make peace with an autonomous group inside its borders. We should respect those who disagree with us, for in this instance we face a genuine 'argument for the sake of Heaven'.

Secondly, the Torah teaches a unique combination of idealism and realism in the political arena. We are neither pacifists nor militarists. We pray for peace but we are prepared to go to war. We say, 'How good and pleasant it is for brothers to live together.' But we also know, from the very beginning of Torah – from Cain and Abel – that brothers are capable of killing one another. We know that a group hitherto dedicated to the destruction of Israel does not change overnight. Maimonides says that nothing in human nature changes overnight. But we are also willing to take risks for the sake of peace, risks taken out of cool political calculations of the lesser of two evils, but risks none the less.

There is a remarkable *midrash* (rabbinic homily) about the creation of the world. It says that when God came to create man, the angel of peace objected because 'man is full of strife'. God ignored the angel and created mankind. The *midrash* raises the question that has hovered over human existence since the beginning of time. Why did God create a being capable of destroying all else He had made? Humanity has consistently disrupted the harmony of the world and engaged in violence and war. What answer did God give to the angel of peace? The answer implicit in the *midrash* is that God had faith that humanity would eventually learn that peace is better than war and that even a difficult peace is better than an easy war. The Holy One, blessed be He, took a risk for the sake of peace. And so at times must we.

Which brings me to the third and final point. There are two words for strength in Hebrew: *koach* and *gevurah*. But they mean quite different things. *Koach* means the strength to overcome your enemies. *Gevurah* means the strength to overcome yourself. Defining *gevurah*, the rabbis said, 'Who is strong? One who is capable of self-restraint.' *Koach* is the strength to wage war. *Gevurah* is the strength to make peace.

For many years the State of Israel has shown unparalleled *koach*. Since it came into existence it has had to fight wars, sometimes against overwhelming odds, merely in order to survive. No other state has faced such opposition from its neighbours. No other state proclaimed by the United Nations has been surrounded by countries who deny its very existence, its right to be. It has fought impossible wars and won. But in recent years Israel has shown that it has *gevurah* as well. It took immense courage for Israel to practise self-restraint during the Gulf War, but it did so. It has taken even greater courage for it to negotiate with its sworn enemies and be willing to pay a high price for peace. But it has done this as well.

There can be no greater contrast between Bosnia, where people who have lived for decades in peace are now engaged in killing one another, and Israel where two peoples who have lived for many years in hostility are coming together to make peace. And there can be no greater sanctification of God's name than this, that in an age of conflict it is the State of Israel, a tiny state surrounded by enemies, which is teaching humanity what it is to show heroism in pursuit of reconciliation.

It will be a difficult peace, fraught with dangers on every side. But for that very reason not only we, but the nations of the world as well, should pay tribute to the courage of those who take this risk in the spirit of Isaiah's vision of a world where 'nation shall not lift up sword against nation, neither shall they learn war anymore'. May the Almighty bless the people and the State of Israel and may He spread over them and us that most fragile but powerful of all dwelling-places: the tabernacle of peace.

II

In the sermon above I had sought, without obscuring my own commitment to the peace process, to give recognition to the conflicts Jews felt about it. In the following sermon, also delivered before the White House signing, I set out another perspective, that of contemporary history seen with the eye of faith.

Uniquely in the religious literature of the ancient world, the Hebrew

*Bible saw God in history. Great events in the chronicles of Israel were
not mere happenings. They were part of a narrative of redemption. To be
a prophet was to have an insight into the course of history, seen as God's
call to the people of the covenant and their response or lack of it.*

*For more than two thousand years we have had no prophets, and to
attempt to see the events of our time from a prophetic viewpoint is full
of dangers. None the less, it is sometimes worth taking the risk. The events
that have befallen Jews this century have too many biblical resonances for
us to ignore them, and this has been felt by secular no less than religious
Israelis. The return of Jews to their land after the darkest night of exile
is central to both the biblical drama of redemption and the experience of
the Jewish people in our time. From this perspective, the peace process
has an altogether larger significance, to which a religious leader must give
expression.*

*The occasion of this address was deeply atmospheric. It was delivered
on 11 September 1993 at the midnight Selichot service at the Bevis Marks
Synagogue, the oldest Jewish place of worship in Britain. It was here that
the Spanish-Jewish community gathered at the beginning of the eighteenth
century to lay the foundations of modern Anglo-Jewry. The synagogue,
which has changed little in almost three centuries, was packed and candle-
lit, and one could almost imagine oneself thrown back in time to those
early Anglo-Jews for whom ancestral memories of the Spanish expulsion
were still vivid. The contrast between then and now, between a Jewry
dispersed and insecure and one that had lived through its rebirth as a
sovereign nation in the land of its beginnings, was overpowering.*

*On this holy night, one of the great moments of prayer and penitence
in the Jewish calendar, I sought to give expression to the religious meaning
of the events through which we had lived.*

'Seek God where He is to be found. Call Him when he is close' (Isaiah
55:6). These seem like simple words. But they are far from simple. Because
it is with these words from Isaiah that Maimonides states one of the great
paradoxes of Jewish life.

'Even though repentance and prayer are *always* appropriate', he rules,
none the less some times are more favourable than others. There is such
a thing as an *et ratzon*, a 'time of favour', a window of opportunity, a
moment of grace. How do we know? Because Isaiah says, 'Seek God
where He is to be found. Call Him when He is close.' There are times
when God is to be found and times when God is not to be found. There
are times when God is close and times when He is far away.

How, though, can this be? A great Hassidic leader once tested his son. He said to him, 'I will give you a rouble if you can tell me where God can be found.' The son, wise beyond his years, replied: 'I will give you *two* roubles if you can tell me where God is *not* to be found.' God is everywhere, in all places and all times. He is as far away as the furthest galaxy and as close as the human heart. How, then, can there be times when God is close and times when God is not close?

The answer is this. The world is full of the light of God, but not always can we see it. There are times when God reveals Himself and times when He conceals Himself. God is always close. But not always do we feel Him to be close. There are special *individuals* to whom God reveals Himself. We call them prophets. There are particular *times of the year* when God reveals Himself. We call them the Days of Awe. And rarest of all, there are *ages*, eras, when God reveals Himself in history, when it as if the entire Jewish destiny emerged from darkness into light. To live in such an age is a privilege that few generations have known. To live in such an age is to seek God and to know that He is to be found, to call on God knowing Him to be close. This year we know we live in such an age.

At the end of his life Moses, the greatest leader the Jewish people has ever known, turned his eyes towards the future and gave his people a solemn warning. He said: There are two roads before you, one of blessing and one of curse. He spoke briefly about the blessings. But about the curses he spoke at length. He listed the fearful sufferings that lay in store for the Jewish people if they turned aside from serving God. So fearful were these curses that to this day, when we read them in the synagogue we say them in an undertone, as if reading them aloud would be too traumatic. But the most fearful curse of all was contained in a simple phrase: 'A day will come [says God] when I will hide My face' (Deuteronomy 31:18).

Defeat, exile, suffering, persecution, are full of pain. But the greatest pain is to seek God and not to be able to find Him. 'God is my light and my salvation', said David in the book of Psalms, 'Of whom, then, shall I be afraid?' 'Though I walk through the valley of the shadow of death, I will fear no evil if You are with me.' But if You are *not* with me – what then? If God's light shines but we cannot see it, if God is close but we cannot feel it, if God speaks and we cannot hear, what then?

Once in the Garden of Eden God called out to man and asked, *ayeka*, 'Where are you?' But for nearly two thousand years we have called out to God, *ayeka*. When the Temple was destroyed, where were You? When Your sages and saints were put to death as martyrs, where were You?

When Your people were dispersed and scattered and exiled and forced to wander homeless across the earth, where were You? When they were tortured and murdered for their faith, where were You? Almighty God, when Your people cried out to You from Auschwitz and Bergen-Belsen and Sobibor and Maidanek, where were You? When one million Jewish children were gassed, burned or buried alive, where were You?

'A day will come [says God] when I will hide My face.' It came. But it was not a day. It was two thousand years. 'You hid Your face, and I was terrified' (Psalm 30:8). We knew the chill, cold fear of darkness. We knew what it was to seek God but not to find Him, to call Him and discover that He was not close. We carried in our souls the words of the book of Psalms:

> You have given us up to be devoured like sheep
> And have scattered us among the nations.
> You have sold Your people for a pittance,
> Gaining nothing from their sale.
> Your have made us a reproach to our neighbours,
> The scorn and derision of those around us.
> You have made us a byword among the nations,
> A laughing-stock among the peoples . . .
> All this has come upon us,
> Yet we have not forgotten You,
> Or been false to Your covenant. (Psalm 44:12–18)

That is what it was for God to hide His face. That is what it was to be a Jew.

Then something began to happen. 'That night, the king's sleep was disturbed' (Esther 6:1). In the midst of darkness, we began to see what looked like the first faint signs of light. One after another, prayers that Jews had said for hundreds of years, more in hope than expectation, began to come true.

'Sound the great Shofar for our freedom.' The ram's horn sounded and in one country after another Jews left the ghetto and were free.

'Raise the banner to gather our exiles.' The banner of Zion was lifted and from across the globe Jews began to return to the land of our ancestors.

'Restore our judges as at first.' The State of Israel was born. The Jewish home was granted independence. For the first time in almost two thousand years, Jews had sovereignty. They could rule over themselves instead of being ruled over by others. They could defend themselves instead of depending on others.

'Return in mercy to Your city, Jerusalem.' In 1967, Jerusalem was reunited. Jews could pray again at the Temple wall.

And they streamed into the land. From Yemen, Iraq and Iran, from Russia and Ethiopia, Jews who had been cut off from their people for decades, for centuries, came home. 'Even if you have been banished to the ends of the heavens, from there the Lord your God will gather you and bring you back.'

Rabbi Joseph Soloveitchik of blessed memory once said that with the birth of the State of Israel there ended the 'hiding of the face' of God. God had re-entered history. It was the beginning of the end of exile. This century, one after another of the prophecies of Moses and Isaiah has come true. All except one. The Jewish people always knew that this would be the last of the promises to come true. Therefore, in our prayers it was always the last: 'Lord who blesses His people Israel with peace.' Has any people ever prayed for peace as we have prayed? The *Amidah* ends with a prayer for peace. So does *Kaddish*. So does the Grace after Meals. So do the Priestly blessings. Peace is always our last prayer, never our first, because we know how hard peace is to achieve.

Jews were always willing, sometimes *too* willing, to make peace with the world. The question was: when would the world make its peace with us? One empire after another, one nation after another, one religion after another, refused to let Jews be. Even when the State of Israel came into being at the decree of the United Nations, its neighbours still refused to let it be. What other nation has had to face this fate, of being unrecognised, deemed not to exist, forced to live in continual fear of terrorism and war? But this year, as if out of nowhere, we are beginning to hear the word 'Peace'. Not from Israel's friends, but from her enemies. Let none of us underestimate the momentousness of this hour. Today our final prayer is no longer a dream. It has become a hope.

The rabbis said that when God revealed Himself in history at the division of the Red Sea, even the simplest Jew was privileged to see what the great prophet Ezekiel did not see. Today God whose name is Peace is revealing Himself in history again. We are living in times the like of which no Jews have known since the days of Solomon. 'I slept but my heart was awake. Listen! My lover is knocking' (Song of Songs 5:2). On our television screens and in our newspapers, if we listen carefully, we can hear the sound of God knocking on the door of Jewish destiny, telling us we live in extraordinary times.

Tonight we feel God very close. It is as if God has emerged from centuries of hiding and is making His face shine on the great events of our time as they touch the Jewish people. Tonight, if we are still, if we open our souls, we will feel ourselves touched by the wings of the Divine presence. And anyone in whom a Jewish heart still beats must know that there can be only one response. 'Seek God where He is to be found. Call Him when He is close.'

III

Yitzhak Rabin's speech on the White House lawn was one of the great political addresses of the twentieth century. It was the speech of a secular Jew. But it was full of biblical echoes, some explicit, others merely hinted at. It was this that gave his words and the occasion itself an epic gravity. None of the commentators fully analysed his speech, and as a result, though they sensed its power and the courage of Rabin's gesture of reconciliation, they missed its profoundly religious undertones.

This was sad for two reasons, one Jewish, the other universal. Jewishly, the birth of the State of Israel has not lessened the sharp divisions between religious and secular Jews. What is forgotten in this war of cultures is that many secular Israelis are driven by a faith that to an outsider seems quite clearly religious. Rabin's speech was a perfect example and a moving instance of how religious faith can surface in the most secular heart.

More generally, religion is often condemned as leading to war rather than to peace. But the Jewish tradition contains a powerful thrust towards peace, not only in its explicit prayers, but in the subtle ways in which Jews are called on to see situations from vantage points other than their own. Peace only comes about when we see the world through other eyes, from the perspective of the stranger, the victim and the rival. One of the most striking examples is an image Yitzhak Rabin invoked in his speech: a mother weeping for her child. This image, taken up in five different ways in the liturgy for the Jewish New Year, forces us to feel the pain of human suffering, even when it is the suffering of our enemies. The fact that Rabin used this phrase in a speech delivered three days before the New Year could not have been accidental. It was a signal reminder that a religious imagination can be one of the most potent forces for peace.

This analysis was published in The Daily Telegraph, *15 October 1993.*

As political ideologies wane in the contemporary world, so the hold of other loyalties grows: racial, ethnic and religious. It is a development full of dangers. Ethnic identities can rapidly descend to the politics of the tribe, exploding as in Bosnia or simmering ominously as in the urban ghettoes of America. Religion in these contexts is rarely a force for reconciliation. It can make conflict more intransigent, lending divine imperative to racial difference. In the course of history, religions have led to war as often as they have paved the way to peace.

Against this background, one recent event has received too little attention: the speech of Israel's Prime Minister Yitzhak Rabin at the White House on the signing of the peace agreement with the Palestinians. It was an historic moment. But it was also a *religious* moment, full of biblical resonances. President Clinton set the tone, speaking of Israel and the Palestinians as the latest chapter in the drama of 'the children of Abraham, the descendants of Isaac and Ishmael'. Both he and Shimon Peres quoted verses from the book of Isaiah about peace.

But it was Yitzhak Rabin's speech that broke through the boundaries of political rhetoric. What was striking was not his overt religious references. He quoted the book of Ecclesiastes about 'a time for war and a time for peace'. He ended his speech with a famous Jewish prayer for peace, and invited the assembled politicians to say Amen. These were moving gestures, but perhaps no more than a sense of moment demanded.

It was not these, but his oblique allusions that made me sit up and take notice. There was the moment when he turned to the Palestinians and spoke about their common humanity. He said, 'We, like you, are people, people who want to build a home, to plant a tree, to love.' This sequence of images was not accidental. It was a reference to a striking biblical passage.

The twentieth chapter of the book of Deuteronomy specifies that when the Israelites prepared to wage war, three groups of people were to be offered military exemption: those who had built a new house, planted a new vineyard, or had become engaged but not yet married. War must not destroy these three scenes of human creativity. Rabin's allusion was precise and powerful.

The most stunning example, though, was when he spoke about the suffering of war. He used a single image. He spoke about the pain of a land where 'mothers weep for their sons'. As soon as I heard this phrase, I knew that it was a reference to the verse in Jeremiah (31:15), 'A voice is heard in Ramah, mourning and great weeping, Rachel weeping for her sons and refusing to be comforted, because her sons are no more.'

There were other biblical mothers who wept for their sons, and I listed them. There was Hagar who wept for Ishmael as he lay dying in the desert (Genesis 21). There was Hannah who wept for the son she could not have (1 Samuel 1). There was Sarah who, according to rabbinic tradition, wept when she learned that Isaac was about to be offered as a sacrifice (Genesis 22). There was the mother of Sisera who wept when her son was killed in battle against the Israelites (Judges 5).

With a shock of recognition, I realised that these five texts were connected. The peace agreement with the Palestinians was concluded three days before the Jewish New Year. Four of the texts were taken from the biblical readings for the New Year. The fifth is the symbolism behind the festival's great religious act, the blowing of the ram's horn. Its sound, says the Talmud, is meant to represent the weeping of the mother of Sisera. In a single phrase, Israel's Prime Minister had evoked five biblical echoes, all drawn from the synagogue service of the forthcoming holy days. This was more than rhetoric. It was the voice of a great religious tradition.

Yitzhak Rabin is a secular Jew. What moved him, at that moment, to speak in the language of the prophets? Surely this. He was taking the most risk-laden decision in the history of the State of Israel. He was making peace with a group which has no tradition of moderation or peace. He was shaking hands with a man previously dedicated to violence and terror. He may have had no alternative. But what a risk it was.

Risk demands courage and courage needs faith. At the heart of the Hebrew Bible is a faith in peace. The Bible sometimes speaks of the necessity of war. But it unsparingly records its human cost *on both sides*. On the Jewish New Year we remember the tears shed not only for Israel, but also for Israel's rivals, Ishmael and Sisera. Behind Rabin's decision, and woven into his words, was the most powerful literature of peace the world has known.

Religion can fuel conflict. But it can sometimes move us beyond it. In the year of Bosnia, it is no small thing that in another troubled area of the world a religious vision led the secular government of Israel to take a momentous risk for peace.

15

After Hebron

On the morning of Purim 5754 (25 February 1994) the world was shocked to hear the news of the massacre of Muslims at prayer in the mosque in Hebron. The perpetrator was a religious Jew. I felt that the strongest possible condemnation was called for, and within an hour I had issued the following statement, which was carried by the national press:

I am shocked and grieved by the devastating criminal act perpetrated in Hebron today which has cost so many lives. Such an act is an obscenity and a travesty of Jewish values. That it should have been perpetrated against worshippers in a house of prayer at a holy time makes it a blasphemy as well.

Our hearts go out to the families who have been bereaved. As a religious leader I unequivocally condemn all acts of violence against the innocent, regardless of by whom and against whom they are committed.

Violence is evil. Violence committed in the name of God is doubly evil. Violence against those engaged in worshipping God is unspeakably evil. In the name of God I pray that in the light of today's tragedy no effort is spared to ensure the safety and security of the three great world faiths to express themselves freely in the Holy Land.

I issued similar statements after the tragic reprisal attacks at Afula and Hadera.

Three days later, on 28 February 1994, Jewish and Catholic leaders met in London to mark the establishment of diplomatic relations between the Holy See and Israel, and I used the occasion to make a further statement about the events in Hebron. It was difficult not to sense the historic resonances of the moment. On the one hand was a significant move to mend the troubled relationship between the Catholic Church and the Jewish people. On the other were the still-fresh reverberations of Jewish-Arab violence. In my address I said this:

We are gathered tonight to celebrate a moment of light in what has been a long history of darkness. In diplomatic terms, perhaps the establishment of relations between the Holy See and Israel is not a major event. But set against the centuries of a relationship between the Catholic Church and the Jewish people which the Pope has described as one of 'internecine enmity and oppression' it is a powerful gesture of reconciliation.

It carries to its logical conclusion the process set in motion by *Nostra Aetate* and taken further by the present Pope when, in the synagogue in Rome, he spoke of the Jewish people as Christianity's 'beloved elder brothers'.

It extends the new relationship from Jews as individuals to Israel as the sovereign state of the eternal people in their ancestral home. As Jews we salute the courage with which the Church has wrestled with her teachings in the aftermath of the Holocaust, knowing – as we all must know – that in our battle against evil we must do our utmost to ensure that our own most sacred teachings are not unwittingly the cause of a legacy of hatred and contempt.

Every faith must wrestle with itself in this century of unprecedented destruction of human life. The Catholic Church has done so with a determination that is both admirable and exemplary. It did so in *Nostra Aetate* (the 1965 Vatican II Declaration on the relation of the Church to non-Christian religions), and it has continued to do so since. I extend my congratulations to those on both sides who made this agreement possible, and to those many others who have worked so hard to create a climate of goodwill and mutual respect between our two faiths.

But in the light of the terrible event in Hebron let me say one more thing. We live, we say, in a secular age. And we, Jews and Catholics alike, know only too acutely the price humanity pays in fragile relationships, broken dreams and the impoverishment of human aspiration when we exile God from the moral and spiritual horizons of mankind.

But we forget at our peril one fact. The secularisation of society began when people of goodwill came to the conclusion that religion brought war, not peace; conflict, not conciliation; intolerance, not love; closed minds instead of open hearts. And incredibly, after all we know about the devastating cost of religious and racial conflict, in which there are no winners, only losers, there are still too many areas of the world where people are prepared to kill other human beings, created in the image of God, and to do so in the name of God.

In the name of God it must end. And it must be brought to an end by men and women of God who have the courage to say that hatred, triumphalism, violence, murder, the estrangement between peoples, and the imposition of truth by force, have no part to play in the life of faith. Between brothers, there must be love; and between enemies, peace. There is no other way.

If the massacre at Hebron has taught us one thing, it is this: that each of us, within our own faiths and across the boundaries between faiths, must double and redouble our efforts for reconciliation and peace. If religion is part of the problem, then religion must be part of the solution. As a religious leader I say, loudly and unequivocally, that violence and vengeance blaspheme the name of God in an age when God is calling on us not to destroy the world He made.

Against this darkness, the establishment of diplomatic relations between the Holy See and Israel is a small candle of light. But as the Jewish mystics said: even a little light banishes much darkness. And there is still much darkness we need to banish. May this agreement be the herald of others between different peoples and faiths. And let us pray that other estranged brothers may yet meet and talk and find reconciliation.

Despite these statements and those of Israeli leaders, religious voices were heard in Israel defending the massacre. This, to me, was profoundly disturbing. There may be legitimate concerns about the wisdom, consequences and detailed provisions of Israel's peace process. But these cannot be addressed by acts of terrorism or threats of civil disobedience without damaging the very structure of Israel as a democratic state and undermining the credibility of Judaism as a religion of peace. Hebron exposed deep tensions at the heart of contemporary religious Zionism. Accordingly I felt the need to reiterate some fundamental Judaic principles in my pastoral letter before Passover. The following section was published in The Times *on 26 March 1994.*

The rabbis said that in telling the story of Passover, 'we must begin with the shame and end with the praise'. There is no doubt this year as to what constitutes the shame. Its name is Hebron.

We know the pain that lay behind the atrocity and some responses to it. Jews have suffered much this century, perhaps too much for a people to bear. The Holocaust. The persecution of Jews in Communist and Arab lands. Israel's wars. The terrorist attacks by Palestinians since the signing of the peace agreement.

We say in the Haggadah, the Passover compilation of readings, 'It was not one man alone who rose against us to destroy us. It happens in every generation.' This year, even after the film *Schindler's List*, we know that anti-semitism did not die at Auschwitz. It merely went underground to sprout again in new and hybrid forms.

Against the backdrop of constant violence against Jews, a mood of fear and anger and resentment is understandable. But in Judaism to understand is not to forgive. What is unforgivable is not merely the act itself – the brutal murder of worshippers at prayer – but failure in some quarters to condemn and in others even to endorse an act of pure barbarity. That a murderer should be spoken of as a hero, a saint, a Samson; that a rabbi should declare that a million Arab lives are not worth a Jewish fingernail – these are a disgrace to Judaism and enough to make us hang our heads in shame.

For there is a question that haunts the festival of Pesach. *Why* did God bring it about that the Jewish people should be born in exile, forged in slavery, and made to suffer brutal oppression? To this the Bible gives an unequivocal answer. *You shall not do what others have done to you.* 'Do not oppress the stranger, because you know what it feels like to be a stranger: you were strangers in the land of Egypt.' What you suffered, you shall not inflict. You experienced injustice, therefore practise justice. You know what it is like to be a slave, therefore do not enslave others. You have been victims, therefore you may not be oppressors. You have been murdered, therefore do not join the ranks of the murderers. Until we have understood this we have not understood Judaism, however religious we are.

There is a moment of transcending moral majesty in the Seder, the service of Passover evening. We spill drops of wine at the mention of the plagues as symbolic tears for their Egyptian victims. We do not say Hallel during the last days of Pesach because, say some authorities, we mourn for the Egyptians drowned at the Red Sea. The midrash, or traditional homily, says that at the Sea, when the angels began to sing a hymn of victory, God stopped them with the words, 'My creatures are drowning, and you wish to sing?' The Egyptians were Israel's persecutors, tyrants and child-murderers. Yet the Torah says, 'Do not hate an Egyptian, because you were once a stranger in his land.'

This is not Diaspora mentality, nor is it the ethic of a timorous minority. It is Judaism plain and simple. It is what gave us the moral strength which proved to be, as the prophets said it would, more powerful than any military might. Everyone has a duty to live by this truth; above all, religious Jews.

Yes: innocent Jews have been murdered by Arab terrorists and few Islamic voices have been raised in protest. Yes: Israel must negotiate peace through strength and not yield to moral double standards.

But we did not survive two thousand years of powerlessness to become brutalised by power. We did not outlive our enemies so that we could become like them. We did not survive Pharoah so that we could become like Pharoah. That is one of the messages of Passover, and we forget it at our peril.

16

The Vatican and Israel

By any standards, the agreement made between Israel and the Vatican on 30 December 1993 to move towards full diplomatic links was an historic turning point in the relationship between two of the world's great faiths. It lacked the obvious drama of the handshake between Yitzhak Rabin and Yasser Arafat on the White House lawn. But when set against almost two thousand years of tragedy between Synagogue and Church it counts as one of the great interfaith achievements of the century.

On the surface, the agreement is no more than another episode in the series of events set in motion by the Gulf War and the subsequent peace process. Since 1991 nearly thirty countries, including China, India and the republics of the former Soviet Union, have established or renewed diplomatic links with Israel. The Vatican could be seen as a belated participant in this re-alignment. But that would be to ignore the unique and troubled relationship between Christianity and Judaism.

From at least the third century their encounter had been set on a tragic course by what the historian Jules Isaac called the 'teachings of contempt' of the Church for the Jews. For these were not two unrelated religions. Christianity had originally been a Jewish sect. It laid claim to the Hebrew Scriptures and to the covenant with Israel. The fact that the majority of Jews did not become Christians was a source of continuing perplexity.

It was resolved by a series of stereotypes that were to have a tenacious hold on the Christian imagination. Jews had rejected salvation. They were an obstinate, accursed people. Their defeat by Rome was to be seen as divine punishment. Far from being a challenge to Christianity, the Jews – dispersed and powerless as they were – were its living proof.

These attitudes persisted long into the modern world, and reached their dénouement in what was widely perceived as the silence of Pope Pius XII during the Nazi Holocaust. Might anti-Judaism have given passive assent

The Daily Telegraph, 31 December 1993

to anti-semitism? That disturbing thought prepared the way for *Nostra Aetate* (1965), which sought to remove official teaching that the Jews were a people 'rejected or accursed by God'.

Many saw the declaration as the beginning of a new era. But they became frustrated when it led no further. The most significant development in Jewish life since the Holocaust was the creation of the State of Israel. For Jews, it meant return to their historical birthplace and an affirmation of life against the decree of death. But *Nostra Aetate* contained no statement about Israel, and the Vatican continued to withhold diplomatic recognition.

Explanations were offered. Rome was concerned about Israel's disputed boundaries, the status of Jerusalem, Palestinian refugees and the position of the Church in Arab lands. But to Jewish and even some Catholic observers, the Vatican's reticence contained traces of ancient theological prejudice. Homelessness – the Church had taught – was the divine judgement against Jews for not becoming Christians. Therefore a Jewish homecoming was impossible.

Shortly before his death in 1904, Theodor Herzl met Pope Pius X and explained his dream of a Jewish state. The Pope replied, 'The Jews have not recognised our Lord, therefore we cannot recognise the Jewish people.' Such sentiments were surely untenable after Auschwitz. How could the Vatican recognise Jewry without including its most powerful collective expression, its State?

So the agreement fulfils a process begun twenty-eight years ago in Vatican II, and will help to heal a wound that has festered for centuries. There can be no doubting the courage with which the Catholic Church has wrestled with its texts and teachings, and for this there can only be Jewish admiration.

On Israel's side too, there has been powerful resistance to overcome. Many Jews, religious and secular, argue that there are injuries too deep to be forgotten. The history of Jewish suffering in the Crusades, blood libels, inquisitions, ghettoes, and expulsions cannot be unwritten. There are, they say, relationships that cannot be normalised. The Vatican and the Jewish people cannot meet in friendship: not yet, perhaps not ever.

Understandable though they are, I believe these views are mistaken. If faith is to meet the challenge of this destructive century it must be prepared to move beyond the antagonisms of the past. Jews cannot ignore a Church with 900 million members and immense influence throughout the world. The Vatican cannot ignore the political rebirth of the Jewish people after two thousand years of powerlessness and dispersion. Above all, neither can forego the imperative of reconciliation after witnessing the full cost of religious conflict.

The story of the covenant begins with two sibling rivalries, between Isaac and Ishmael, and Jacob and Esau. Jewish tradition traced Ishmael to Islam and Esau to Rome. The year 1993 will be seen in retrospect as the year in which Israel exchanged a handshake with its own Ishmael and Esau, the Palestinians and the Catholic Church.

These were secular, political events. But behind them on both sides are centuries of religious tension. At a time when old ethnic sores have been re-opened, these two gestures are momentous signals of hope. Ancient hostilities do not die overnight. But neither are we condemned to replay them for ever. The year 1993 may yet be seen as the year in which Jerusalem sent a message of peace to the world.

17
Democracy and Religious Values

As religion once again becomes a power in the contemporary world – often allied with ethnicity and nationalism – it becomes important to re-examine the relationship between democracy and religious belief. The connection is far from obvious. To a religious believer, democracy can look as if it locates authority in the wrong place: with fallible mankind instead of infallible God. It involves compromise. It is built around the wrong kind of freedom: 'freedom from' rather than 'freedom to'. So at least, it can be argued. Religion has not always been democracy's friend. At times it can be its implacable enemy.

None the less, it was from the Hebrew Bible that the great architects of British and American democracy drew their inspiration. The ethical arguments for democratic government carried force precisely because they were based on biblical principles and values. Those principles now need restating.

But I begin from the opposite direction, because the strength of a religious argument *for* democracy depends on the honesty with which we are able to confront the contrary case. The religious argument *against* democracy is this. Democracy, or rule by the people, is directly opposed to theocracy or rule by God. We owe our western political traditions not to the Hebrew Bible, but to the Greek city states of the fifth century BCE. The Bible by contrast sets out its ideal political system in terms of monarchy, the king anointed by the prophet as the representative of God.

Religion and democracy represent two conflicting visions of the social order, and this can be seen by their respective answers to a set of ultimate questions. Is authority vested in God or in humanity? Do we owe obedience to a higher will or to the collective determination of the human will? Is the ideal society one in which a single vision prevails of the common good, or

Lecture to the Inter-Faith Conference on Democracy, Westminster Abbey,
17 November 1993

is it one in which plural visions co-exist and compete for our allegiance? Democracy tends to emerge from secularisation, while ecclesiastical power has historically been associated with authoritarian regimes.

There is enough truth in this argument to make us cautious about too easy an identification between ancient faiths and contemporary political structures. None the less there is a route to be charted from biblical principles to democratic government. Democracy is not prescribed in the Bible, nor is it an end in itself. But it is the best means currently available for protecting the values at the heart of a biblical vision of society.

Political Structures as Means, not Ends

Our most important starting point is the realisation that neither the Hebrew Bible nor the rabbinic tradition idealise any specific political order. Judaism has known rule by magistrates, judges, elders, kings, patriarchs, exilarchs and community leaders of all kinds. Jews have experienced the complete spectrum of political power, from national sovereignty to local autonomy to voluntary association. They have constructed political systems ranging from monarchy to oligarchy to representative democracy. That same variety is evident today as we survey the Jewish world from the sovereign State of Israel to the highly variegated governance of diaspora communities.

This calls for explanation. The Hebrew Bible is intensely concerned with the political domain. A large part of it is devoted to what we might call political history. Jewish law covers the spectrum of social, economic and environmental concerns. Why then does it not articulate an ideal form of government? The answer surely is this. Systems of government do not form a proper subject of revelation. Revelation is concerned with spiritual and moral truth, with principles that apply at all places and times. Political structures are not of this kind. They are means, not ends. A form of government appropriate in one context may be inappropriate in another. A tribal society is different from a unified kingdom. A sovereign state is different from a scattered diaspora. Systems of government meet specific needs, and those needs change from age to age. Democracy itself is not the same phenomenon in the small Greek city state of antiquity and in the large European nations of today. Revelation contains a set of principles against which any particular political order can be tested. But it is not a timeless formula for constructing governments.

Nowhere is this conveyed more dramatically than in the sequence of events in chapters 18–20 of the book of Exodus. In Exodus 19–20 we read of the great revelation at Mount Sinai. The Israelites are convened as a people and they hear, directly from God, the core of their constitution, the Ten Commandments. Immediately prior to this, however, they institute their first system of governance. This does *not* come directly from God, but from Moses' father-in-law, the Midianite priest Jethro, who advises Moses to appoint a hierarchy of officials – leaders of thousands, hundreds, fifties and tens – who will judge and apply the law. The principles are established of delegation and subsidiarity.

The contrast is clear. Israel receives its constitution from God, but it learns its system of government from the experience of other people. In other respects, the Bible lays down a code of difference for the people of the covenant. They are to be a holy people, which is to say, separate, distinct, set apart. The sole exception is government. Even monarchy, one of the few political structures to be divinely commanded, is described in Deuteronomy and the book of Samuel as an imitative gesture, something Israel will seek in order to be 'like the nations' around them.

From this we can draw a fundamental conclusion. All attempts to confer transcendental justification on a particular system of government – be it the Divine Right of Kings or the Thousand Year Reich or the Communist utopia – is at best mistaken, at worst a form of idolatry. Revelation is eternal. Politics is not.

The Primacy of the Individual

Religion does not uniquely specify an ideal form of government. Instead it provides us with a set of values or principles against which a system can be judged. What are they?

The first is the epic statement of the opening chapter of the Bible, that the human individual is created 'in the image of God'. This is a religious and ethical proposition. But it is also a political one. The person is prior to the collectivity. The starting point of political theory must lie in the rights, freedom and dignity of the individual, not in those of the State. It is this that forms the biblical basis of modern political theory, and an eternal protest against totalitarianism.

To this must be added two other propositions. The idea that humanity is created in the image of God is a subtle one, because central to the Hebrew Bible is the idea that God has no image. His very name, God tells Moses, is *ehyeh asher ehyeh*, 'I will be who I will be'. God is Being in its infinite, open-ended unpredictability. What is divine about humanity is its diversity, not its uniformity. The rabbis of the Mishnah put it simply. They said: when coins are minted in a single mould, they are all alike. But when people are created in the image of God they are all different. What they hold in common is simply their infinite value, from which the rabbis derived the rule that one who saves a single life is as if he had saved an entire universe.

But the individual is not self-sufficient. Each of us lacks some gift that someone else has. The Bible presents this proposition in an arresting way. The first chapter of Genesis describes the stages of creation, each ending with the phrase 'and God saw that it was good'. There is one thing which God declares *not* to be good: 'It is not good for man to be alone.' To achieve anything we must form associations, and this gives rise to the political process. The great twelfth-century Jewish thinker, Moses Maimonides, puts it thus:

> It has already been fully explained that man is naturally a social being, that by virtue of his nature he seeks to form communities; man is therefore different from other living beings that are not compelled to combine into communities. He is, as you know, the highest form in creation, and he therefore includes the largest number of constituent elements; this is the reason why the human race contains such a great variety of individuals, that we cannot discover two persons exactly alike in any moral quality, or in external appearance . . . This great variety and the necessity of social life are essential elements in man's nature. But the well-being of society demands that there should be a leader able to regulate the actions of man; he must complete every shortcoming, remove every excess, and prescribe for the conduct of all, so that the natural variety should be counterbalanced by the uniformity of legislation, and the order of society be well established. I therefore maintain that the Law, though not a product of nature, is nonetheless not entirely foreign to nature. (*The Guide of the Perplexed*, 2:40)

People are different, but they must be able to form societies. This requires laws, and hence a legislator, and therefore a source of legislative authority. Humanity needs political structures.

Covenant

The key word underlying such structures in the Bible is *brit*, 'covenant', and it is this which gives Judaic politics its distinctive character. The idea of covenant presupposes that all parties to a political order have independent integrity, that associations are formed on the basis of reciprocal under-takings, and that they are freely assented to by all their members. Daniel Elazar describes covenant as a compact 'usually meant to be perpetual between parties having independent but not necessarily equal status, that provides for joint action or obligation to achieve defined ends . . . under conditions of mutual respect, in such a way as to protect the integrity of all parties involved.'

Crucial to the idea of covenant is *consent*, and this remains so even when one of the parties is God Himself. Prior and subsequent to the great covenant at Sinai, Moses assembles the people, who signal their willingness to be bound by its terms (Exodus 19:8; 24:3,7). National assemblies are convened subsequently to ratify the covenant at critical moments of change, as in the days of Joshua or Ezra (Joshua 24; Nehemiah 8–10). Similar assemblies are gathered to institute the monarchy (1 Samuel 8) and to confirm the transfer of kingship to David (11 Samuel 5:3).

The idea of the consent of the governed is central to the defence of liberty. Hobbes and Locke, for example, took the biblical concept of covenant as the starting point of their political theory. For the Hebrew Bible itself, covenant is rooted in a vision of the human being as a moral agent for whom freedom and responsibility go hand in hand. God and man are linked in a shared enterprise. They are, as the rabbis put it, 'partners in the work of creation'. Axiomatic to the Hebrew Bible, therefore, is the idea that God never acts to restrict human freedom. As Moses Maimonides explained, though God may miraculously change the course of nature, He never changes human nature. To do so would vitiate the entire purpose of the law, which is predicated on free human choice. When a fourth-century rabbi hypothesised that the Israelites in the wilderness may have had no choice but to accept the covenant, a rabbinical colleague immediately countered that this would constitute a fundamental flaw to its authority since obligations cannot be binding if accepted under duress. Even the moral authority of a Divine covenant ultimately rests on its initial free acceptance.

The Limits of Power

Covenant itself, though, is set within a wider context: the supremacy of morality. Justice constitutes a limit on all power, even that of God. This gives rise to the momentous dialogue between God and humanity in the form of the great challenges of Moses, Jeremiah and Job, reaching a crescendo in Abraham's question: 'Shall the judge of all the earth not do justly?'

According to the Bible, therefore, no authority is absolute, even if initially endorsed by the people's will. David is wrong to arrange for the death of Uriah. Ahab is wrong to seize Naboth's vineyard. Governmental authority is circumscribed by the moral law. Accordingly rabbinic law recognises *in extremis* the duty to disobey illegal or immoral orders, a principle already foreshadowed in the biblical account of the Hebrew midwives who refused to carry out Pharaoh's decree that male Israelites be drowned at birth.

How, though, is justice to be secured against the inevitable corruptions of power? Crucial to biblical politics is the division of leadership into three domains, those of the king, the priest and the prophet. They were later called by the rabbis the three crowns: of government (*keter malkhut*), priesthood (*keter kehunah*) and Jewish law and moral teaching (*keter Torah*). This separation of powers, later developed and modified by Montesquieu, seems to have been a consistent feature of Jewish political organisation at most times. It does not correspond to a division between secular and spiritual authority, since each domain drew its ultimate mandate from God and was bound by the Divine law. Rather, it represents three different aspects of the life of society, the king embodying its civic and political governance, the priesthood its organised worship, and the prophet or sage its commitment to the eternal principles of the Divine law as translated into daily life.

There were and are constant struggles between these domains, but attempts to combine them in a single person or institution were resisted. This was the criticism levelled by the sages against the later Hasmonean kings, who combined monarchy and priesthood. The independent voice of the prophet was particularly important in guarding against the temptations of power. It served as a continual reminder that power must be tempered by justice, and that all authority is constrained by the sovereignty of God.

These principles did not entail democracy in the modern sense of the word, but they did contain the seeds from which it could evolve. The Bible, as well as containing a mandate for monarchy, includes a sustained prophetic critique, never surpassed, of the ways in which governmental power can be abused. This led the great fifteenth-century Jewish scholar and diplomat, Don Isaac Abrabanel, to review the whole Judaic political tradition and conclude that monarchy was not so much commanded by the Bible as temporarily conceded. It was, he says, one of those concessions the Bible makes to the shortcomings of human nature and is not in any way to be regarded as an ideal form of government.

Abrabanel's remarks, written five hundred years ago, are still of interest. The arguments for monarchy in his day were that the concentration of authority in a single individual made for unity, continuity and absolute power. The king stood in the same relationship to the people as the heart to the body, or as God to the universe. Abrabanel dismisses this argument in the following words:

[As to unity,] it is not at all impossible for a people to have many leaders conducting the state and its laws in unison and concurrence. [As to continuity,] I know of no reason why their leadership should not be temporary, changing from year to year, or at other intervals, and thus making their actions subject to control and, if need be, to the punishment of those who follow them in office. [As to the benefit of absolute power,] I do not see any reason why their power should not be limited and regulated according to established laws and customs. Common sense dictates that one man in the position of a monarch is more likely to do wrong than many people acting together. For if any one of them is inclined to commit a crime, his colleagues will prevent him from doing so, knowing very well that all of them will be called to account after a short while and will be subject to the punishment meted out by their followers and to public disgrace. (*Commentary to Deuteronomy* 17:14)

The case for democracy could hardly be put better.

Perhaps the greatest testimony to the power of the democratic idea in Judaism is the fact that the modern State of Israel was from the beginning and remains a vigorous democracy, despite the fact that the overwhelming majority of its population come from countries in which democratic government was unknown. Of few other states created since the Second World War can this be said.

Religion and Democracy

The Judaic tradition thus suggests a distinctive approach to questions often posed about religion and democracy. Is there not a conflict between religious and democratic concepts of authority? From a Judaic perspective, this question is based on a fallacy. There is a sharp distinction between matters of right and wrong, which for the biblical monotheisms are the subject of revelation, and matters such as defence, the economy and the preservation of order, which are the domain of politics or the 'crown of government' (*keter malkhut*). Judaism has always seen authoritarianism in this second sphere as an assault on the essential dignity of the individual. Government is a partnership between those who govern and those who are governed. That partnership must be honoured both in the manner in which the government is chosen and in the substance of the policies which it pursues. Democracy, as the most effective form we know of accountability to those affected by government policies, has powerful biblical support, and it was within the biblical context that the early theorists of democracy both in Britain and the United States constructed their arguments.

It is true to say that democratic regimes are now in favour. Is this a passing phase in the progress of civilisation, or is democracy a value to which we are committed unconditionally? Prior to the ultimate redemption – which is to say, within the terms of human history as we have known it – no political achievement is final. The struggle between power and justice will continue. So will the search for a proper balance between the individual and the collective. There are many kinds of democracy; none is perfect. Nor is democracy alone the guarantor of a healthy society. None the less it is the best system we have thus far evolved to ensure the accountability of governments, the protection of the individual, and the freedom within which we can grow to maturity as autonomous moral agents. It is in ongoing danger of erosion, and as a result constant vigilance is required.

Is democracy an end in itself or is it a means (perhaps the least unreliable we know) for securing the values of freedom, the rule of law and protection of the weak and vulnerable? The Judaic answer would be that, being a political structure, democracy is a means, not an end. As Maimonides put it, the highest forms of human perfection lie within the domain of the individual soul. However, to achieve those perfections, we must secure certain physical needs, which we can only do by constructing societies and hence political systems. These require the ceding of individual entitlements to a central body (property, as in the case of taxation; liberty, as in the case of a judicial system backed by punishments). The individual must have a say in both the process and product of that transfer of rights. Democracy is therefore the least unreliable form of government, which is itself only a framework of human flourishing, not the flourishing itself.

Do religions have a role in safeguarding democratic values against corruption? They do, but in two distinct ways, corresponding to the biblical realms of prophecy and priesthood. Prophecy has a critical function. Ezekiel defined his role as 'watchman' to the house of Israel, giving warning of impending catastrophe. But priesthood is about constructing communities where the life of faith is given tangible expression: the role given its classic sociological analysis by Emile Durkheim. Without prophecy a society can become corrupt at the top. But without priesthood, it can erode from below. It can lose its structures of family and community life, within which the civic virtues are learned and enacted. Prophecy is dramatic, priesthood is not. Prophecy makes headlines, priesthood rarely does. But both are necessary to the civil order. Without the matrix of institutions within which individual responsibility and the moral sentiments are nurtured, no freedoms are secure for long. In an age in which those institutions are rapidly dissolving, the priestly function is no less important than the prophetic.

Can Religions Endorse a Plural Society?

These are some of the questions commonly posed about religion and democracy. But there is another and more fundamental tension between our great religious traditions and the contemporary political environment. The modern democratic state is built on quite different foundations than Athens or Sparta in ancient Greece. Those were hierarchical societies, in which only some groups, not all, were enfranchised. Women were not; slaves were not; nor were long-term resident aliens. Greek democracy would today be regarded as intolerably undemocratic. It was less rule by the people than rule by a subsection of the people, and it left large groups outside the political process.

Greek democracy was predicated on cultural *homogeneity*. Modern democracy faces the problem of cultural and religious *diversity*. In its purest form, it proposed to solve the problem by drawing a sharp distinction between individuals and groups. Individuals were to be enfranchised, groups were not. A person's religion or culture was irrelevant to the political process. He or she participated not as a Protestant or Catholic or Jew but as a person. Church and State were, either formally or in effect, to be separated. Politics was to become a neutral arena where conflicting interests were resolved.

We now know that this vision did an injustice to the human need for identity: a sense of the past, of belonging, and of common purpose. It understated the connection between political structure and a nation's history and traditions. It also neglected the degree to which members of religious and ethnic minorities felt part of their group and its loyalties, and not merely disembodied citizens. The ground was set for a tense conflict between a coherent national identity and a culture of different faiths and ethnicities.

The modern democratic nation state is built on more than the concept of government by the collective will for the collective good. It is based on the idea that there is a domain of public life in which a multiplicity of communities with different traditions can join together in the collective enterprise of citizenship. It is not merely a democracy. It is a plural democracy. And it is this idea – a difficult one, calling for a most delicate balance of restraints – which is today in danger. As the neutral state fails to answer the most basic questions of personal identity, so we see larger societies disintegrate into religiously, culturally or ethnically defined entities: in the break-up of the Soviet Union, the possibility of French-Canadian secession, the divorce between Czechs and Slovaks, and most tragically in bloody ethnic war in Bosnia.

The most important conflict in today's political landscape is less between religion and democracy than between religion and pluralism, an essential component of the ethnically diverse state. Religions often embody a yearning for a unitary social order which overcomes the dichotomy between the rich traditions of the individual, the family and the group, and the relative neutrality of the state and its 'naked public square'. How can a genuine religious believer tolerate the indignities of a pluralist democracy in which, though the members of his group have rights, so too do the members of other groups who reject and even ridicule the values he holds dear? Religious conviction finds itself in conflict less with democracy as such, than with the jangling discord of voices which a plural society inevitably broadcasts. In such a society, there is no one dominant voice. As Michael Novak puts it, 'In a genuinely pluralistic society, there is no one sacred canopy. *By intention* there is not. At its spiritual core, there is an empty shrine.'

The question that has suddenly become acute in today's fragmenting political order is: can a strong religious presence tolerate this empty shrine, and with it a society which confers equal rights to members of other faiths or of none? If the answer to this is no, then a religion might tolerate democracy in the Athenian but not in the modern sense. It would reject the essential premise that different groups should have an equal share in defining the common good.

The defence of pluralism has usually been constructed in secular terms, and therein lies its weakness. It can be derided as secularism and the 'moral bankruptcy of the West.' But there is a powerful religious defence. The Bible contains just one description of a unitary social order. It speaks of a time when all humanity shared a single language and a common speech. There was no religious, cultural or ethnic diversity. The name the Bible gives to it is Babel. The Tower of Babel is our eternal symbol of the hubris of attempting to construct a uniform society. After Babel, it is our duty to realise that God has created many languages and civilisations, many paths to His presence. Our task is to be faithful to our own heritage while being a blessing to others, willing if we are of the majority faith to make space for others to pursue their own vision of the truth, and willing too, if we are of a minority faith, to 'seek the peace and prosperity of the city' to which the Lord has carried us, knowing that in its welfare lies the possibility of ours (Jeremiah 29:7).

Religions are at their best in constructing communities of shared vision, societies of the like-minded. They are at their worst in tolerating diversity. Religious passion tends to sectarianism, and sectarianism translated into political reality leads to the ethnically cleansed or *Judenrein* state. Against such a tendency, one must invoke the highest biblical principle of all: the transcendence of God.

God makes a covenant with the children of Israel. But He makes other covenants. 'Are not you Israelites the same to me as the Cushites? says the Lord. Did I not bring Israel up from Egypt, the Philistines from Caphtor and the Arameans from Kir?' (Amos 9:7). God is universal, but religions are particular. Hence Solomon's remarkable prayer at the dedication of the Temple: 'As for the foreigner who does not belong to Your people Israel . . . when he comes and prays towards this temple, then hear from heaven, Your dwelling place, and do whatever the foreigner asks of You, so that all the peoples of the earth may know Your name and fear You, as do Your own people Israel' (1 Kings 8:41–3). And hence the prophetic vision, not of the conversion of the nations, but of a world of co-existence and peace.

Just as there is political, so there is religious totalitarianism, and it comes from eroding the distinction between religion and God. God is the covenantal partner to particular forms of religious living. But beyond this He is the author of all being in its irreducible diversity. A plural society tests to the limit our ability to see God in religious forms which are not our own.

18

Pluralism

Pluralism is a compelling idea, but it is not a simple one. In my Reith Lectures I strongly defended a plural society – what I called a 'community of communities'. At the same time I pointed out that pluralism is a more complex doctrine than is usually realised, and can rise to contradictory or unacceptable positions. Consider, as an example, Joseph Raz's award-winning exploration of pluralism, *The Morality of Freedom.*

Raz values the principle of autonomy, the right of individuals to make their own choices. But he notes that this poses a problem in relation to 'communities whose culture does not support autonomy' such as immigrant communities or religious sects. The problem is this: 'Since they insist on bringing up their children in their own ways they are, in the eyes of liberals like myself, harming them. Therefore can coercion be used to break up their communities, which is the inevitable by-product of the destruction of their separate schools, etc.?'

To this question, Raz is prepared to answer in the affirmative. He writes: 'The perfectionist principles espoused in this book suggest that people are justified in taking action to assimilate the minority group, at the cost of letting its culture die or at least be considerably changed by absorption.' In practice, to be sure, it should be done slowly. But if it should become clear that the religious or ethnic minority is not assimilating, merely dwindling, then 'assimilationist policies may well be the only humane course, even if implemented by force of law'.

Raz has the great virtue of honesty. He is a liberal pluralist, but as a philosopher he recognises that liberalism is not, as is often claimed, a value-neutral public policy. It has, he says, a 'cultural imperialism' of its own. To me, those words have a chilling ring. They recall the demands of late eighteenth and early nineteenth-century European liberals who argued that if Jews were to be admitted to society as citizens, they would first have to

The Jewish Quarterly, Autumn, 1991

abandon the Yiddish language, the dietary laws, the Jewish Sabbath and religious divorce, and assimilate into the dominant culture. On this, Samuel Heilman's judgement seems to me to be correct, that 'These changes brought about, in a sense, a new version of the age-old Christian efforts to convert Jews. Now instead of demanding conversion to Christianity, the Christians were demanding a Jewish conversion to secular citizenship.'

Raz's argument was brought home to me recently. In the course of a *Desert Island Discs* programme, Sue Lawley asked me what I would say to my son if he was thinking of marrying a non-Jewish girl. I said that I would try to discourage him. I would hope that Judaism and its continuity would mean enough to him to wish to create a Jewish family and raise Jewish children.

This, as I thought, uncontroversial proposition brought an extraordinary response from a journalist on the London *Evening Standard*. He wrote that 'The closed nature of the Jewish faith must be one of the reasons for its frequent persecution', and went on to say that the Jewish opposition to intermarriage explained the Nazi accusation of a 'Jewish conspiracy' (the text was modified between earlier and later editions of the paper).

I was not inclined to see the article as anti-semitic. It was a sincerely voiced expression of the view that if Jews are to be part of a multi-cultural Britain they must be prepared to be indifferent to intermarriage. That view has been expressed by Jews as well, most famously by Israel Zangwill in his play, *The Melting Pot*. It was at the heart of Napoleon's questions to the Assembly of Jewish Notables in 1806, and the notables were forced into a tortuously diplomatic reply.

It is important to remember that the demand for Jewish assimilation, from the nineteenth century to today, has come not from conservatives but from liberals. The argument of the *Evening Standard* journalist was essentially that of Joseph Raz, namely that for the sake of an open, pluralist and autonomy-supporting society, 'people are justified in taking action to assimilate the minority group, at the cost of letting its culture die or at least be considerably changed by absorption.' Yet it was precisely this approach that led Martin Buber to lament, on the eve of the Holocaust, that emancipation had failed because it emancipated Jews *individually*, not *collectively*. Jews, to become citizens, had to relinquish the structures of group-identity. It was just this problem that pluralism was intended to address.

Pluralism, unlike the liberal individualism that preceded it, focused not on the individual but on the group. It recognised the integrity not only of persons, but also of the cultures, ethnicities and religious traditions to which they belonged. Horace Kallen, the first philosopher of pluralism, recognised that individuals are not abstractions. They have identities, forged by history, ancestry, religion, culture and ethnicity. The matrix of identity is the group. Therefore if the individual is to be respected in his or her individuality, so too must be the group of which he or she is a part. As a Jew, I believe this to be true. That is why I am a pluralist rather than a liberal individualist.

But political pluralism is a complex idea. It designates not a solution but a range of problems. What happens when the integrity of the group conflicts with the integrity of the individual? The Salman Rushdie affair illustrates the problem, as does the demand for state support for certain denominational schools. Both sides to both disputes defend their stance by reference to pluralism. In a plural culture, argues one side, *all* religions, not just Christianity, should be protected by the law of blasphemy. In a plural culture, argues the other side, *no* religion should be protected by the law of blasphemy. In a multi-faith society, argues one side, *each* religion should have its own schools. In a multi-faith society, argues the other side, *no* religion should have its own schools: every child should learn a little of every faith. When both sides to an argument invoke the same concept to justify opposing views, that is a clear sign that the concept is problematic.

The liberal individualist is at least lucid and consistent. I understand his view and oppose it. It rests, I believe, on a mistaken view of the individual, identity, morality and society. Philosophically, I take my stand alongside such recent critics of liberalism as Alasdair MacIntyre, Michael Walzer, Michael Sandel, Stuart Hampshire, Robert Bellah and Peter Berger. Jewishly, I am committed to a continued group identity against the arguments and pressures for assimilation. That is why I am a pluralist. But intellectual integrity forces me to recognise and articulate the problems.

My argument in the Reith Lectures was that there is no neat solution. Instead, there is a delicate interplay between our second languages of identity and our first language of common citizenship. If we recognise only the first language, we are in effect calling for the disappearance of minorities. If we insist on second languages to the exclusion of a common culture, we risk moving to a society of conflicting ghettoes. Tom Wolfe's *The Bonfire of the Vanities* describes a New York that has reached this stage. Two recent critiques of American society, Arthur Schlesinger's *The Disuniting of America* and Robert Hughes' *Culture of Complaint*, reinforce the same concern. Neither alternative does justice to the subtle problems of creating a society that is both cohesive and diverse.

Jews are used to living with the tension. For the past two centuries we have negotiated an equilibrium between Jewish and British identities. We know what it is to speak two languages, to strive to be true to our traditions while contributing to the common good. It is not easy, but it can be done. In a plural society, the modern Jewish condition becomes the human condition *tout court*. What is needed is a balance between the conflicting claims of the individual, the group and society as a whole. What I reject as cultural imperialism is any approach that takes one of the three to be determinative and to cancel out the claims of the other two.

The Judaic Case for Pluralism

The other error against which we must guard is the claim that a plural society must necessarily be a secular society, one where religion is banished from the public domain. The argument is this. Religions cannot tolerate diversity. Each claims exclusive access to the truth. The public domain is plural, religious truth is not. Therefore religion must be confined to the private domain. This dogma deserves to be challenged. Pluralism can flow from a religious vision. In the case of Judaism it does.

Judaism is pluralist with respect to the claims of other religions. Crucial to an understanding of Jewish faith is the fact that God's first words to Abraham, setting the destiny of Israel into motion, do not appear until the twelfth chapter of the book of Genesis. They are prefaced by chapter eleven, which recounts the story of the Tower of Babel. That narrative is the classic text of pluralism. It defines our this-worldly situation as one of an irreducible multiplicity of languages and cultures. Therein lies our diversity and our occasional tragedy, that we 'do not understand one another's speech'. Judaism is predicated on this, that prior to the end of days there is no universal religion or language. Or as Mary Midgely once put it: the thing about universal languages is that no one speaks them.

Consistently throughout its history, Judaism has understood the relationship between Jews and God to be *covenantal*. A covenant is inherently pluralist. It does not negate the possibility of other covenants with other peoples. There were times when the prophets strove to remind Israel of this fact. Malachi declared, 'From where the sun rises to where it sets, My name is honoured among the nations' (1:11). Isaiah spoke of the day when God will say, 'Blessed be Egypt My people, Assyria My handiwork and Israel My inheritance' (19:25). Israel has no monopoly of virtue or God's love. These remain radical and important statements.

To be sure, Judaism is not open-endedly tolerant. It opposes idolatry. It imposes obligations on Jews. But it sets severe limits on what Jews might demand of non-Jews. The Torah opposes the sexual conduct of the Canaanites and the Egyptians, but it nowhere prescribes norms other than for Israel itself. Maimonides recognised in Islam a legitimate monotheism. The Tosafists denied that their Christian contemporaries were idolators. The fourteenth-century Talmudist, Rabbi Menahem ha-Meiri, ruled that *all* members of cultures 'governed by the ways of religion' had the halakhic status of *ger toshav*, meaning that they were to be accorded full equality of rights.

Nor does the existence of many faiths relativise them all. That mistake was made recently by Sir Hermann Bondi in *The Times*. How, he asked, could religions claim absolute truth when there are so many of them, each believing in something else? The question confuses *absoluteness* with *universality*. To give an analogy: I am absolutely bound by marriage, but not universally bound. To the contrary, marriages are inescapably particular. The opening of *Anna Karenina* notwithstanding, no two marriages or happinesses are alike. As a moral descendant of those who stood at Sinai I am absolutely bound by its continuing claims. But that is not to deny that others whose relationship to God is mediated by other texts, traditions and languages may experience the same absoluteness in their own way. Like a marriage, a covenant may be both absolute and particular.

That is a distinctively Jewish way of understanding the plural character of faith. For it flows from Judaism's distinction between universal and particular covenants, the covenant with Noah and humanity on the one hand, and with Abraham and the children of Israel on the other. Zvi Werblowsky notes that the universal monotheisms that came in the wake of Judaism had 'a fundamental unwillingness to accept, let alone respect or appreciate, the specific individuality and integrity of other religious groups'. A particularist faith such as Judaism, by contrast, contains 'possibilities of a pluralistic respect for . . . other religious configurations'. Perhaps each religion has to arrive at pluralism in its own way, through its own beliefs and categories. None the less, Jews have an important statement to make in the contemporary world: that pluralism can be a religious orthodoxy.

What, then, are the ethical and political implications of such a view? The rabbis made a fundamental distinction between the 613 commands of Judaism and the moral requirements of mankind as such – the 'seven Noachide laws'. They distinguished between the ethical system of Judaism and the shared morality of a religiously plural world. There is, in other words, a first language of citizenship whose minimum requirements are set by the Noachide laws. And there are diverse second languages of religious identity: in the case of Jews, the language of Jewish law and faith. That distinction, central to Judaism, is essential to any society which values the integrity of a multiplicity of faiths.

Freedom of expression, too, has a religious value. Rabbinic Judaism encouraged what one writer has called a 'culture of argument'. Truth, especially religious truth, is multi-faceted. Its pursuit requires the freedom to articulate alternative and sometimes dissenting perspectives. The one rabbi of Mishnaic times who sought to limit freedom of argument – Rabban Gamliel II – was temporarily deposed from his position as head of the Jewish community. 'Argument for the sake of heaven' is one of the oldest Jewish traditions.

Three centuries before John Stuart Mill's *On Liberty*, Rabbi Judah Loewe (the *Maharal*) of Prague, wrote:

It is proper, out of love of reason and knowledge, that you do not summarily reject anything that opposes your own ideas, especially so if your opponent does not intend merely to provoke you, but rather to declare his own beliefs. And even if such beliefs are opposed to your own faith and religion, do not say: 'Speak not, close your mouth.' If that happens, there will take place no purification of religion . . . For one who causes his opponent to hold his peace and refrain from speaking, demonstrates thereby the weakness of his own religious faith. This is therefore the opposite of what some people think, namely that when you prevent someone from speaking against religion, that strengthens religion. That is not so, because curbing the words of an opponent in religious matters is nothing but the curbing and enfeebling of religion itself.

This testimony of one of the great masters of the rabbinic tradition is still germane. But it is not unique. It echoes Maimonides' dictum, 'Accept the truth from whichever source it comes', which in turn recalls Ben Zoma's aphorism, 'Who is wise? He who learns from all.' The point was made earlier still. Asking why the views of the school of Hillel gained acceptance over those of the school of Shammai, the rabbis answered: 'Because the disciples of Hillel were kind and modest, and studied not only their own teachings but those of their opponents, and *recited the views of their opponents before their own.*'

Lastly, there is the religious value of religious liberty. The Torah, with its radical opposition to paganism and mythology, rests on the existence of a free God who desires the uncoerced worship of free human beings. The principle of free will, says Maimonides, is the foundation of Torah. Without it there would be no point to the commandments and no justice to punishment and reward.

Religious freedom is not a matter of metaphysics alone. It is striven for in history. It determines economic and political structures. The definitive event of Jewish history, the exodus from Egypt, is a journey from slavery to liberty. Biblical legislation restricts slavery, and rabbinic law comes close to abolishing it. Shabbat is a weekly exercise in liberation. On it, all hierarchies are suspended. No one – not a slave or an employee or even an animal – is subject to a master's command.

But what, then, of law? Laws are enforcible constraints, and Judaism is a religion of law. Central to the Hebrew Bible, though, is the proposition that the covenant between God and Israel is only binding because it was voluntarily accepted and repeatedly re-affirmed. Two centuries ago Moses Mendelssohn added a further observation in his classic defence of religious liberty, *Jerusalem*. He distinguished between the law of the state and religious law, or commandments. 'The state', he said, 'prescribes *laws*, religion *commandments*. The state has physical power and uses it when necessary; the power of religion is love and beneficence.'

Religion, he argued, was an essential component of society. It was a 'pillar of civic felicity'. Its task is to teach people 'the truth of noble principles and convictions; to show them that duties toward men are also duties toward God, the violation of which is in itself the greatest misery; that serving the state is the true service of God; that charity is His most sacred will; and that true knowledge of the Creator cannot leave behind in the soul any hatred for men.' But it cannot avail itself of civil law and its sanctions. 'Religious society lays no claim to the right of coercion, and cannot obtain it by any possible contract.' Mendelssohn's example was Judaism. Since the destruction of the second Temple, Jewish courts had relinquished the power to enforce punishments and fines. For seventeen hundred years Judaism had been, in effect, a voluntary allegiance. To be sure, Jewish communities still had the right to excommunicate dissident members. But Mendelssohn urged them to give it up. Within a century, throughout Europe, they did.

Equally significant is the halakhic argument against religious coercion cited by the great Rabbi Meir Simcha of Dvinsk. Maimonides had ruled, in accordance with Talmudic law, that there are circumstances in which a Jewish court can coerce a recalcitrant husband into granting his wife a divorce. How so? One of the conditions of a divorce is that it be freely given. In this case, apparently it is not. Maimonides answered as follows. Since the husband wishes to be a Jew and to fulfil the commandments, he genuinely wishes to do what rabbinic law requires, namely that he divorces his wife. Underlying the power of coercion is a presupposition of voluntary assent to the law. But this, so a nineteenth-century rabbinic scholar argued, cannot be assumed in the case of someone who has relinquished Judaism.

Coercion, in short, presupposes but cannot produce assent. Just such an argument, transposed into secular terms, was later used to fine effect by Sir Isaiah Berlin in his 'Two Concepts of Liberty'. Sir Isaiah is a secular Jew. But the libertarian conclusion had already been arrived at in religious thought.

In my introduction to *The Persistence of Faith* I quoted John Plamenatz's remark that 'Liberty of conscience was born not of indifference, not of scepticism, not of mere open-mindedness, but of faith.' None the less, we have tended to believe that pluralism, freedom and the right to dissent are secular ideas. It is not so. The absolute dignity of otherness is a spiritual proposition. Religious commitment may yet prove to be its best defence.

PART III
HOLY DAYS

19

Introduction: Sharing Time

One of the most unusual things I ever did was to save television's 'God slot', if only for a few years. It came about like this.

British broadcasting had long carried the imprint of John Reith's days at the BBC. The Reithian tradition had a specific moral vision. British society had a shared core of ethical and religious values – predominantly though not exclusively Christian – and it was the responsibility of broadcasting to reflect and even strengthen them. So the BBC's *Handbook* for 1928 could state that 'The BBC is doing its best to prevent any decay of Christianity in a nominally Christian country', and twenty years later the then Director-General, Sir William Haley, was moved to say, speaking of Christian values, that the BBC 'seeks to safeguard those values and foster acceptance of them'.

One of the legacies of those early days was the so-called 'closed period'. Initially this meant that no television at all was broadcast between 6 and 7 p.m. on weekdays and between 6.15 and 7.30 p.m. on Sundays, so as not to compete with religious worship. Inevitably, as Britain became more secular and diverse, the convention was whittled down. The weekday pause vanished. The Sunday interval shrank and became, instead of a time without television, a period in which both major channels (BBC1 and ITV) showed religious programmes. This – the time between 6.40 and 7.15 p.m. on Sundays – was affectionately if irreverently known as the 'God slot'. In the competitive, commercial mood of the 1980s it could hardly survive without a challenge, and the challenge duly came.

In September 1988, London Weekend Television proposed ending the closed period. Religious broadcasting would be moved to other times of the day, and against the BBC's *Songs of Praise* it would show a news magazine programme. Because the proposal involved an issue of principle about the relationship between broadcasting and religion, it was sent by the Independent Broadcasting Authority to the Central Religious Advisory Committee, of which I was then a member.

As it heard the arguments for and against, the members of the Committee were divided. The commercial programmers made the case that by moving religious broadcasting to earlier and later times they would secure a younger and more varied viewing audience. I was not persuaded. The closed period attracted a remarkably large following. The programme about to be abolished, *Highway*, had viewing figures of some eight million, a considerable achievement for early Sunday evening. As I listened to the programmers, it seemed to me that they were driven less by concern for religion than by an intense hostility to it. The closed period was like a church in the middle of a shopping centre, an embarrassing reminder of eternal values in a fast-moving consumer age. It was bad for business and should be replaced as soon as possible by a supermarket.

Minor though the issue was, it raised a serious question about the nature of our public culture, of which television has become the most important vehicle. As it happens, the Committee met for its deliberations on the day after Yom Kippur, the Jewish Day of Atonement. I felt strong words were needed, and I said something to the following effect:

The Jewish community has become highly secularised. Yet yesterday every synagogue in the world was full. Even Jews who have little to do with Judaism during the rest of the year come to synagogue on Yom Kippur, despite the fact that it is the most difficult day of the year to observe. It is a day of fasting. It is a day spent exclusively in prayer. Why then do they come? Because the Day of Atonement is *holy time*. Almost every Jew knows that at least one day of the year is *kadosh*, holy, set aside. It is part of the rhythm and structure of our lives. It is an almost instinctual pause for reflection and self-examination. Without holy times, there is no framework or architecture of time, merely the rush and press of random events. A civilisation needs its pauses, its intervals, its chapter-breaks if it is to be a civilisation at all.

The closed period on television, I argued, makes a similar statement, if inevitably shorter and less intense, about British culture. It says that there is a period of time, no more than half-an-hour, in which the normal thrust of news and entertainment is held back and fifteen million viewers think about more ultimate values. It is one of the last fragments of holy time left in our public life. Ending it, I said, would not be a small decision about programming schedules. It would be a significant step towards marginalising religion in the public domain.

The Committee was persuaded and voted against the proposal. A week later its recommendation was endorsed by the IBA. The closed period was saved. But it could not last.

Under the 1990 Broadcasting Act, radio and television were deregulated. By the beginning of 1993 the new authority for commercial television, the Independent Television Commission, could no longer require its companies to honour the closed period agreement, and it immediately lapsed. By 1994 a more significant defeat had been inflicted on the concept of holy time. Sunday trading was deregulated. Shopping had won its battle with prayer as our age's most compelling form of collective worship.

Like my predecessor Lord Jakobovits, I have found arguments like these the strangest in which I have been involved. We have both found ourselves as Jews defending Christian institutions: religious education, Sunday rest and the established Church. That is not because Jewish interests are at stake. If anything, Jews benefit from being able to shop on Sundays and watch alternatives to Christian worship on television. What is at stake is not interests but religious principle, in this case a principle that goes far beyond Judaism itself. Not only as Jews but as citizens we believe that faith is not private but shared. It is nurtured, cultivated and receives its finest expression in communities. Faith is a public good. That is at the heart of the idea of holy time.

The clearest contrast between communal faith and an individualistic culture is between a *luach*, the traditional Jewish calendar, and that symbol of contemporary time, the personal organiser. A personal organiser represents time as a private project. Into it go our appointments, social events and leisure activities carefully prioritised by goals and objectives. Its message is that how I spend my time is who I am. A *luach* is something else. It speaks of holy days to be shared with family and community, days where time is not mine to do with as I like but ours to live out together the truths we share and the history of which we are a part, and to join our hopes to those of others in praise and prayer. The *luach* is time as collective experience. Its message is that there is public time just as there is public space: time in which we merge our private concerns with the larger community of which we are a part.

Judaism, as theologians have noted, is a religion of time. The first thing the Bible declares holy is not a place or a person but a day: the Sabbath. The first commandment given to Israel as a people was 'This month shall be for you the beginning of the months' (Exodus 12:1), the verse from which tradition derived the mandate to determine the calendar and thus the dates of the festivals. Rabbi Abraham Pam once asked why the fixing of the calendar should have been the first instruction given to the Israelites as they were preparing for the exodus from slavery. He answered: the difference between a slave and a free human being is that the latter has control over his time. Time is the medium within which we work out our inner freedom. It is canvas on which Judaism paints its religious landscapes.

Whether it was because of Judaism's strong sense of God's transcendence or our long experience of exile, Jews found God in the *when* rather than the *where*. Perhaps it was neither of these things, merely the simple practical truth that religious faith needs regular rehearsal, dedicated time. Whatever the reason, Jewish theology is less to be found in systematic treatises than in the Jewish calendar with its regular enactment of the great principles of our faith and history.

There is a profound difference between the mentalities of ancient Greece and Judaism. Greek thought is *logical* while Jewish thought is *chronological*. Logical systems are ideally timeless. Chronological systems are embedded in time. Logical systems are contemplated. Chronological systems are lived. Thus for Jews the creation of the universe is not a metaphysical truth to be accepted. It is an experience to be lived one day in seven. The exodus from Egypt is not a historical truth to be recorded. It is a dramatic episode to be re-enacted every year. The calendar – the musical score of the symphony of time – is how we take truths from the abstract heavens or the distant past and make them real in our shared lives.

In his *Spheres of Justice*, Michael Walzer points out the difference between vacations and holy days. 'What is crucial about the vacation is its individualist (or familial) character...Everyone plans his own vacation, goes where he wants to go, does what he wants to do.' The biblical Sabbath, by contrast, is a collective good. It is 'enjoined for everyone, enjoyed by everyone'. Walzer notes, too, the paradox of holy days. They are an abridgement of liberty. A holy day is not one in which we are free to do what we like. None the less, 'the historical experience of the Sabbath is not an experience of unfreedom. The overwhelming sense conveyed in Jewish literature, secular as well as religious, is that the day was eagerly looked forward to and joyfully welcomed – precisely as a day of release, a day of expansiveness and leisure.' It is expansive the way a public park is expansive: by not being private property. The Sabbath is time we, not I, own.

The fate of the closed period on television, like the fate of Sunday itself, suggests that Britain is now too fragmented to share collective time. I lament this, as I lament every move towards what John Kenneth Galbraith called 'private affluence and public poverty'. The more we move from public to private time, the less egalitarian we will be as a society and the more abrasive the workings of our economic system will become. The Sabbath is a day without work or spending. Within it the rich and poor, the employed and unemployed, are equals, members of the same community standing before God. No weekend of leisure and shopping offers the same sharing of dignity. We become what we can afford to buy. That is too limited and random a measure of the human condition to sustain a society in the long run.

The chapters in this section had their origin in broadcasts or speeches about the holy days of the Jewish year. Their message, I hope, reaches out beyond the Jewish community. They are about time as the vehicle of collective memory and aspiration, and about days made more precious by being shared.

20
Shabbat / The Sabbath Day of Delight

'Come, let us sing joyously to the Lord;
Let us shout for joy to the rock of our salvation.'

With these words every Friday night, Jews welcome *Shabbat*, the Sabbath – day of rest and delight. What *is* Shabbat? The Bible tells us that for six days God created the world and on the seventh day He rested. So we were instructed that for six days we too should labour to create, and on the seventh day we should rest. Why, though, does the Bible include rest in the scheme of creation and set aside a day in every week to celebrate it? Does an all-powerful God *need* to rest? And if we sometimes need to relax, can we be said to be imitating God?

Perhaps the simplest answer is this. All of nature is creative, but only God and humanity create consciously for a purpose. So that for us, unlike the plant or animal kingdoms, creation is not a process of ceaseless activity. It involves moments of contemplation when we reflect on *why* we act. We need time for thinking as well as for doing. So the Sabbath is holy time, meaning time set apart, time out from the relentless pressures of activity: a day dedicated to thinking about the purpose of what we do.

As we pause to contemplate, we see that the natural world is not just an infinite collection of atoms endlessly colliding in random ways. Seen through the eyes of science that may be all there is. But heard through the ears of faith, it too has a purpose. The universe sings a song of praise to its Creator. The mere fact that it exists, testifies to the One who spoke and brought it into existence, endowing it with majesty and meaning.

One of the Psalms we say on the Sabbath gives voice to this 'song of the earth':

'The heavens declare the glory of God;
The skies proclaim the work of His hands.
Day pours forth speech unto day,
Night imparts knowledge to night.
There is no speech or language
Where their voice is not heard.

Their voice goes out through all the earth,
Their words to the ends of the world.'

৯

The landscape of Shabbat is vast: creation and our purpose in it. And yet for most Jews, myself included, the mood of the day is intimate. It is a time in which we celebrate family and children, the home, and just being together.

Imagine the experience of coming home on Friday afternoon. The week has flown by in a rush of activity. You are exhausted. And there, in all its simplicity and splendour is the Sabbath table: candles radiating the light that symbolises *shalom bayit*, peace in the home; wine, representing blessing and joy; and the two loaves of bread, recalling the double portion of manna that fell for the Israelites in the wilderness so that they would not have to gather food on the seventh day.

Seeing that table you know that until tomorrow evening you will step into another world, one where there are no pressures to work or compete, no distractions or interruptions, just time to be together with family and friends.

So, after the Friday evening service, we bless our children. Jewish husbands say to their wives that lovely passage of praise from the book of Proverbs, 'A wife of noble character who can find? She is worth far more than rubies.' And after we have said the blessings over the wine and bread, we take turns to speak about the weekly Bible reading, and we sing *zemirot*, family songs in praise of God.

Relationships take time, and Shabbat is when we give them time – to listen to one another, praise each other, share in a meal, sing together, and sense the blessedness of one another's company. Adam and Eve, said the rabbis, were spared one day in the Garden of Eden before they were exiled into the world of toil. That day was Shabbat. And for those who observe it Shabbat becomes a way back into Eden, paradise temporarily regained.

Peace in the home is where world peace begins, so that for Jewish mystics the seventh day was a kind of cosmic wedding and the Sabbath itself was the bride. And in our Friday evening prayers, as we finish Psalm 29 with its promise of peace, we sing the mystical song, *Lekha dodi*:

'Come my beloved to meet the bride.
Together let us welcome the Sabbath.'

133

&

The great Hassidic master, Rabbi Levi Yitzhak of Berdichev, was once looking out of his window watching the crowds of people rushing as they went about their business. He leaned out and asked one of them, 'Why are you rushing?' The man replied, 'I'm running to work to make a living.' 'Are you so sure', asked the rabbi, 'that your livelihood is running away from you and you have to rush to catch it up. Perhaps it's running *toward* you, and all you have to do is stand still and let *it* catch up with *you*.'

I understand what the rabbi meant. We can sometimes work so hard that we forget why we work at all. We don't live in order to labour. We labour in order to live. And the Sabbath is the day we stand still and just live, and let all the blessings we have accumulated catch up with us.

The Sabbath was and remains a revolutionary idea. Many ancient religions had their holy days. But none had a day on which it was forbidden to work. The Greeks and Romans were frankly perplexed. Seneca said it was because Jews were idle that they devoted a seventh of their time to rest. Rabbinic tradition says that when the Hebrew Bible was first translated into Greek, the translators changed a sentence to make it comprehensible. Instead of 'On the seventh day God finished the work He had made', the translators wrote 'On the sixth day . . .'. It is as if they knew that the Greeks could understand that in six days God made the universe, but not that on the seventh He made rest – that rest itself is a creation. But the rabbis knew otherwise. 'After six days, what did the universe lack? It lacked rest. So when the seventh day came, rest came and the universe was complete.' Rest is the creation which allows us to enjoy all other creations. Just as clear space surrounds a page or frames a picture, so clear time is the frame in which we set our work, giving it the dignity of art.

The Sabbath has been part of Judaism from the beginning, one of the first of the biblical commands. In the three thousand years of its history the world of work has been transformed from labour to industry to technology. But Shabbat has renewed its meaning in each generation. For my grandparents it meant rest from sheer physical exhaustion. For my contemporaries it means release from psychological fatigue, from stress and the pressures to compete and win. Shabbat today is a world in which there are no phones or faxes, no urgent messages, no deadlines. It remains an oasis of serenity, the still centre at the heart of time.

&

Shabbat is more than family time. It is collective time. Even those who have been too busy to come to the synagogue during the week do so on Shabbat, joining others in prayer and listening with them to the weekly Bible reading. If the synagogue is the centre of community space, Shabbat is the centre of community time.

I used to be the rabbi of a synagogue in the centre of London. It was near many hotels, so that on Shabbat our congregation would not merely be local. We would be joined by visitors from across the world. There would be Jews from Texas and Australia, from India and Gibraltar and South America, many from Israel, some from Eastern Europe. Each week, as I said the Friday afternoon prayer just before the holiness of the day began, I used to say with special devotion the phrase, 'Blessed are You, O Lord, who gathers together the dispersed of His people Israel.' Only two things draw Jews together in such a way: the land of Israel and Shabbat, one a place, the other a time. I used to marvel at this strange congregation of people who dressed and spoke so differently, converging from so many parts of the world on this place at this time, never having met before, many never having been here before, yet instinctively belonging: for they were fellow citizens of the world of Shabbat, at home in its rhythms and words and melodies. Shabbat turns strangers into friends.

We would pray together, and then after the service we would make *Kiddush* (Sanctification) together over wine and fishballs and cake, for much of Judaism is about turning physical pleasures into spiritual pleasures: 'Taste and see that the Lord is good.' Then we and other members of the congregation would invite the visitors back to our homes for a meal. Since the days of Abraham, who sat at the entrance of his tent looking for passers-by to whom to offer hospitality, we have known that a home must be open, and friends and strangers invited in. 'Welcoming visitors', said the rabbis, 'is greater than receiving the divine presence.'

Shabbat is not private time, but shared time, a time for sharing, not owning. I discovered, when we moved from the suburbs to the heart of London, that the places of densest population can also be the loneliest, that in the blocks of flats surrounded by traffic and crowds and noise there were all too many people living alone. Shabbat brought us together and redeemed us from our isolation. It was time without walls.

ṣ❧

Not working on the seventh day is more than relaxing and meeting. The

Hebrew Bible sees the Sabbath as the education of a people in two fundamental truths.

Today we would probably call the first *environmental*. The Sabbath reminds us that the universe is created – meaning that ultimately it belongs to God and we are merely its guardians. Adam was placed in the Garden to 'serve and protect it', and so are we. One day in seven we must renounce our mastery over nature and the animals, and see the earth not as something to be manipulated and exploited, but as a thing of independent dignity and beauty. It too is entitled to its rest and protection. More powerfully than any tutorial or documentary, the Sabbath makes us aware of the limits of human striving. It is a day, if you like, of ecological consciousness.

But it is also a day of history and politics. The Bible tells us to rest because of the exodus from Egypt and liberation from slavery. It is a time of freedom, and the greatest freedom is the freedom to be masters of our own time. On Shabbat we may not work, meaning that one day in seven we are no one's servant except God's. Nor may we force anyone to work for us. Even our servants should be able to rest the way we do.

Tyrannies make people slaves by making them forget the taste of freedom. But no one who observes the Sabbath can ever forget what it is to be free. Jews know more than most what it is to have spent long centuries in homelessness and persecution. Yet every week, for a day, however poor they were, they gathered their possessions and celebrated like royalty. The Sabbath was their political education, a regular reminder of liberty.

ès

The Jewish mystics tell the story of the rabbi who once asked his son, 'Where does God live?' The child could not understand the question. Where does God live? Where does he *not* live? 'Surely', said the child, 'he fills the heavens and the earth?' 'No', said the rabbi. 'God lives *wherever we let Him in*.' Perhaps that is the religious secret of the Sabbath. It is the day when we cast off our own devices and desires and let God in.

For centuries philosophers and scientists argued over the existence of God, as if it were a matter of speculation or hypothesis that could be proved or disproved. What they held in common was the idea that if God existed, it should be obvious to everyone. But it was the prophet Elijah who discovered that God was not in the fire or the hurricane or the earthquake but in the still small voice. To hear God we have to learn to listen, and to listen we need to create a kind of silence in our soul.

During the week our lives are filled with noise: radio and television, the pulse and press of daily events, the hectic sound of secular time. But stand in the streets of Jerusalem on the Sabbath and you can hear the silence. In it I have sensed the sheer wonder of existence and the mystery at the heart of all living things. Which is why the greatest command of Judaism is not to prove or know or believe, but simply *Shema Yisrael*, 'Hear', or better still, '*Listen*, O Israel. The Lord our God is One.'

The Sabbath is not just a day of leisure and relaxation. It is *holy time*. We are used to the idea of holy places and holy people. But the first thing the Bible calls holy is not a place or a person. It is a day: 'And God blessed the seventh day and made it holy' – as if to say that God has given us one precious gift, time itself, that fleeting span of years which makes up a human life. The Sabbath is our moment of eternity in the midst of time. Within the cycle of the week it creates a delicate rhythm of action and reflection, making and enjoying, running and standing still. Without that pause to experience family, community and God we risk making the journey while missing the view.

Jewish thinkers have called the Sabbath many things: a day of light and joy, a sanctuary in time, a period in which we feel as if we have been given an 'extra soul'. The prophet Isaiah said simply: 'You shall call the Sabbath a delight.' A delight it is to all those who enter its world.

21

Pesach / Passover
Celebrating Freedom

Pesach, or Passover, is the Jewish festival of freedom. I can remember as a child the vivid atmosphere that used to build up as it approached. The house was frantic with activity. During Pesach not only are we not allowed to eat any leavened food; we cannot have any in the house. So for weeks in advance we would be turning out rooms, getting rid of any crumbs that might be lying about, and getting out the special cutlery and crockery reserved for the festival days. With all the cleaning and packing and unpacking, it was almost as if we were getting ready for a great journey. In a sense we were, because Passover is more than just a festival. It is the journey each of us is invited to take from slavery to freedom, tracing out the route of one of the most powerful events ever to have fired the human imagination.

The story of Passover is set out in the book of Exodus and it begins in Egypt more than three thousand years ago. There, in that great centre of ancient civilisation, was a group of immigrants from the land of Canaan. They were known to others as Hebrews and to themselves as the children of Israel. Being strangers and outsiders with different customs and beliefs they were easy targets of prejudice, as outsiders have always been. Eventually they became victims of a tyrannical Pharaoh. They were turned into slaves, an expendable labour force press-ganged into building the great cities whose ruins you can still see today. Things got worse. Hebrew children were thrown into the Nile to drown. Slavery began to darken into genocide.

And then something happened, something we have remembered ever since. An Israelite who by chance had been brought up as an Egyptian saw what was happening to his people. He himself was not at risk. But he knew he could not go free when those around him were enslaved. One day tending his sheep at the edge of the desert he heard the call of God speaking from a burning bush, telling him to go back to Egypt and say to Pharaoh, 'Let my people go'. The man was Moses, and although his mission had many setbacks and disappointed hopes, eventually he led the Israelites to freedom and to the brink of the promised land.

There the story might have ended, were it not that from the very outset the Bible seems to sense that the journey from slavery to freedom is one we need to travel in every generation. So we were commanded to gather our families together every year at this time and tell the story of what it was like to be a slave and what it felt like to go free. Not just tell the story but act it out as well. We eat *matzah*, the unleavened 'bread of affliction'. We sample *maror*, the bitter herbs, so that we can experience the taste of suffering. And we drink four cups of wine, each one a stage on the road to liberation. We tell the story in such a way that each of us feels as if we had lived through persecution and come out the other side as free human beings – as if history had been lifted off the page to become recent memory. That is how we learn to cherish freedom.

The story of the exodus has inspired not only Jews. When Oliver Cromwell made the first speech of his parliament, when Thomas Jefferson and Benjamin Franklin chose their images for the Great Seal of the United States, when black Americans struggled for civil rights and when South American Catholics shaped their liberation theologies, they chose the model of Moses leading the Israelites towards the promised land. The story of the exodus has inspired the search for freedom in many places and times. It does not belong simply to the chronicles of an ancient people. It is a journey each of us must trace and retrace, because freedom is fragile and needs defending. That is why, every year, we taste slavery and suffering, and understand again why God wants us to be free.

৯৯

What has freedom to do with faith or religion or spirituality? Freedom, after all, is about politics and society, not about religion and the soul. Karl Marx used to argue that religion keeps us slaves by allowing us to live with our lack of freedom, seeing it as the will of God. He called it the opium of the people.

But that is not the religion of the Bible. The redemption brought about by Moses was not something that happened in the privacy of the soul. It was a political revolution, an event that changed the history of a people. They had been slaves in Egypt. Now they were free human beings, travelling through the desert on their way to their own land.

A free God wants the free worship of free human beings. That is the message the Bible sounds again and again through its verses. And because freedom is created or destroyed by the political system, God wants us to worship Him at least in part by the kind of society we build and the laws we enact. That is why the books of Moses are not just about miracles and revelation and faith. They contain laws, commandments and rules by which we build a just and free society.

God, as He speaks to us through the words of the Bible, asks us to take special care of the widow, the orphan and the stranger, those who are vulnerable and without power. He tells us to give part of what we produce to those in need and to cancel debts every seventh year so that no one becomes caught in the trap of poverty. These rules, first stated three thousand years ago, are still capable of moving us today even though we sometimes forget their origin in the story of the exodus.

Beyond them, there are laws whose simple purpose is to remind us of what it feels like to be free, none more so than the institution of the Sabbath. One day in every seven, no one was allowed to work or force anyone else to work. Everyone – servants, employees, even animals – was given a taste of absolute freedom. It is hard to overestimate what this did to keep the spirit of Jews alive.

My grandparents came to this country eighty years ago from Poland. They arrived in London's East End with nothing. They knew no English. They had no skills. They found themselves in the heart of London's poorest district, strangers in a strange land. I sometimes wonder how they and their many neighbours kept alive the burning hope that one day things would be different. But in my heart of hearts I know it was the Sabbath that was their inner strength.

However desperate things had been during the week, that day they would set the table with a shining white cloth and light the candles in their silver candlesticks and relax as if they were guests at God's own banquet. The Sabbath preserved their dignity and kept them from being crushed by the burdens life had loaded on their frail shoulders. The Sabbath – and Pesach itself with its declaration that 'This year we may be slaves, but next year we will be free'. You could taste the hope in those four glasses of wine, and from hope came energy and determination.

One of Judaism's most powerful messages is that *redemption is of this world*, and every time we help the poor to escape from poverty, or give the homeless a home or cause the unheeded to be heard we bring God's kingdom one step closer. The best way never to forget this message is every year to eat the bread of affliction and taste the bitter herbs so that we never forget what it is like to be unfree. 'Do not oppress the stranger', says the Bible, 'because you know what it feels like to be a stranger. You were once strangers in the land of Egypt.'

చ∾

Mah nishtanah halaylah hazeh mikol haleylot, 'Why is this night different from all other nights?' Those must have been the first words of Hebrew I ever said. If I strain my memory I can still see my grandparents' dining table with all the uncles and aunts and cousins gathered round on those Passover nights in Seven Sisters Road many years ago. Pesach was the great family gathering and all very daunting to me, the youngest, three or four years old. But I quickly learned that it is in fact the youngest who has the best lines: the four questions with which the whole service begins. Why is this night different? Why the unleavened bread and bitter herbs? Why do we dip the vegetables and why lean when we drink the wine?

The answers came much later in the evening. But meanwhile there was much to keep a young child awake. My favourite part came when my grandfather broke the middle *matzah* in two and gave me one half to hide until the end of the meal. This kept me in a state of pleasant suspense for several hours because I knew that when the time came for us to eat the broken *matzah*, custom decreed that the adults would put on a show of searching for it, they would fail, and I would then be entitled to a present in return for disclosing its whereabouts. It was an elaborate charade, but it worked.

And then there were the rousing songs with which the evening ended, usually after midnight. The last one was my favourite, the one about the young goat that father bought, which got eaten by a cat, which was eaten by a dog, which got hit by a stick, which got burned by a fire, and so on in a manic crescendo until in the last verse God Himself came and defeated the angel of death. Mortality duly vanquished, we could go to bed.

Judaism has always had a genius for attracting the interest of a child, never more so than on Passover night. Nor is this accidental, because if you turn to the book of Exodus, you find that on the brink of Israel's liberation Moses repeatedly speaks to the people about children and how, in generations to come, they should be taught the significance of that event. Only slowly did I come to understand why. Freedom is not born overnight. It needs patience and training and carefully acquired skills. It needs an education in freedom. Without it, a society can all too quickly lapse into chaos or conflict, rivalry and war.

The Israelites of Moses' day were unprepared for liberty, and the Bible faithfully records their quarrels and disorders. It took a new generation to be ready to cross the Jordan and enter the promised land. As the Rabbi of Kotzk put it: 'It took one day to get the Israelites out of Egypt. But it took forty years to get Egypt out of the Israelites.' That is why on Pesach we begin with the youngest child, as if to say to him or her: This is what affliction tastes like, and here, by contrast, is the wine of our hard-earned freedom. This is the heritage of our historical experience, and tonight we begin to hand it on to you.

No less importantly, the first lesson we teach our children is how to ask questions. Religious faith is not uncritical. It does not only ask us to take things on trust. It encourages us to look at the world, and ask, why are things as they are? Could they be otherwise? The great prophets took nothing for granted, least of all the injustices of the world. They asked questions of God, deep and searching questions. And God asks questions of us. Why do we allow evil to prosper? Why are we passive in the face of suffering? For God and mankind are partners in the work of redemption, and every step on the way begins with a willingness to question why we are as we are.

As I read the Bible I sense the link between Moses' two great passions, for justice and for teaching children. What we learn as children shapes the society we make when we become adults. And so on Pesach we turn to our children and say: Here is the freedom God has given us. Take it and make it yours.

ﻉ

In the Kovno ghetto in the early 1940s an extraordinary scene took place one morning in the makeshift synagogue. The Jews in the ghetto had begun to realise the fate that lay in store for them. They knew that none of them would escape, that the work camps to which they would be transported were in fact factories of death. And at the morning service, the leader of prayer, an old and pious Jew, could finally say the words no longer. He had come to the blessing in which we thank God for not having made us slaves. He turned to the congregation and said: 'I cannot say this prayer. How can I thank God for my freedom when I am a prisoner facing death? Only a madman could say this prayer now.'

Some members of the congregation turned to the rabbi for advice. Could a Jew in the Kovno ghetto pronounce the blessing thanking God for not having made him a slave? The rabbi replied very simply. 'Heaven forbid that we should abolish the blessing now. Our enemies wish to make us their slaves. But though they control our bodies they do not own our souls. By making this blessing we show that even here we still see ourselves as free men, temporarily in captivity, awaiting God's redemption.'

The hardest question I am asked is: where was God at Auschwitz? Where was God when his faithful servants were being turned to ashes and dying as martyrs in their millions? Where was God when more than a million children were murdered, not for their faith but for the faith of their grandparents? Where was redemption when the Jews of Europe were gassed and burned and God was silent?

That question haunts us on the night of Passover, because on that night we remember that slavery in Egypt was not the only, or even the worst, chapter of the suffering of the people of the covenant. We say, in a moment of painful memory, 'It was not one alone who rose up against us to destroy us.' Pharaoh was not the only person who sought to put an end to Abraham's children. There have been Pharaohs in every generation. And not only Jews have been their victims. There are peoples today who live under the threat of genocide. There are populations subject to that terrifying phrase, 'ethnic cleansing'. If God redeems – not in heaven but here on earth – where is His redemption?

The greatest prophets asked that question and received no answer. None the less there is a fragment of an answer, and it was given by the rabbi in the Kovno ghetto. God has chosen only one dwelling place in this finite, physical universe and that is the human heart. Whenever we banish God from the human heart, tragic things happen. When rulers set themselves in place of God, they begin by taking other people's freedom and end by taking other people's lives. There is a direct line from tyranny to idolatry to bloodshed. Our greatest defence is the knowledge that above all earthly powers is the supreme king of kings, God Himself, who has endowed all human beings with His image. No absolute ruler has ever succeeded in extinguishing that spark from the souls of a people, which expresses itself in a passion for freedom. That is why all tyrannies have failed and will always fail.

Where was God in the Kovno ghetto? In the hearts of those who, though they were prisoners in the valley of the shadow of death, insisted on pronouncing a blessing as free human beings. Their story had no simple happy ending, but they left us an immortal legacy: the knowledge that the human spirit cannot be killed, and that therefore freedom will always win the final battle.

Judaism tends to be a mystery to observers. It is a religion of the spirit, but it seems to be about very physical things. There is nothing abstract about Pesach. It is about the hard, dry unleavened bread, and the sharp horseradish of the bitter herbs, and about drinking wine and telling stories and singing songs. Nor is it about solitude, the lonely soul in communion with God. Go to a Pesach meal and the one thing you will not find is solitude. You will find a table crammed with grandparents, parents and children, uncles, aunts and cousins. Even those who are lonely at other times are tonight here as guests, sharing in the crowded celebration.

The reason is simple. God created the world as a home for mankind, and He wants us to create a world that will be a home for Him. There may be rare saints for whom suffering is spiritual. But for most of us, affliction turns us in upon ourselves. Slavery which begins by imprisoning the body can end by narrowing the soul. We need freedom, a sense of inner spaciousness, to be able to reach out beyond our own immediate needs and breathe the air of a larger reality. So, though it does not end there, the religious journey starts in the here-and-now of daily life, the society we build and the relationships we make.

For many years I was puzzled by the first words we say on Pesach: 'This is the bread of affliction which our ancestors ate in Egypt. Let all those who are hungry come and eat it with us.' What kind of hospitality is it to offer the hungry the bread of affliction? Finally, though, I think I understood. The unleavened bread represents two things. It was the food eaten by slaves. But it was also the food eaten by the Israelites as they left Egypt in too much of a hurry to let the dough rise. It is the bread of affliction, but it is also the bread of freedom.

When we eat it alone, we taste in it all the suffering of the human condition. But when we offer to share it, we can taste in it something else: the sense of a freer world that God has promised us we can create. One who fears tomorrow does not share his bread with others. But one who is willing to divide his food with a stranger is capable of fellowship and hope. Food shared is no longer the bread of affliction. Whenever we reach out and touch other people's lives, giving help to the needy, and hope to those in despair, we bring freedom into the world, and with freedom, God.

22

Shavuot / Pentecost
Israel's Wedding

In Judaism, mysteries have a habit of becoming controversies, none more so than in the case of Shavuot, otherwise known as Pentecost or the Feast of Weeks. Shavuot generated one of the great arguments in Jewish history. It is not too much to say that on its outcome the future of Jewish people turned.

The mystery of Shavuot is twofold. The first is that uniquely among the Jewish festivals it has no date; the Bible gives it no explicit place in the Jewish calendar. Instead, it is to be arrived at by counting seven weeks after the beginning of the *Omer*, the offering brought from the barley harvest, the first crop to ripen in the spring. 'And from the day on which you bring the sheaf of the wave offering – the day after the sabbath – you shall count seven weeks' (Leviticus 23:15).

The second is that alone of the pilgrimage festivals it has no overt historical content. The Jewish festivals have a double character. They belong to cyclical time – the seasons of the year. And they belong to linear time – they recall formative moments in Jewish history. So Pesach is the festival of spring and also the time when we re-enact the exodus from Egypt. Sukkot is the festival of the autumn harvest and the time when we re-live the journey through the wilderness in temporary dwellings or tabernacles. But as we read the biblical description of Shavuot, half of the festival seems to be missing. Its seasonal significance is clear. It is called the 'Feast of the Harvest' and the 'Day of Firstfruits'. But the historical dimension is absent. So Shavuot raised two questions that were to become the subject of deep controversy: *when* was it celebrated, and *why*?

The argument became acute in the days of the second Temple when Jews were divided into several groups, most notably the Sadducees and Pharisees. We know all too little about this period, but we can say this. Of the two groups, the Sadducees were the more affluent and influential. They were closely connected to the Temple hierarchy and to the political élite. They were as near as Jewry came to a governing class. The Pharisees drew their support from the poorer groups of the population, and they had a distinctive ethos. Whilst the Sadducees saw Jewish identity in terms of the State and its institutions, the Pharisees saw it in terms of personal piety and scrupulous observance of the Law. In particular, they had a passion for education. They built academies and schools and devoted their days to the study of Torah.

There were several doctrinal differences between the two groups, but one in particular was crucial. The Pharisees gave equal authority to the twin sources of Judaism, the Written Torah (especially the Mosaic books) and the Oral Torah, the unwritten traditions which accompanied the biblical text, interpreting and supplementing it. The Sadducees accepted only the Written Torah, not oral tradition. This was to become the key issue in the debate over the date of Shavuot.

The Torah had specified that the counting of seven weeks should begin on 'the day after the sabbath'. The Sadducees took this literally. The counting should begin on Sunday, so that Shavuot would always fall on Sunday seven weeks later. The Pharisees invoked tradition and argued instead that in this case 'sabbath' meant 'festival', specifically the first day of Pesach. The counting should begin on the second day of Pesach, so that the dates of Pesach and Shavuot were linked. The argument between them became acute – inevitably so, since there can be few more divisive situations than one in which two sections of the population are celebrating the same festival on different days.

When we read about religious controversies, we are often surprised and even dismayed that so much passion should be spent on matters that seem so slight. This is usually because we fail to understand the deeper issues at stake, issues rarely spelled out by the protagonists at the time. Between the Sadducees and the Pharisees, I suspect, lay an argument that had little to do with the meaning of the word 'sabbath' and everything to do with the nature of Jewish history and character.

The Sadducees read the message on the surface of the Bible. This said that Shavuot was an agricultural festival whose date was determined by the barley harvest. There were even Sadducees who argued that the Almighty must have had farmers in mind when He decided to fix Shavuot on Sunday: at the end of the harvest it gave weary workers a long weekend! The religion of Israel was the religion of a people in and on its own land. It was about kings and priests, the Temple and sacrifices, farmers and fields, the seasons and their celebrations.

The Pharisees, though, read not only the text but also the subtext. They sensed the link between the two great events with which the history of

Israel began: exodus and Sinai, liberation and revelation, the going out from Egypt and the giving and receiving of the Law. That was what the mysterious counting of seven weeks was about. It represented not the duration of the harvest, but the forty-nine days between Moses leading the people out of Egypt and their assembly at the foot of the mountain to receive the Torah. Shavuot was not simply an agricultural festival. It was a historical festival with a precise date and content. It was the anniversary of the revelation at Mount Sinai, the day of the Giving of the Law.

Occasionally there are arguments that are decided by history, and this was one. In the year 70 of the Common Era, the Temple was destroyed by the Romans. Jewish autonomy in the land of Israel came to an end and a millennial exile began. The movement represented by the Pharisees became the dominant force in Jewish life for the next eighteen hundred years. Of the Sadducees almost nothing remained: no literature or philosophy, no lasting trace of their influence. The once ruling class vanished within a generation. It could hardly have been otherwise. The things on which they based their identity – the Temple and its priesthood, the land and its farmers, Jerusalem and its seat of power – were gone. Had Judaism been nothing but these, it too would have disappeared. Jews would have argued (as Spinoza did, many centuries later) that the end of their sovereignty meant the end of the covenant. God had given Israel a law and a land, a law *for* the land. The loss of one spelled the demise of the other. You could not celebrate Shavuot, the harvest festival, when you had no fields to harvest. You could not observe your own law when you had no country over which you ruled.

Judaism owes its continued existence to the fact that, two thousand years ago, the Sadducees were not the only force in Jewish life. There were others, the Pharisees, who did more than read the Torah's written text. They *listened* to it with an inner ear. In it they heard Moses' warning that the people of Israel would suffer exiles. They understood that the Law had been given in the wilderness to signal that it applied everywhere, outside the promised land as well as within. They knew that this was the crucial fact about Israel, that even without a land it still had a Law, and even in exile it still had the covenant. When you can no longer celebrate Shavuot as an agricultural festival, you can still observe it as the anniversary of the giving of the Law.

The controversy over the date and significance of Shavuot – fought over the meaning of a single word – was nothing less than an argument about the terms of Jewish history, about whether the key event in the

Hebrew Bible was the giving of the land or the Law. That there has *been* Jewish history for the past two thousand years is due in no small measure to those who successfully argued that Shavuot was more than a celebration of the land. There is something left even when the land is lost, and that is what Shavuot recalls: the giving of the Torah, text of the eternal covenant between God and His people.

ҙ๑

My earliest memories are of the time when we lived together with my grandparents in Finsbury Park. My maternal grandfather, a stout and gentle man with a rich head of silver hair, owned his own synagogue – I never discovered why. He was not a rabbi, though he was the son of one, and he presided over a little house of prayer a few doors away from where we lived. As his grandson I was given a special privilege during the Sabbath morning services. When the reading from the Torah scroll was over, and the scroll had been raised and rebound in its velvet covering, I would take the silver bells which were its ornamentation and, lifted by my father (I was two at the time), I would place them on its wooden handles. The scroll was then ready to be placed back in the ark.

From that day to this I have been awed by the love Jews have for the Torah. Generally speaking, we are not a reverential people nor is ours a religion of holy objects – with one exception: the Torah scroll itself. In its presence we rise. On the day we complete its reading, we dance with it as if it were a bride. The Torah alone comes near to the sanctity we attach to human beings. If, God forbid, a Torah scroll is dropped, the congregation fasts. If, even worse, a scroll is desecrated or destroyed we mourn as if someone had died and we bury it as if it were a person. My great-grandfather once travelled, in the 1870s, from Lithuania to Jerusalem, a long and hazardous journey in those days, carrying with him a Torah scroll he had commissioned so that he would have one from which to read in the Holy Land. He spent the whole journey carrying it, never letting it out of his sight so that it should not fall. It stayed there, in one of the little synagogues in the Old City, until the Jordanians destroyed it and the synagogue in 1949. I never knew my great-grandfather. He died before I was born. But from photographs (he had stern eyebrows but otherworldly eyes) I can imagine him cradling the scroll in his arms as if it were a child.

Jewish spirituality is quite simply the story of a tempestuous love affair between God and a people: the story of a marriage whose contract is the

Torah. Every weekday, Jewish men bind the strap of their phylacteries around their finger as if it were a wedding ring, and recite the moving words of Hosea:

> I will betroth you to me for ever
> I will betroth you in righteousness and justice,
> In love and compassion
> I will betroth you in faithfulness
> and you will know the Lord. (Hosea 2:21–2)

But it has not been an easy marriage. The prophets speak of Israel's infidelities, and were they alive today they would do so again. Abraham, Moses, Jeremiah and Job contend with God for His apparent injustices, and had they foreseen the Holocaust what would they have said? There is argument, even long periods of estrangement. Yet, said Isaiah, there is no divorce. And for the prophets and the rabbis the Torah itself was the proof. It was Israel's never-to-be-rescinded marriage contract with God.

So Jews studied it and wrote commentaries to it. Wherever they were, and however harried and distressed, they gathered together to debate and meditate on its words. In the *shtetl*, the small township of Eastern Europe, when Jews met, one would say to the other: '*Zog mir a shtickl Torah* – Tell me a little Torah.' Its words were their intimations of infinity, its letters the solid shapes of mysteries to be decoded. They would stay up long into the night arguing over its meaning, each hoping to hear a *chiddush*, a 'new' interpretation, 'new' in inverted commas because all true interpretations had already been revealed to Moses at Mount Sinai. But especially on Shavuot they would stay awake all night, for as the mystical treatise, the *Zohar*, said: All the wedding guests must stay with the bride on the night before her wedding, rejoicing with her in her preparations for the great day. Shavuot was the wedding day between God and Israel.

In our prayers every day we say:

> Blessed be our God . . .
> Who gave us the Torah of truth
> And planted in us everlasting life.

Those who study Torah become part of an unbroken conversation that has continued throughout the centuries in which all Israel's prophets and sages participated. To become a sentence in that conversation, a letter in the scroll, is what we and our ancestors understood as everlasting life.

23
Sukkot / Tabernacles
The Canopy of Faith

Sukkot, or Tabernacles, is the most joyous of all the festivals. We call it the 'season of our rejoicing'. And like Pesach much of the celebration lies in the preparation. For a week, we leave the security of our houses and live in huts or booths to remind us of the tabernacles in which the Israelites sheltered during the forty years of wandering on their way to the promised land. For several days beforehand – beginning immediately after the Day of Atonement – Jewish families become teams of builders, putting up the fragile structure, roofing it with leaves, and decorating it so that it becomes a temporary home where we eat and study and welcome guests.

There is no more potent symbol of Jewish history than the *sukkah*, the temporary dwelling. For that, for the greater part of four thousand years, is where Jews lived. From the time of Abraham, we have travelled towards the land of Israel. But we have been destined to live there all too briefly. Instead our story has been one of exiles and dispersions, as if wandering in the wilderness was not the fate of Moses' generation alone but a recurring theme of Jewish life. In the Middle Ages alone, Jews were expelled from England in 1290, from Vienna in 1421, Cologne in 1424, Bavaria in 1442, Milan in 1489 and most traumatically from Spain in 1492. A century ago the wave of pogroms in Eastern Europe sent millions of Jews into flight to the West, and these great migrations continue even today among the Jews of the former Soviet Union. Jewish history reads like a vast continuation of the stages of the Israelites' journey in the thirty-second chapter of the book of Numbers: 'They travelled ... and they encamped ... They travelled ... and they encamped.' The very name *ivri*, or Hebrew, means one who wanders from place to place. More than most, Jews have known insecurity, whether in the land of Israel or else-where. Too often home turned out to be no more than a temporary dwelling, a *sukkah*.

Yet with its genius for the unexpected, Judaism declared Sukkot to be not a time of sadness but the 'season of our rejoicing'. For the tabernacle in all its vulnerability symbolises faith: the faith of a people who set out long ago on a risk-laden journey across a desert of space and time with no more protection than the sheltering divine presence. Sitting in the *sukkah* underneath its canopy of leaves I often think of my ancestors and their wanderings across Europe in search of safety, and I begin to understand how faith was their only home. It was fragile, chillingly exposed to the storms of prejudice and hate. But it proved stronger than empires. Their faith survived. The Jewish people has outlived all its persecutors.

At the end of his *History of the Jews* Paul Johnson wrote:

> The Jews were not just innovators. They were also exemplars and epitomisers of the human condition. They seemed to present all the inescapable dilemmas of man in a heightened and clarified form . . . The Jews were the emblem of homeless and vulnerable humanity. But is not the whole earth no more than a temporary transit camp?

Those words go to the heart of Sukkot. To know that life is full of risk and yet to affirm it, to sense the full insecurity of the human situation and yet to rejoice: this, for me, is the essence of faith. Judaism is no comforting illusion that all is well in this dark world. It is instead the courage to celebrate in the midst of uncertainty and to rejoice even in the transitory shelter of the tabernacle, the Jewish symbol of home.

৵

Twenty years ago I built my first *sukkah*. It was almost a catastrophe. It happened like this.

My wife and I were newly married and had just settled in to our new home. One morning, leaving the synagogue, a friend said, 'I'm just off to the local timber yard to buy wood to build a *sukkah*. Would you like to come with me?' Delightedly, I said yes. We didn't have a car, and I had been wondering how to buy and transport the materials to make a hut. The offer was providential. We went back to his home to get the list of things he required.

The contrast between us, though, could not have been greater. The friend – who was later to become one of Anglo-Jewry's great rabbis – was superbly organised. He had drawn up architectural plans for his temporary dwelling. It was to be a stand-alone structure with windows and a door, and it was going to require considerable skill in carpentry. He had made a long and precise list of the materials he needed, and was ready to begin. I was shame-faced. I had no idea how to make anything, let alone a *sukkah*. In school, I had always come bottom of the class in woodworking, and when it came to practicalities, changing a light-bulb was the limit of my ability. Humbled, I followed him into the car, hoping that inspiration would come.

In the timber yard, he rattled off his list of requirements and ended up with an impressive pile of beams and planks and hinges and screws. I settled for an impromptu list of a few sheets of hardboard, some wooden supports and a bag of nails. We went off to our respective homes and began hammering away. Before the festival began we visited each other to see the results of our efforts. His was a thing of beauty, a summer house in which anyone could have faced wandering in the wilderness with equanimity. Ours was modest by any standards. I had joined the hardboard to the beams to make three square walls, nailed them to one another, and rested them against the back wall of the house. It looked like a large packing case. There was a hole for a door.

The festival arrived, and as luck would have it, there was a storm on the second night. The wind howled and blew itself into a gale. In synagogue the next morning my friend sat dejected. His *sukkah* had blown down. 'What', he asked, 'happened to yours?'

'It's still standing', I said. He could hardly believe it. His elaborate tabernacle had been overturned while my makeshift hut survived.

'I must come round and see it', he said. 'I don't understand how any *sukkah* could have stayed standing after that storm.' So we went to my home together to investigate the mystery. We soon found the answer.

Unlike his, our *sukkah* did not stand alone. It had three walls, and for the fourth we had rested it against the house. To stop it collapsing, I had joined one corner to the wall of the house with a single nail, and it was that nail which had held firm during the gale. My friend laughed and said: 'Now I understand the meaning of Sukkot. You can plan and construct the most sophisticated building, but if it is not joined to something stable, one day the winds will come and blow it down. Alternatively, you can make an improvised shelter which looks frail and probably is. But if it is joined even at only one point to something immovable, it will hold fast in the worst storm.'

'That nail in the corner', he said, looking at it with a smile I have never forgotten, 'is faith.'

❧

No other festival brings us so closely into contact with nature as does Sukkot. It is not merely living in the tabernacle that exposes us to the sun, the wind and the rain. It is also the other ritual of Sukkot, the 'four kinds'. The Torah commands us to 'take the fruit of the goodly tree (the *etrog* or citron), branches of palm trees (the *lulav*), boughs of leafy trees (*hadassim*) and willows of the brook (*aravot*), and you shall rejoice before the Lord your God for seven days' (Leviticus 23:40). These fruits of nature form a central part of the synagogue service. We hold and wave them during *Hallel*, the psalms of praise, and proceed around the synagogue holding them and chanting the special prayers called *Hoshanot*, hosannas, with their refrain, 'Help us, please, O Lord'.

Judaism has a complicated relationship with nature. While other ancient peoples identified gods with the forces of nature, the Hebrew Bible spoke of the one God who stood above nature, bringing it into being and establishing its laws and boundaries. It was a huge revolution of thought. God was not *in* but *above*; not immanent but transcendent. Ultimate reality was not to be found in the contending elements of the natural world. Instead it lay in something beyond, in the Creator, Ruler and Judge of all things. One creation alone – humanity – was destined to experience the tension between the natural and supernatural. We were and are, as the Bible puts it, a mixture of dust of the earth and the breath of God (Genesis 2:7).

It took an outsider and one who was deeply unsympathetic to Judaism to see what this entailed. Friedrich Nietzsche wrote of Jews that 'they made of themselves an antithesis to *natural* conditions – they inverted religion, religious worship, morality, history, psychology, one after the other in an irreparable way into the *contradiction of their natural values*.' He added: 'For precisely this reason the Jews are the most *fateful* nation in world history.' He was correct, for Judaism represents the polar opposite of what he believed in: justice as against power, right instead of might, reverence rather than domination, compassion not control. The state of nature is a war of all against all. It is not where we find God or grace. In nature the weak are preyed on by the strong. In the Torah the strong have responsibilities to the weak. The ethics of Nietzsche and the Hebrew Bible are stark alternatives, and much of human civilisation was and continues to be the story of the conflict between them.

So it is no accident that Sukkot, the festival of nature, is built around the idea of *rain*. The 'four kinds' are plants which need rain to grow. In Temple times Sukkot was marked by an elaborate 'water drawing' ceremony, for at this time of the year, according to rabbinic teaching, 'the rainfall of the world is judged'. And in a remarkable speech at the end of his life, Moses explains to the Israelites why rain will be important to them in the years to come. Until now he has spoken of the promised land as a 'land flowing with milk and honey'. Now, for the first time, he explains that its fertility is not so simple. It depends not on rivers but on rain:

The land you are about to enter and possess is not like the land of Egypt, from which you have come, where you planted your seed and irrigated it by foot as in a vegetable garden. But the land you are crossing the Jordan to possess is a land of mountains and valleys that drinks rain from heaven. It is a land the Lord your God looks after; the eyes of the Lord your God are continually on it from the beginning of the year to its end. (Deuteronomy 11:10–12).

The Nile delta was naturally fertile. Israel was not. In the book of Genesis we read repeatedly of how the patriarchs had to leave because of famine and drought. Even today, water is Israel's scarcest resource. In a land of rivers, fertility comes from the ground. In a land like Israel, fertility comes from the sky in the form of rain. Nothing in such a land is predictable, nothing can be taken for granted. Instead your eyes turn towards heaven. The promised land turned out to be, not a place of natural security, but one whose inhabitants would be constantly aware of their vulnerability to forces beyond their control. Daily survival would demand a leap of trust. It still does. Climatically and militarily, Israel has always been peculiarly exposed: a dry land that depends on rain, a small country surrounded by great empires; never a fortress, always a *sukkah*. If nature prevailed, Israel would not survive. Perhaps that is why faith is engraved on our souls.

ষ♥

With a final and glorious touch of paradox, custom ordained that in the middle of this 'season of our rejoicing' we should read Ecclesiastes, on the face of it the most gloomy and unexpected book in the entire Bible. Its author is the man who has had and done everything. He has read books, studied the accumulated wisdom of mankind, built palaces and planted pleasure gardens, acquired wealth and all its trappings and 'denied myself nothing that my eyes desired'. Now, like all true hedonists, he has grown weary with life. 'Meaningless, meaningless', he says repeatedly, 'Everything is meaningless.'

The Talmud records the great debate that took place before Ecclesiastes was admitted into the biblical canon as a holy book. Understandably so, for the world according to Ecclesiastes is not what we expect from a man of faith. Wisdom, he says, only begets sorrow. Wealth creates anxiety. Politics is an arena of corruption. All striving under the sun ends in disillusion. One thing alone is certain, and that is death: 'Man's fate is like that of the animals; the same fate awaits them both; as one dies, so dies the other, for both have the same breath. Man has no advantage over the animals for everything is meaningless.' If it is strange that so bleak a testimony should have been included in the Bible, it seems doubly ironic that it should have been chosen as a reading on the festival of joy.

But I sense in Ecclesiastes a surprising affirmation. It is a meditation about mortality, one of the most poignant ever written. The word Ecclesiastes uses to describe the human condition is *hevel*, usually translated as 'meaningless' or 'futile' or 'vain'. But it means something else: a breath. The words the Hebrew Bible uses to describe the spirit or soul – words like *nefesh*, *ruach* and *neshamah* – are not abstract nouns. They are all terms which refer, each with its own nuance, to the act of breathing. The word *hevel* signifies the fragility of life, as if to say that the entire horizon of our experience is bounded by a mere breath. That insubstantial puff of air is all that separates us from death. *Hevel* is the almost-nothing which is life itself. Whenever I read it in Ecclesiastes I think of King Lear's lament as he holds the dead Cordelia in his arms: 'Why should a dog, a horse, a rat have life, and thou no breath at all?'

Ecclesiastes is a song of life – life in and of itself, frail, transitory, vulnerable, but all there is. No one saw more clearly than its author how we waste our time in the vain pursuit of immortality, as if by accumulating wealth or power we could cheat death of its final victory. Ecclesiastes has taken all those routes and seen where they end. From his many journeys its author has arrived at a deeply religious conclusion. God has given us one thing – life – and too many of our human strivings lead away from it. Life is the breath of God that transforms the handful of dust, and we serve God by celebrating it and not the counterfeit substitutes of human devising. 'I know that there is nothing better for men than to be happy and do good while they live. That every man may eat and drink and find satisfaction in all his toil – this is the gift of God' (Ecclesiastes 3:12–13).

Sukkot is a complex set of variations on the theme of life: life stripped of all illusions of security. It tells us that home, like immortality, is in *how* we live, not where or for how long. It is the festival of a people who have known more starkly than any other that the canopy of faith is the only shelter we have. And it is no small testimony that we can gather beneath its shade, and sing.

24
Rosh Hashanah / New Year
The Courtroom of the World

Rosh Hashanah, the Jewish New Year, is a kind of clarion call, a summons to the Ten Days of Penitence which culminate in the Day of Atonement. The Torah calls it 'the day when the horn is sounded', and its central event is the sounding of the shofar, the ram's horn.

More than any other, the sound of the shofar has been the signal of momentousness in Jewish history, italicising time for special emphasis. It was the ram's horn that sounded at Mount Sinai when the Israelites heard the voice of God and accepted the covenant that was to frame our religious destiny. It was the ram's horn that accompanied them into battle in the days of Joshua. And it would be the ram's horn that would one day signal Israel's return from exile, gathered once again in the promised land.

On Rosh Hashanah the shofar becomes a herald announcing the arrival of the King, for at this time of the year God is seen not as a father or creator or redeemer, but as the Sovereign of life enthroned in the seat of judgement. The imagery of the prayers is royal and judicial. The world has become a vast court, and its creatures pass before the King of Kings awaiting his verdict.

> With trumpets and the blast of the ram's horn
> Raise a shout before the Lord, the King . . .
> For He comes to judge the earth. (Psalm 98:6, 9)

Before Him are the books of life and oblivion, and we pray to be written in the book of life.

At times the imagery of the day can seem remote, because monarchy has become for us less judicial, majestic and grand. Kings and queens no longer enter palaces to the sound of trumpets and preside over issues of life and death. None the less, Rosh Hashanah still conveys a sense of expectancy and moment. Its two days are Days of Awe in which we are conscious of standing before God, our past exposed to scrutiny, our future unknown and in the balance.

The New Year and the Day of Atonement are vivid enactments of

Judaism's greatest leap of faith: the belief that the world is ruled by justice. No idea has been more revolutionary, and none more perplexing. There are questions that challenge faith, and there are questions that come from faith. Those who asked about the apparent injustices of the world were not figures of doubt. They were Judaism's supreme prophets. Moses asked, 'O Lord, why have You brought trouble upon this people?' Jeremiah said, 'Right would You be, O Lord, if I were to contend with You, yet I will speak with You about Your justice: Why does the way of the wicked prosper? Why do all the faithless live at ease?' They did not ask because they did not believe. They asked because they *did* believe. If there were no Judge, there would be no justice and no question. There *is* a Judge. Where then is justice? Above all else, Jewish thought through the centuries has been a sustained meditation on this question, never finding answers, realising that here was a sacred mystery no human mind could penetrate. All other requests Moses made on behalf of the Jewish people, says the Talmud, were granted except this: to understand why the righteous suffer.

As tenaciously as they asked, so they held firm to the faith without which there was no question: that there is a moral rule governing the universe and that what happens to us is in some way related to what we do. Good is rewarded and evil has no ultimate dominion. No Jewish belief is more central than this. It forms the core of the Hebrew Bible, the writings of the rabbis and the speculations of the Jewish mystics. Reward and punishment might be individual or collective, immediate or deferred, in this world or the next, apparent or veiled behind a screen of mystery, but they are there. For without them life is a tale told by an idiot, full of sound and fury, signifying nothing. The faith of the Bible is neither optimistic nor naive. It contains no theodicies, no systematic answers, no easy consolations. At times, in the books of Job and Ecclesiastes and Lamentations, it comes close to the abyss of pain and despair. 'I saw', says Ecclesiastes, 'the tears of the oppressed – and they have no comforter.' 'The Lord', says Lamentations, 'has become like an enemy.' But the people of the Book refused to stop wrestling with the question. To believe was painful, but to disbelieve was too easy, too superficial, untrue.

So on Rosh Hashanah we live in the presence of this risk-laden proposition, that in goodness is the way of life. Knowing our failings, we come before God asking Him to find in us some act that we have done or that we might yet do for good. 'Write us in the book of life.'

༜

The ram's horn, though, meant something else to Jewish tradition as well as the sound of judgement. It recalled one of the great trials of the Hebrew Bible: Abraham, who was willing to sacrifice his son Isaac for the love of God. This too is a mystery until we read the end. God tells Abraham to put down the knife. He does not desire the sacrifice of human life. Abraham looks round and sees a ram caught in a bush by its horn and offers it instead. This became a motif of Rosh Hashanah:

Rabbi Abbahu said: Why do we blow the ram's horn? The Holy One, blessed be He, said, 'Sound before Me a ram's horn so that I may remember on your behalf the binding of Isaac the son of Abraham and account it to you as if you had bound yourselves before me.'

I sometimes wonder what lay behind this interpretation of Rabbi Abbahu, a great third-century sage. Was it merely the idea of ancestral merit, that God would forgive Israel as He had done in the days of Moses out of love for the patriarchs? Or was it a more recent memory of the Jews who had died as martyrs under Roman rule rather than give up practising their faith and teaching Torah in public? For they had allowed themselves to be bound at the altar of self-sacrifice, and no word had come from heaven to end the trial.

I remember one of the first sermons I was called on to give. I was a student at the time, and the Torah portion of the week was the passage in Exodus which describes how the Israelites in the wilderness made the golden calf. After days of fruitless effort I turned to my teacher for advice. 'I want,' I said, 'to say something positive. But wherever I turn I find something dispiriting: the Israelites' sin, Aaron's weakness, and Moses' anger.' My teacher replied in the following remarkable words:

When Moses prayed for forgiveness for the Israelites, he said, '*Because* this is a stiff-necked people, forgive our wickedness and our sin and take us as Your inheritance' (Exodus 34:9). Was this not a strange thing to say? Their obstinacy was surely a reason to be angry with them, not to forgive them. But the truth is that we *are* an obstinate people. When the Israelites saw God, in the wilderness, they disobeyed Him. But when they could not see Him, throughout the many centuries when Jews were powerless and persecuted for their faith, they were tenaciously loyal to Him. They might have converted or assimilated, but they did not. They chose to suffer as Jews rather than find tranquility by relinquishing their Judaism. Their obstinacy, which was once their greatest vice, became their greatest virtue.

It was with that plea that Jews came before God on the days of judgement. They had known what it was to be Isaac bound on the altar. Already in the Middle Ages, as they wept for the victims of the blood libels and the

Crusades, the authors of elegies recalled that earlier trial. In a penitential prayer once said on the eve of Rosh Hashanah, telling the story of massacre in Mainz in 1096 in which more than a thousand Jews died, many of them children, we read:

When were there ever a thousand and a hundred sacrifices in one day, each of them like the binding of Isaac son of Abraham? Once at the binding of one on Mount Moriah, the Lord shook the world to its base . . . O heavens, why did you not go black, O stars, why did you not withdraw your light, O sun and moon, why did you not darken in your sky?

Long before the Holocaust, Jews knew the risk they took in remaining Jews. But Jews they remained. The ram's horn spoke not only of the majesty of God. It spoke of the obstinate loyalty of the Jewish people, Abraham's children.

ﬞ

Rabbi Levi Yitzchak of Berdichev was one of the most extraordinary figures in the history of Jewish spirituality. Born in Galicia in 1740, he became a disciple of the Maggid of Mezerich, himself a follower of the Baal Shem Tov. These were the early days of the Hassidic movement when it was a revolutionary force in Jewish life. Hassidism belonged to the mystical tradition of Judaism. But unlike previous mystical groups, it was popular rather than esoteric. It emphasised devotion and prayer more than scholarship. It spoke to simple Jews rather than to the rabbinic élite. And it placed at the centre of its world the charismatic leader – the Tzaddik or Rebbe – who watched over the destiny of his followers.

Against the backdrop of medieval Jewish tradition with its emphasis on study and on the rabbi as scholar and teacher, it was a radical departure, and the movement had strong opponents – the *mitnagdim*. Levi Yitzchak found himself frequently embroiled in controversy and was forced to move from town to town. Eventually, in 1785, he came to Berdichev where, as a rabbi and communal leader, he won widespread respect. He served there until he died, in 1810.

No one understood more clearly than he that if the New Year and the Day of Atonement were a time of judgement and the days themselves a kind of trial, the Jewish people needed a defending counsel. For the key to these days was not strict justice but forgiveness. Had God not chosen the Jewish people? And did this not therefore mean that He loved them? And if He loved them, did He not *wish* to forgive them? If so, then the vital task was not to berate the congregation for their sins, but to plead with God to let mercy prevail. This, Levi Yitzchak did. He did so each year in prayers of unprecedented audacity. He spoke directly to heaven. He did so familiarly, using the Yiddish language rather than the formal Hebrew of the prayer book. It was as if the synagogue in Berdichev had become the courtroom of the Jewish world, and in the hush before the judgement Levi Yitzchak approached the Judge and in words of passion sought to have the case dismissed.

One year he said: 'Master of the Universe, Your people Israel have many sins. But You have much forgiveness. I propose an exchange. Let us trade our sins for Your forgiveness. And if You say, That is an unfair exchange, I answer, Without our sins, of what use would Your forgiveness be?'

Another year: 'Master of the Universe, You know that even the humblest Jew, if he saw a holy book lying in the street, would pick it up, kiss it and put it in a place of honour. But we, Your people, *are* a holy book. Your words are written in our lives. And we are lying in the street, crushed by poverty and persecution. Can You pass by and *not* pick us up?'

And on a year on which Rosh Hashanah fell on Shabbat: 'Master of the Universe, You have given us many laws. And You, being just, are bound by those same laws. What we may not do, You do not do. But today is the Sabbath. And on the Sabbath we may not write. How then, as the books of life and death sit before You, can You write? There is only one cause which permits us to write on the Sabbath: to save a life. Write us, therefore, in the book of life.'

Where did they come from, these daring intercessions so close to being in contempt of court? From an ancient Jewish tradition, prophecy itself. For the greatest of the prophets pleaded on behalf of humanity. Abraham prayed for the cities of the plain. Moses, after the sin of the golden calf, said: 'Please forgive them now their sin – but if not, then blot me out of the book You have written.' The prophet was one who loved his people more than he reprimanded them. He knew their faults. But he pleaded their cause, and stood his ground even before the throne of glory. Levi Yitzchak gave fresh voice to one of the great themes of the Jewish spiritual drama, the triumph of forgiveness over justice.

His most daring prayer? Once, on Kol Nidrei night, as the Day of Atonement was beginning, he looked around the synagogue and saw a man whose face was filled with tears. He went up to him. 'Why are you crying?'

'I cannot help it. Once I was a pious Jew. I had a good livelihood, a comfortable home. My wife was devout. Our home was always open to strangers. Then suddenly He intervened. I lost my wife. My business collapsed. I had to sell my home. And I am left poor and homeless with six children to look after. I do not know how to pray any more. All I can do is come to the synagogue and weep.'

Levi Yitzchak comforted the man and brought him a prayer book. 'Will you pray now?'

'Yes,' said the man.

'Do you forgive God now?'

'Yes', he replied. 'Today is the Day of Atonement; I must forgive.'

Then Levi Yitzchak turned his eyes upward towards heaven and said, 'You too must do the same, Master of the Universe, You too must forgive.'

ஐ

Caught up in this drama of sin and repentance, justice and forgiveness, estrangement and reconciliation, I begin to realise that being a Jew – being a human being – is not a matter of the here-and-now only. My life is more than this place, this time, these anxieties, those hopes. We are characters in a long and continuing narrative. We carry with us the pain and faith of our ancestors. Our acts will affect our children and those not yet born. We neither live our lives nor come before God alone. In us, the past and future have resided their trust. The battle of good against evil, faith against indifference, is not won in a single generation. Never in earthly time is it finally won, and must be fought each year anew. In each of us the faith of Abraham and Sarah and Isaac still echoes. The pleas of Levi Yitzchak still resonate. The question is: Will we hear them? On Rosh Hashanah we ask God to remember. But on Rosh Hashanah God also asks us to remember.

Before God lie two books, and one of them is the book of life. It was many years before I understood that before us, also, lie the same two books. In one is written all the things to which human beings have instinctively turned: appetite and will and self-assertion and power. It was Judaism's most fateful claim that this is not the book of life. The other book is not without these things, but it comes with a condition: that they must be sanctified, used responsibly, turned to the common good. From beginning to end Judaism teaches us to enjoy and affirm life. But it teaches that this is not an easy thing if we are to enjoy and affirm other people's lives as well as our own. There is a code, a law, a covenant, a discipline, and without these things pleasure turns to ashes and life into a passing shadow that leaves no trace. In the ram's horn is a plea, from heaven and from Jewish history: Choose life.

25

Yom Kippur / The Day of Atonement Coming Home

Yom Kippur, the Day of Atonement, is the supreme moment of Jewish time, a day of fasting and prayer, introspection and self-judgement. At no other time are we so sharply conscious of standing before God, of *being known*. But it begins in the strangest of ways.

Kol Nidrei, the prayer which heralds the evening service and the beginning of the sanctity of the day, is the key that unlocks the Jewish heart. Its melody is haunting. As the cantor sings, we hear in that ancient tune the deepest music of the Jewish soul, elegiac yet striving, pained but resolute, the song of those who knew that to believe is to suffer and still to hope, the music of our ancestors which stretches out to us from the past and enfolds us in its cadences, making us and them one. The music is sublime. Tolstoy called it a melody that 'echoes the story of the great martyrdom of a grief-stricken nation.' Beethoven came close to it in the most otherwordly and austere of his compositions, the sixth movement of the C Sharp Minor Quartet, opus 131. The music is pure poetry, but the words are prosaic prose.

Kol Nidrei means 'all vows'. The passage itself is not a prayer at all, but a dry legal formula annulling in advance all vows, oaths and promises between us and God in the coming year. Nothing could be more incongruous, less apparently in keeping with the solemnity of the day. Indeed, for more than a thousand years there have been attempts to remove it from the liturgy. Why annul vows? Better, as the Hebrew Bible and the rabbis argued, not to make them in the first place if they could not be kept. Besides which, though Jewish law admits the possibility of annulment, it does so only after patient examination of individual cases. To do so globally for the whole community was difficult to justify. From the eighth century onwards we read of *geonim*, rabbinic leaders, who condemned the prayer and sought to have it abolished. Five centuries later a new note of concern was added. In the Christian-Jewish disputation in Paris in 1240, the Christian protagonist Nicholas Donin attacked Kol Nidrei as evidence that Jews did not feel themselves bound by their word, a claim later repeated by anti-semitic writers. In vain Jews explained that the prayer had nothing to do with promises between man and man. It referred only to private commitments between man and God. All in all, it was and is a strange way to begin the holiest of days.

Yet the prayer survived all attempts to have it dislodged. One theory, advanced by Joseph Bloch in 1917 and adopted by Chief Rabbi J H Hertz, is that it had its origins in the forced conversion of Spanish Jews to Christianity under the Visigoths in the seventh century. These Jews, the first *marranos*, publicly abandoned their faith rather than face torture and death, but they remained Jews in secret. On the Day of Atonement they made their way back to the synagogue and prayed to have their vow of conversion annulled. Certainly some such reason lies behind the declaration immediately prior to Kol Nidrei in which the leaders of prayer solemnly grant permission 'by the authority of the heavenly and earthly court' for 'transgressors' to join the congregation in prayer. This was a lifting of the ban of excommunication against Jews who, during the year, had been declared to have placed themselves outside the community. That, surely, is the significance of Kol Nidrei in the Jewish imagination. It is the moment when the doors of belonging are opened, and when those who have been estranged return.

The Hebrew word *teshuvah*, usually translated as 'penitence', in fact means something else: returning, retracing our steps, coming home. It belongs to the biblical vision in which sin means dislocation, and punishment is exile: Adam and Eve's exile from Eden, Israel's exile from its land. A sin is an act that does not belong, one that transgresses the moral boundaries of the world. One who acts in ways that do not belong finds eventually that he does not belong. Increasingly he places himself outside the relationships – of family, community and of being at one with history – that make him who he is. The most characteristic sense of sin is less one of guilt than of being lost. *Teshuvah* means finding your way back home again.

That, on this night of nights, is what Jews do. The synagogue is full of the faces of those who rarely visit it. During the year – albeit less dramatically than their medieval predecessors – they may have been *marranos*, hidden Jews. They have worn other masks, carried different identities. But tonight the music of Kol Nidrei has spoken to them and they have said: here is where I belong. Among my people and its faith. I am a Jew.

ले

In ancient Israel there were holy places. The land itself was holy. Holier still was the city of Jerusalem, and in Jerusalem the holiest site was the Temple. Within the Temple was the supremely sacred place known as the Holy of Holies.

There was holy time. There were the festivals. Above them was the Sabbath, the day God himself declared holy. Above even that was the one day in the year known as the Sabbath of Sabbaths, the most holy day of all, the Day of Atonement.

There were holy people. Israel was called 'a holy nation'. Among them was a tribe of special sanctity, the Levites, and within it were individuals who were holier still, the *cohanim* or priests. Among them was one person who was supremely holy, the High Priest.

In ancient times the holiest man entered the holiest place on the holiest day of the year and sought atonement for his people.

Then the Temple was destroyed. Jerusalem lay in ruins. Devastated, too, was the spiritual life of Israel. There were no sacrifices and no High Priest. None of the rites of the Day of Atonement, spelled out in the book of Leviticus, could be performed. How then could sins be purged and the people of Israel annually restore their relationship with God?

One saying has come down to us from that time, a sentence which rescued Judaism from the ruins. Its author, Rabbi Akiva, lived through the destruction. His early years were spent as an illiterate shepherd. Tradition tells us that he fell in love with Rachel, daughter of one of the wealthiest men in Jerusalem. She agreed to marry him on condition that he studied and became a Torah scholar. Her father disinherited her, but she remained devoted to Akiva, who eventually became the supreme scholar of his day and one of the architects of rabbinic Judaism. He died, a martyr, at the hands of the Romans.

Rabbi Akiva was a remarkable man. It was at his insistence that the Song of Songs was included in the biblical canon. He framed a number of enactments to foster love as the basis of marriage. He said, 'Beloved is mankind for it is created in the image of God' and declared that 'Love thy neighbour as thyself' is the fundamental principle of Judaism. But above all he could see through catastrophe. When others wept at the destruction of the Temple, Rabbi Akiva preserved a spirit of hope, saying that since it had been prophesied, the rebuilding of Jerusalem, which had also been prophesied, would also come to pass. 'Whatever God does is for the best.' About the Day of Atonement he said this:

Happy are you, O Israel! Before whom are you purified and who purifies you?

Your Father in heaven, as it is said, 'And I will sprinkle clean water upon you and you shall be purified' (Ezekiel 36:25).

Israel did not need a Temple or a High Priest to secure atonement. It had lost its holiest place and person. But it still had the day itself: holy time. On that day every place becomes a holy place and every person a holy individual standing directly before God. By turning to Him in *teshuvah* it is as if we had brought an offering in the Temple, because God hears every cry that comes from the heart. When there is no High Priest to mediate between Israel and God, we speak to God directly and he accepts our prayer. So it has been for almost two thousand years.

So we fast and remove our shoes and dress in white shrouds and spend the day in prayer and confession as if each of us stood in the Holy of Holies in Jerusalem, because God heeds not who or where we are, but how we live. And though we no longer have a Temple and its offerings, we have something no less powerful: prayer, the 'service of the heart'.

> Hear our voice, Lord our God,
> Have pity and compassion on us,
> And with compassion and favour accept our prayer.

ह

At the core of the day's prayers is *vidui*, confession. Through all the letters of the Hebrew alphabet we enumerate, admit and apologise for our sins. But it is at this point that we encounter one of Judaism's most striking phenomena. Instinct would suggest that confession and repentance are best done alone. It is painful to undergo self-criticism in the privacy of our souls; doubly so in the company of others. But on Yom Kippur we confess together, publicly and aloud. We say not 'I have sinned' but 'We have sinned'.

The practice clearly recalls the time when the High Priest atoned collectively for all Israel. But the problem is obvious, then and now. If I have sinned, only I can put it right. If I have wronged, lied, cheated or humiliated, it does not help if you make amends and apologise. The wrongs we do, we do alone. You cannot atone for my sins and I cannot atone for yours. How then could the High Priest atone for the sins of all Israel, sins he did not commit? How can we in our prayers turn the singular into the plural and atone not as individuals but as a community?

Judaism has a strong sense of individual dignity and responsibility. But it has an equally strong sense of collective responsibility. 'All of Israel', says the Talmud, 'are sureties for one another.' The great sage Hillel used to say, 'If I am not for myself, who will be for me? But if I am only for myself, what am I?' The 'lonely man of faith' is a figure almost unknown to Judaism. Ours is not a religion of hermits or monks or ascetics, living apart from society and communing solely with God. The heroes and heroines of the Hebrew Bible are fathers and mothers, people set in the context of their families and societies. In the second chapter of Genesis the Bible states its view of the human condition: 'It is not good for man to be alone.'

So the faith of Israel is constructed in the first person plural. Indeed the very basis of the covenant – of Judaism as a religion of divine law – rests on this assumption. Every commandment in Judaism, every 'Thou shalt' and 'Thou shalt not', is a way of putting the 'We' before the 'I'. When we rest on the Sabbath, for example, we do not engage in private relaxation. If we did, we would spend the seventh day playing golf or listening to records or whatever else we chose. The Sabbath is instead a day of public rest. It is a day of 'We' not 'I'. Judaism is a faith less of individual salvation than of collective redemption.

Correspondingly, every transgression in Judaism is a way of putting the 'I' before the 'We'. Whenever we put personal advantage over collective interest, or private inclination before the laws of the community, sooner or later we sin. That is why the severest punishment in Judaism is *karet*, literally being 'cut off' from the community. Atonement consists in reconnecting ourselves with the community, and that is why Yom Kippur is of its essence a shared, collective day.

When the Temple stood, the Jewish people was embodied in its supreme religious representative, the High Priest. When he atoned, all Israel shared in his act. Now that we have no High Priest, we share in one another's atonement, each gaining moral strength from one another.

There is a moving prayer that we say at the climax of Yom Kippur, in the concluding service called Neilah. It speaks of the fragility of human achievement, the smallness of humanity in the face of the Infinite:

> What are we?
> What is our life?
> What is our piety, our righteousness, our helpfulness? . . .
> What shall we say before You,
> O Lord our God and God of our fathers?
> Are not all the mighty ones as nothing before You,
> The men of renown as if they had never existed,

The wise as if devoid of knowledge,
The intelligent as if without discernment?

Under the eye of eternity our lives are a shadow's shadow. Said at the end of the Day of Atonement, this prayer stands in its unrelieved austerity. But when we recite it at other times we follow it with a momentous 'nevertheless':

Nevertheless we are Your people,
The children of Your covenant . . .

Individually we are small. But collectively we are capable of greatness. Such at any rate is our belief. It is the 'I' that sins, the 'We' which atones.

ॐ

In 1798 the great Hassidic leader, Rabbi Shneur Zalman of Ladi, was imprisoned for spreading religious faith (and thus subversion) amongst the Jewish population. It is told that while he sat in prison awaiting trial, his warden, conscious of being in the presence of a holy man, asked him a question that had long been troubling him. He said: 'We read in the book of Genesis that when Adam and Eve sinned, they hid themselves amongst the trees of the Garden of Eden, and God called out, "Where are you?" What I want to know is this. If God knows and sees everything, surely He knew where they were. Why did He need to ask: Where are you?'

The rabbi replied: 'The words of the Bible were not meant for their time alone but for all time. So it is with the question God asked Adam and Eve. It was not addressed to them alone but to each of us in every generation. We do wrong and then we believe that we can hide from the consequences. But always, after we have done wrong, we hear the voice of God in our heart asking: What have you done with your life? *Where are you?*'

That is the great question of Yom Kippur. God has given us one thing: life itself, this all-too-brief span of years. There may be days, weeks, even months when we lose ourselves in the pace of daily routine, never looking upwards. We can even go through the motions of a religious way of life without the divine presence ever really penetrating to our core of consciousness. We hide. But on the Day of Atonement there is no hiding. We read the book of Jonah, whose message is that one cannot escape the call of God. And we become Jonah: summoned, addressed. God speaks a question. How have we spent our life? Where are we?

Yom Kippur is a day of awe. Yet the Talmud calls it one of the most joyous days of the year. Rightly so, for its message is that as long as we breathe, there is no final verdict on our lives. 'Prayer, penitence and charity have the power to turn aside the evil decree.' God has given us free will, and thus the strength to turn from bad to good. He has granted us a Day of Atonement, and thus the chance to unwrite our wrongs and find forgiveness. There is no equivalent in Judaism to the Greek ideas of *fate* and *tragedy*, the decree that cannot be averted and the futility of our attempts to escape it. Those concepts are utterly alien to the Jewish mind, along with all theories which see our behaviour as determined by causes outside ourselves. Instead, we believe that there is always a chance to begin again. For though we may lose faith in God, God never loses faith in us. On this day of days we hear His voice, gently calling us to come home.

PART IV
JEWISH ETHICS AND
SPIRITUALITY

26

Introduction: Sharing Fate

Between October and December 1988, I recorded a series of broadcasts on Jewish spirituality for the BBC World Service series, 'Words of Faith'. The texts form the first and longest chapter in this section. In them I try to give expression to the powerful and living relationship between a people and a book: Jews and the Torah, the Hebrew Bible.

That relationship is neither simple nor naive. Jews are not fundamentalists. For the most part, they have not read the Bible as a scientific text or a set of deterministic predictions, as if it contained factual information of a kind otherwise unavailable to the human mind. It is not a short cut to knowledge or a magical disclosure of the fate of the universe. That is not how Judaism understands the search for knowledge or the challenge of history.

Instead, reading Torah is a way of experiencing Jewish history as the interplay between a moral and challenging God, and the often disobedient but ultimately loyal people He chose to be the bearers of His special covenant. It is a particular way of seeing our fate and destiny – what happens to us and what we are called on to do in response. It is the Book which gave and continues to give shape to the Jewish imagination, and frames our interpretation of events. It is this which makes Jews a distinctive people, and gives Jewish history its special character.

To a remarkable degree, scenes that occur in the Hebrew Bible *recur* at critical moments in post-biblical Jewish history, and continue to do so to the present day. That is no accident. For human history, as we understand it, is not a blind sequence of events, operating on one another as causes and effects, as if human beings were billiard balls struck by others and striking others in their turn. It is made by how we understand what we suffer and what we do. And it makes a great difference when we set these events in the context of a narrative and a tradition, as if, far from being isolated individuals, we were characters in a drama that had its origins long before our birth and will continue far beyond our lifetime.

To be a Jew is, in part, to respond to the Hebrew Bible as the book of our destiny, the text which tells us who we are, where we came from, and what we are called on to do. That is what I was later to call a 'covenantal reading' of the text. So long as Jews read and respond to the Hebrew Bible in this way, our history will continue to have the strange, even epic, character of an ongoing commentary to the Book. The past helps us to understand the present. The present discloses new dimensions in the past. That vital connection between text and life is, for me, what gives Jewish life throughout the millennia its singular character, and these talks are my portrait of Jewry's 'habits of the heart'.

To them I have added chapters on the Jewish ethics of business, the ecology, handicap and leadership, less to sum up Jewish teachings than to give examples of the *feel* of moral reflection in the Jewish tradition, and to show how this too is a matter of wrestling with texts in the context of life. The section ends with chapters on two of the more perplexing questions of our time: Jewish identity and Jewish reflection after the Holocaust.

The Baal Shem Tov, founder of the Hassidic movement, used to describe Jews as letters in a Torah scroll, and the image is as apt as any. A letter on its own has no meaning. But as it is joined to others in words, sentences, chapters, and books, it takes its part in something that *has* meaning – in the case of Torah the extended dialogue between God and the covenantal people that began at Mount Sinai and has continued uninterrupted ever since. Jewish life is part destiny, part fate; *writing* and *being written* in the narrative that spans our distant ancestors and generations yet to come: the scroll of the covenant. To be a letter in that text is what it is to be a Jew.

27

Images of Jewish Spirituality

Abraham's Children

The Jewish people has had a history longer than most, and it encompasses an extraordinary number of wanderings and reversals. Yet to Jews, that history is experienced not so much as the story of things that happened in the past but as the shape of things that happen in the present. Key moments that may have taken place long ago seem to recur again and again. It is as if Jewish history were a set of variations on a theme, or as if some events had so implanted themselves in our mind that we carried them with us wherever we went.

Consider the words of God to Abraham that set Jewish history in motion:

Leave your country, your birthplace and your father's house and go to the land which I will show you. I will make you into a great nation, I will bless you and I will make your name great, and you shall be a blessing. I will bless those who bless you, and whoever curses you, I will curse; and all the peoples of the earth will be blessed through you. (Genesis 12:1–3)

First, Abraham was told that he would have to break with the usual securities of life. A country, a birthplace, a father's house, are what make us feel at home. They are where we belong. But Abraham, in the words which set him on his way, was commanded to leave these assurances behind. He was to become an *ivri*, a Hebrew, meaning one who wanders from place to place, whose sole security is his faith. To be a Jew since Abraham has often meant just that, travelling geographically from country to country across a vast diaspora, and spiritually, from trial to trial: a history redeemed from tragedy by faith alone.

Secondly, there was that unnamed destination: 'the land which I will show you'. Where was Abraham travelling? We discover soon enough that it was the land of Canaan, later to become the land of Israel. But no sooner does Abraham arrive than famine forces him to leave. Throughout the Bible the land of Israel is never a simple destination, a place at which you simply arrive. It is indeed a geographical location, a country on the map, but it is more than that. It is the place we travel towards, symbol of a not-yet-realised future. That future, mapped out in greater detail in the book of Deuteronomy and in the visionary images of the prophets, is the perfect society: what Judaism was to call the Messianic Age. There are religions whose golden age is in the past, a paradise lost. Judaism's golden age is in the future, a paradise not yet reached.

Lastly there is that simple phrase, half promise, half command: 'You shall be a blessing.' Abraham, unlike Adam and Noah, is not a symbol of humanity as a whole. He is an individual singled out for a particular destiny. His children, too, become a people singled out for a particular destiny. Why Abraham was chosen, we never discover. That is one of the great enigmas of the Bible. But to what end he was chosen, we discover at the very beginning: to be a blessing. Not to his family or to God alone, but to all the peoples on earth. Somehow he would enrich the lives of others, of cultures and faiths very different from his own. Some would bless him for this, others would curse him. That much was known in advance. But the lives of his descendants would be peculiarly interwoven with the history of many nations, and they would leave their mark, hopefully for blessing, on many cultures. That too has been a recurring theme of Jewish experience.

It is strange and not a little awe-inspiring to think how much of Jewish history – its exiles, its messianic hopes, its singular destiny – was foreshadowed in those few words. To be a Jew is to be one of Abraham's children. His fate goes with us, and his challenge too.

Choosing Life

The story of the binding of Isaac is surely the most powerful and most perplexing in the Bible. Abraham and Sarah had waited years for a child, so long, in fact, that when they were told by God they would have a son, they could hardly believe it. They laughed.

But Isaac was born, the child of their hope, the son of the promise. And then, incredibly, came the command to Abraham: 'Take your son, your only son, the one you love, Isaac, and go to Moriah and offer him up as a sacrifice.' Early the next morning, Abraham rose and saddled his donkey, and he and Isaac set off on their journey. Three days later they arrived and walked to the fateful place. Abraham built an altar, and arranged the wood, and bound his son, and lifted his knife. Then we read these words:

The angel of God called to him from heaven and said: 'Abraham, Abraham.'
'Here I am,' he replied.
'Do not lay a hand on the boy', the angel said. 'Do not do anything to him. Now
I know that you fear God, because you have not withheld from Me your son,
your only son.' (Genesis 22:11–12)

So the trial ends, and we are left wondering why. Why was Abraham
put through so cruel an ordeal? Why was Isaac made to suffer such a
torment? Why make the life on which the future of the covenant rested,
seem to hang in doubt? Why did God issue a command that He never
meant Abraham to fulfil? Those questions have been with us almost from
that day to this. But generations of Jews understood that the point of the
story lay in its *end* – in the voice from heaven that stopped the trial and
said: Choose life, not death.

Death has often held a religious fascination, whether in the form of
sacrifice or martyrdom. Against this, the binding of Isaac stands as a
definitive protest. Death is not sacred in Jewish law. Instead, it defiles.
'Choose life', said Moses, summarising his teachings. When Jews raise a
glass of wine they still say *lechaim:* 'To life.'

This idea was one of the turning points of Jewish history. In the first
century of the Common Era, a group of Jews surrounded by the Roman
army on the mountain fortress by the Dead Sea called Masada, chose to
die at their own hands rather than be taken captive. They were courageous
martyrs, but they did not enter Jewish memory as heroes. In the early
second century, under Hadrian's religious persecution, many rabbinical
leaders chose to resist his decrees and be killed. They too, though they
are remembered with reverence, did not become models whose example
was to be followed. There are times when it needs as much courage to
live as to die. At such times, Judaism teaches: Choose life.

One of the great mysteries of the Jewish people is its survival through
tragedies that seemed to spell its end: the destruction of two temples,
exiles, medieval massacres, the Spanish Inquisition, and most fearfully of
all, the Holocaust. After each blow, the Jewish people has begun again,
choosing life. Where did it come from – this tenacity, this determination
to survive, that has puzzled so many historians? Surely from the binding
of Isaac. For if Jews felt that they were living through a trial, they were
equally certain it would stop before its end. The God of Abraham desired
life, not death. Isaac would survive and have children. The covenant
which had seemed to hang in doubt would continue.

So it has continued, from Isaac, the first Jewish child, to the children of the Holocaust survivors. Jewish existence is bounded by a covenant fraught with trials. But it is a covenant, despite everything, of life.

The Argument with Heaven

The town of Sodom epitomises what the Hebrew Bible regards as evil. God confides in Abraham that He is about to destroy it. But Abraham does not accept the verdict and its rightness. Instead he begins one of the most remarkable conversations in the history of man's relationship to God:

Abraham came forward and said: 'Will You sweep away the innocent with the guilty? What if there should be fifty innocent people in the city? Will You then wipe it out and not forgive it for the sake of the fifty innocent people who are there? Far be it from You to do such a thing, to kill the innocent as well as the guilty, treating innocent and guilty alike. Far be it from You! Shall not the Judge of all the earth deal justly?' (Genesis 18:23–5)

God agrees that if there are fifty righteous people, He will spare the town. But Abraham, admitting that he has no right to speak, that he is but dust and ashes, continues to plead until it is agreed that the town will be saved even if there are only ten innocent people.

As it turns out, there are not, for we read next that the entire population of Sodom surrounds the house of Abraham's nephew Lot and attempts to assault his two visitors. But a quite unprecedented tone of voice has entered the dialogue between earth and heaven, one that was to leave a permanent mark on Jewish spirituality. We hear it again when Moses says to God after the first failure of his mission to Pharaoh, 'Why have You brought trouble to this people?' And again, when he pleads for the Israelites after they have made the Golden Calf. 'Please forgive their sin, but if not, then blot me out of the book You have written.' It continues through the prophets and reaches a climax in the book of Job.

Judaism has been called a religion of holy argument. The rabbis spoke of 'argument for the sake of heaven'. But in these passages there is argument with heaven itself. Nor was it confined to the prophets. The rabbinic literature took it further still, and it continued through the elegies of the Middle Ages and the prayers of the eighteenth-century mystics called the Hassidim. It exists today in Jewish writings about the Holocaust. It takes the form of the question 'Why?' Why do the righteous suffer? Why does evil have power? Why, in this world in which God reigns, are there innocent victims? Jews have never stopped asking these questions, and in asking them they have not turned away from, but towards heaven, saying, with Job, 'I desire to speak with the Almighty and to argue my case with God.'

What is it based upon, this daring conversation that began with Abraham? God, after all, is infinite and man a handful of dust. God redeems. Man cannot. How then can we ask questions of God? It originates, surely, in two central ideas of the covenant: that justice is not mystical but ethical, to be sought on earth, not only in heaven; and that God and humanity are partners in achieving it. Injustice cannot be accepted as an illusion. It is a reality that must be protested. And in turning to God, we find new resources within ourselves to change the world.

The argument with heaven does not end with easy answers from God. It ends with a challenge to humanity. It is a prelude to action, and to that passion for justice which is the driving force of the Bible's message to humanity.

Jacob's Struggle

The biblical Jacob had dressed in Esau's clothes. He had stood before his blind father Isaac and taken his brother's blessing. The result was tragic for all three. Isaac suffered the pain of deceit. Esau felt cheated. Jacob had to run away from home in fear that Esau would kill him.

Twenty-two years passed until Jacob decided to return home, hoping perhaps that Esau's anger was spent. As he approached, though, he discovered that Esau was coming to meet him with four hundred men. Was this going to be a brutal confrontation? Jacob was 'very afraid and distressed'. He divided his camp so that some at least would survive. He prayed to God for help. He sent messengers to Esau bearing gifts. Then, after all the precautions had been taken, we read:

Jacob was left alone, and a man wrestled with him until daybreak. When the man saw he could not overpower him, he touched the socket of Jacob's hip so that it was strained as he wrestled with the man.
Then the man said, 'Let me go. It is daybreak.'
But Jacob replied, 'I will not let you go until you bless me.'
The man asked him, 'What is your name?'
'Jacob', he replied.
Then the man said, 'Your name will no longer be Jacob but Israel, because you have struggled with God and with men and have overcome.' (Genesis 32:25–9)

Who was the stranger who wrestled with Jacob? Rabbinic tradition said that it was the guardian angel of Esau. It went on to identify Esau with Rome, the reigning non-Jewish power of the time. In so doing, it turned a biblical episode into a lasting image of the relationship between Jews and gentiles.

At one level, the rabbis were alluding to the uneven struggle between Jews and powerful empires that often threatened their religious freedom, sometimes even their continued existence. Jews would never live totally at peace with the world. Their very name, 'the children of Israel', suggested conflict and struggle. But the image of Jacob signalled that they would survive, even if, like Jacob, they would afterwards limp.

But at a deeper level, and reaching to the heart of the biblical story, they were hinting at the struggle that would have to take place within the people of Israel itself. Jews have often been fascinated by other cultures. The Bible is full of warnings against adopting the religions of neighbouring peoples. Israel was to be singular, different, a people that dwells alone. But it was not easy. Some two hundred years before the Christian era, there were Jews who became devoted to the culture of the Greeks. Centuries later there were others who opted for the sophistication of the Romans. In the modern age, there were many who felt that Judaism was as narrow as the ghetto walls, and who chose secularism instead.

Encounters like these have always led to a crisis in Jewish identity, as if Jacob was once again putting on the clothes of Esau. In each case there had to be a long night of struggle before Jacob could defeat the inner Esau and become himself again. But the biblical story held a promise. The next morning, after the struggle was over, the two brothers met. Jacob's fears proved groundless. Esau ran to greet him. They embraced and wept. Each spoke of his contentment with what he had. No longer did they envy one another's gifts.

That sublime note of reconciliation perfectly describes the relationship between Jews and the non-Jewish world at its rare moments of blessedness, when Jews and Christians, or Jews and Muslims, accepted their differences and enriched one another's lives. The story of Esau and Jacob begins in conflict and ends in peace. They start as rivals but end, simply, as brothers.

Exodus and Revolution

Moses, an Israelite brought up among Egyptians, is in exile. He is tending his sheep when a vision appears to him from a bush that bursts into flame, and he hears these words:

I am the God of your father, the God of Abraham, Isaac and Jacob . . . I have indeed seen the misery of my people in Egypt. I have heard them crying out because of their slave drivers, and I am concerned about their suffering. So I have come down to rescue them from the hand of the Egyptians, and to bring them up out of that land into a good and spacious land, a land flowing with milk and honey. (Exodus 3:6–8)

Of all events that have shaped the Jewish mind, none has been more powerful than this, the beginning of the exodus from Egypt. God, heard by Moses in those words, revealed three characteristics that have moulded Jewish spirituality ever since.

First, He was a God of history, not the abstract God of philosophy, nor even the intimate God of personal salvation. He was concerned with the behaviour of mankind, with society, freedom and the politics of suffering. The consolation He offered lay in historical and political change: the exodus of a people and the building of a new social order.

Secondly, He was a God who cherished freedom. Often the Mosaic books return to the theme, and always with reference to the exodus. Free your slaves in the year of release. Do not let them work for you on the seventh day. Remember that you were once a slave in the land of Egypt. It is as if any loss of freedom is an assault on the image of God that is man.

Thirdly, He was a God who wanted His people never to forget the experience of being a minority without power. Do not oppress a stranger, commands the Bible, because you understand the heart of a stranger – you were once strangers yourselves. Plead the cause of the widow and the orphan, the underprivileged. Power corrupts, the Bible seems to argue, unless we carry in our memories the thought of what it is to be without power. Social justice is born not so much of political theory as it is of the sharp pain of injustice and the decision, having felt it, never to inflict it.

The exodus showed religion to be political and not on the side of the established power. Ever afterwards it has been a text to which prophets, reformers and revolutionaries have turned when they sensed that their task lay in defending the oppressed and righting social wrongs. It appeared in the pamphlets of the German Peasants' Revolt. It was cited by John Calvin and John Knox in their political writings. It was a key text of the Puritan Revolution. It figured largely in the thought of the founders of American society, who saw themselves as a new Israel. It played a role in the early writings of Moses Hess, friend and colleague of Karl Marx. Moses' words, 'Let my people go', were the inspiration of black activist movements in the United States and in South Africa. The exodus story lies behind the powerful movement of Latin American Christian thought known as Liberation Theology.

The story of the exodus has been one of the Bible's most powerful influences on human civilisation. It gives those who reflect on it a focused moral energy. It forces us to realise that the task of religion is not to reconcile us to the world as it is, but to change the world into what it might and should be. That command is always with us, for neither freedom nor justice occur naturally. Nor do they last without prophets reminding us of their importance. Small wonder, then, that the Bible commands us to remember the exodus from Egypt in each generation, all the days of our lives.

Promised Land

There is a strange and recurring feature about the story the Bible tells of Abraham, Isaac, Jacob and then Moses. Almost from the beginning, Abraham is promised the land of Canaan, the land we know as Israel. So is Isaac, and so is Jacob. Yet when Sarah dies, Abraham still has no land of his own. He has to negotiate to buy a burial place. He calls himself an alien and a stranger. Isaac cannot dig a well without a quarrel with the local residents. Jacob has to leave the land more than once, and dies in exile. By the time we reach the end of the book of Genesis, the promise is still just a promise.

As we begin the book of Exodus, we seem to be approaching the fulfilment. Moses is told by God to lead the people out of Egypt and into their land. But again the moment is deferred. On the brink of entry, the people lose heart and are condemned to wander in the desert for forty years. Even as we reach the end of the Mosaic books, the moment has not yet come. Moses prays to be allowed to set foot in the land, but the request is refused. The last picture we have of his life sums up the entire biblical narrative thus far:

Moses went up from the plains of Moab to Mount Nebo, to the top of Pisgah, opposite Jericho. There the Lord showed him the whole land . . . And the Lord said to him:
'This is the land I promised to Abraham, Isaac and Jacob when I said: I will give it to your descendants. I have let you see it with your own eyes, but you shall not cross over into it.' (Deuteronomy 34:1-4)

And there Moses died.

There is something fateful about that image of Moses seeing the land from a distance, the land to which his whole life as leader had been a journey, one he was destined not to complete. Historians have noted the paradox of Jewish history. On the one hand, the land of Israel is central to the Jewish journey. It is where we began and where we were destined to return. It is the place where we are summoned to create the just society. On the other hand, most of Jewish history has been spent outside Israel. It was outside Israel that Abraham received his call, and outside Israel that the Torah was given at Sinai. It was in Babylon that the prophet Ezekiel had his visions. It was there too, a thousand years later, that the great monument of rabbinic Judaism, the Babylonian Talmud, was compiled.

For some 1800 years, between the fall of the second Temple and the late nineteenth century, Jews throughout the world were like Moses, seeing the land from a distance, but for the most part unable to enter. They felt the full pain of those early exiles who said: 'By the rivers of Babylon we sat and wept when we remembered Zion . . . If I forget you, O Jerusalem, may my right hand forget its skill.' They mentioned the land in all their prayers. Wherever they were, they built their synagogues to face Jerusalem. At the holiest moments of the Jewish year they said, 'Next year in Jerusalem', as if they, like Moses, were at its very borders.

It is sometimes difficult to explain what the last forty years have meant to Jewish life – the years in which Israel has become again a Jewish home. They have not been easy. They have been years of wars and strife between Israel and her neighbours. Israel has faced ethical dilemmas to which no solution has yet been found. But religiously, it is hard to overestimate their significance. The promise which neither Abraham nor Moses lived to see fulfilled has come true again. The longest journey ever travelled by a people has reached its destination. However deep the difficulties, a new era in Jewish history has begun.

The Ever-dying People

One of the great themes of Jewish history is announced early in the pages of the Bible:

God's word came to Abram in a vision, saying, 'Fear not, Abram. I am your shield. Your reward will be very great.'
But Abram said, 'O Lord, God, what can You give me, since I remain without a child?'
Abram continued: 'You have given me no children. A servant in my household will be my heir.'

Suddenly God's word came to him. 'That one will not be your heir. Instead a son born to you shall be your heir.'
He took him outside and said, 'Look at the sky and count the stars. See if you can count them.' He added, 'So shall your descendants be.' (Genesis 15:1–5)

In retrospect we think of Abram as the first Jew. But he feared that he would be the last. Would there be another generation to carry on the covenant?

The theme stays with us in countless variations. Sarah and Rebekah and Rachel are unable to have children, other than by a miracle. At the beginning of the book of Exodus, the picture is reversed. Suddenly the Israelites are fertile and prolific. Their numbers increase. Then Pharaoh decrees: Let all the male children be drowned. Again the people of Israel seem to be reaching an end. Again it is averted only by a miracle.

A Jewish historian once called Israel the ever-dying people. 'The world', he said, 'makes many images of Israel, but Israel makes only one image of itself – that of a being constantly on the verge of ceasing to be, of disappearing.' It has often seemed as if the end was in sight. Before the Israelites had even entered the land, Moses had already prophesied catastrophe and exile. It came. After King Solomon, the people split in two. In the eighth century BCE, the northern kingdom was defeated by the Assyrians. Its people were deported and eventually assimilated – the so-called lost ten tribes.

Little more than a century later the southern kingdom too was overwhelmed, this time by the Babylonians. In a terrifying image, the prophet Ezekiel saw his people as a valley of dry bones. But as he foresaw, they came to life again. They returned, renewed the covenant and rebuilt the Temple. But by the second century of the Common Era, with the Temple once again in ruins and Israel under repressive Roman rule, the rabbis made a remarkable confession. 'If we were rational', they said, 'we would decide not to marry and have children, and let the family of Abraham come to an end.'

Fortunately reason did not prevail. Instead, faith did. But throughout the religious persecutions of the Middle Ages, above all the Spanish expulsion, it seemed as if the Jewish drama was drawing to its close. In the nineteenth century, as Europe opened the doors of emancipation, the end was predicted for the opposite reason. Judaism would be killed by kindness. Jews would assimilate into oblivion. Almost all the thinkers of this period saw themselves as the last guardians of a dying tradition. In the twentieth century a different and unprecedentedly brutal ending was announced, Hitler's Final Solution, in which a third of the Jewish people died. Even today, in a period of rebirth, we speak the language of crisis. Jewish conversations are about schisms and divisions, the decline in religious observance, and low birth rates. We are, as Abba Eban said, 'the people that can't take Yes for an answer'.

Anxiety, pessimism and fear about the future have been a constant theme of Jewish reflection since Abraham confessed his doubts as to whether there would be a next generation of the covenant. But there was always the answering promise, stated most memorably by the prophet Jeremiah: that the Jewish people would live as long as there was a sun by day and stars by night. The ever-dying people has proved to be the people of eternity.

Though He may Slay Me, Yet I will Trust in Him

For Jews of the Middle Ages the Spanish expulsion was a tragedy that turned the world upside down. For centuries Spain had been the scene of Diaspora Jewry's golden age. Jews flourished and became poets, philosophers, scientists and statesmen. Then from 1391 to 1492 came an escalating series of persecutions and massacres. Jews, terrified at what was happening, began to convert to Christianity, though in secret they remained Jews. *Marranos*, they were called. But this brought an even greater terror, the Inquisition. Finally in 1492 those that remained were expelled. It was the worst disaster in Jewish history since the second Temple had been destroyed.

Could fate have anything yet worse in store? It could. The historian Solomon ibn Verga, who lived through those events, tells of an incident that occurred to one of the ships carrying Jews away. An epidemic developed among the passengers and the captain refused to carry on the journey. He made for the nearest land and put them ashore. There, most of them died. The survivors began to search for the nearest town, among them a young Jew with a wife and two children. After a few days of wandering, the wife died. The man continued his journey, carrying his children, until he fainted from hunger. When he regained consciousness he found that they too had both died.

Ibn Verga continues:

In great grief, he rose to his feet and said: 'O Lord of all the universe, You are doing a great deal that I might desert my faith. But I say to You that – even against the will of heaven – a Jew I am and a Jew I shall remain. And neither that which You have brought upon me, nor anything You may bring upon me in the future, will be of any avail.'

183

He gathered some earth and grass and buried his sons, and went forth in search of a settlement.

That remarkable speech, which overwhelms us by the sheer power of its faith, is itself an echo of far more ancient words – words spoken by the biblical Job. Job too had lost everything, his property and then his sons. He too had reason to believe that heaven had turned against him. 'God has wronged me and drawn His net around me', he said, 'but I know that my Redeemer lives.' He cursed the day he was born, but he said: 'Though God may slay me, yet I will trust in Him.'

Those words echoed again this century. A Jewish writer tried to describe the last hours in the life of a pious East European Jew, Yossel Rackover, who died in the Warsaw ghetto. He imagined him saying this anguished prayer: 'And these are my last words to You, my wrathful God ... You have done everything to make me renounce You, to make me lose faith in You, but I die exactly as I have lived, a believer.'

Why do the innocent suffer? The question is asked many times in the Bible, and if Moses and Jeremiah and Job were not given the answer, neither are we. But in Job and the refugee from Spain and Yossel Rackover we hear a faith deeper than questions or answers. It is the knowledge that God is with us even in the valley of the shadow of death. He can be spoken to, even when the world is falling apart. In that knowledge is a terrible strength: the strength to live through tragedy with the human spirit unbroken.

The words I have quoted, spoken in some of the deepest darkness ever known to man, are to me the most awe-inspiring proof that faith is stronger than any doubt, and that God has lit a flame in the human soul that no force on earth can extinguish.

The Teacher as Hero

In the fifth century before the Common Era an event occurred that was to have a decisive effect on the character of Jewish life. In the previous century the kingdom of Judah had suffered conquest and exile at the hands of the Babylonians. The Temple had been destroyed. The country was in ruins. But the Babylonians in turn were defeated by the Persians. Gradually the Judeans, or Jews as they came to be called, were allowed to return. They began rebuilding the country and the Temple. The greatest moment came when the people assembled in Jerusalem and rededicated themselves to the covenant. Ezra, a priest and scribe, stood in front of the people and read to them from the Torah scroll, the book of the teachings of Moses. This is how the Bible describes the event:

When the seventh month came and the Israelites had settled in their towns, all the people assembled as one man in the square before the water gate. They told Ezra the scribe to bring out the book of the Teaching of Moses, which God had commanded for Israel. On the first day of the seventh month, Ezra the priest brought the Teaching before the assembly, which was made up of men and women and all who were able to understand. He read it aloud from daybreak until noon . . . All the people listened attentively to the book of the Teaching . . . As he opened it, the people all stood up. Ezra praised the Lord, the great God; and all the people lifted their hands and responded, 'Amen, Amen.' Then they bowed down and worshipped the Lord with their faces to the ground. (Nehemiah 8:1–6)

Ezra was assisted by a group of Levites who acted as interpreters and teachers, explaining the meaning of the Torah to the assembled people. Shortly afterwards the leaders formally pledged themselves to keep the covenant, and fixed their seals to the agreement.

Ezra was a distinctive kind of Jewish hero – not a king or a prophet, not a poet or a general; not even, though he was these things, a priest or a scribe. Ezra was a teacher. Moses too is known by Jews simply as *Moshe Rabbenu*, 'Moses our teacher'. Even God Himself was seen by the rabbis as a sage, discussing Jewish law with the angels, and as the God who had appeared at Mount Sinai to instruct His children in the eternal teachings.

Some five hundred years after Ezra, the Jewish people faced a new loss of land, sovereignty and Temple, this time under the Romans. Eventually they were to trace their survival to the request made by a rabbi, Jochanan ben Zakkai. 'Give me', he is said to have asked the Romans, 'Yavneh and its sages.' Yavneh housed an academy for the study of Torah. There, in that enclave of teachers and disciples, the civilisation of sacred study called rabbinic Judaism was kept alive.

It was one of the most fateful intellectual achievements of all time, because for the next eighteen centuries it united as a people Jews scattered across the face of the earth. They had nothing else in common – not land or language or culture – except this, that they were the 'People of the Book', the Book given by Moses, taught by Ezra, rescued by Jochanan ben Zakkai, and studied unbrokenly in every generation since.

Perhaps each culture has its ideal type of human being: a political leader or a military hero, a charismatic leader or a saint. Judaism's ideal type is a teacher, an interpreter of tradition, surrounded by disciples asking difficult questions. Judaism renewed itself through study. Its teachers did something more lasting than winning wars or ruling states. They kept the teachings alive.

Family Quarrels

There is a scene at the beginning of Moses' career which foreshadows a lasting aspect of Jewish character. Moses had been hidden by his mother at birth, afraid that otherwise he would be killed. He had been found by a daughter of Pharaoh and raised as an Egyptian prince.

One day, when Moses had grown up, he went out to where his own people were and he saw their hard labour. He saw an Egyptian beating a Hebrew, one of his own people. He looked around and saw no-one else. Then he hit the Egyptian and hid him in the sand. The next day he went out and saw two Hebrews fighting, so he said to the one in the wrong, 'Why are you hitting your fellow Hebrew?' The man replied, 'Who made you ruler and judge over us?' (Exodus 2:11-14)

An unpromising beginning. But it signals two things that have been motifs of Jewish history.

The first is a kind of fierce individualism that threatens to make Jews ungovernable. We see two members of this enslaved people fighting one another rather than confronting the Egyptians. When Moses intervenes in the name of justice, they resent it, 'Who are you to be our judge?' Even after Moses has led the people into freedom, they remain obstinate and rebellious, not easily led. Several times Moses yields to despair and has to be persuaded by God to carry on.

At other key moments in our history, Jewish unity has seemed both necessary and impossible. The Maccabean uprising in the second century BCE was as much a conflict between zealous and Hellenising Jews as it was between Jews and Greeks. When the Romans later attacked Jerusalem, the Jews within were bitterly divided, fighting among themselves. Despite the enemy at the gates, there was civil war. When the Romans eventually seized power, one contemporary, Rabbi Haninah, the deputy High Priest, was moved to say: 'Pray for the welfare of the government, for were it not for the fear of it, we would swallow one another alive.' The same tensions mark Jewish society today, in Israel and elsewhere. Jews long for unity. Rarely do we find it. We are a people with a tradition of individual dignity and liberty. We are critical of leaders, and have little reverence for power.

What then has held Jews together? That, surely, is the second element of the scene of Moses' youth. Moses had been brought up as an Egyptian in Pharaoh's court. He had before him a life of comfort. Few people knew him to be a Hebrew, born to the people who were slaves. None the less when for the first time in his life he sees the condition of his kinsmen, he knows he cannot deny his identity. He enters into the Israelites' suffering. He is incensed at its injustice. He belongs to his afflicted people. His destiny lies with them.

That same sense led alienated Jews in the nineteenth century, most famously Theodor Herzl, back to their people. More recently it lay behind the rescue of the Jews of Ethiopia, the worldwide campaign on behalf of Soviet Jewry, and the universal Jewish concern when Israel is in danger. We have an overwhelming sense of kinship when we see other Jews suffering.

How then are we to describe this mystery of Jewish peoplehood, with its inner conflicts on the one hand, and on the other its sense of a common bond, a shared fate? Surely the answer is this, that more than Jews are a nation or a faith, they are a family. The members of a family have quarrels. But they know their destiny is interlinked. Jews began life as a family, the children of Israel. A family, they remain.

Renegade Children

It is not easy to be a heretic in Judaism. We have few principles of faith. Those there are, are open to several interpretations. Jewish faith is expressed more in law than doctrine, more in what we do than in what we believe.

But there was one famous heretic in the rabbinic tradition. His name was Elisha ben Abuyah and he lived in the second century of the Common Era. The rabbis called him *Acher*, 'the other one', the one who became an apostate. Some say he was attracted by Greek culture, others that he was overwhelmed by the injustice of a world in which the righteous died the death of martyrs.

The picture we have of him is fascinating. Before his heresy he was a great rabbi. Among his students was Rabbi Meir, who was to become one of the great Jewish sages. According to tradition, Rabbi Meir remained devoted to his teacher even after his apostasy:

Once Acher was riding on a horse on the Sabbath, and Rabbi Meir was walking alongside him to learn Torah from his mouth. Acher said to him: 'Meir, turn back. I have measured by the paces of my horse that we have reached the Sabbath limit. Beyond here, you are forbidden to walk.'

Rabbi Meir replied, 'You too turn back.'

But Acher answered, 'I cannot turn back. For I heard a voice from behind the veil of heaven saying, "Turn back, O rebellious children – all except Acher." '

It is a remarkable scene. Acher is desecrating the Sabbath by riding a horse. But the bond between teacher and disciple is too strong to be broken. The two of them travel together, arguing and debating. Eventually they reach the city limits, beyond which it is forbidden to walk on the Sabbath. Meir, the faithful Jew, has not noticed. Acher, the heretic, has. He tells his disciple to turn back.

Both of them realise that the point they have reached is not just the border of the city. It is the border of faith. Within lies Jewish tradition. Beyond is the unknown country of apostasy. Meir begs Acher too to turn back, to rejoin the faith. Acher says he cannot. He has already gone too far. It is as if heaven itself had ruled against his repentance. So they go their separate ways.

There is no easy ending. But in the modern age the story has come to represent the tense relationship between Judaism and Jewish intellectuals. Some of the most revolutionary architects of modern thought – Spinoza and Freud, Marx and Trotsky, Einstein and Wittgenstein, Proust and Kafka, Durkheim and Levi-Strauss – were Jews. Most were lapsed or alienated, some were only half-Jewish, others renounced their faith. Perhaps they should not be thought of as Jews at all. None the less, many scholars have found in them something distinctively Jewish.

This may be because being a Jew is not just a matter of religion. It means belonging to a people, and Freud, Einstein and Kafka felt their Jewishness deeply. It may be an ancient tradition, going back to Abraham, Moses and the prophets, that sees Judaism as a protest against the idolatries of the age, as if there is something religious in creating a revolution of thought. It may be the passion for reason, freedom and justice – Jewish values, even when they are turned against Judaism itself. Or it may simply be the profoundly Jewish condition of exile taken one stage further. Many of these figures were exiles from everything, even their own past, and had the unusually clear vision of the outsider.

The alienated Jew is an intriguing phenomenon. He is Elisha ben Abuya talking to Rabbi Meir at the border between faith and heresy. Something deep unites them even as they know they must part company. It is the great paradox of Jewish life these past few centuries that Jews, even when they have rejected their heritage, have kept on carrying it with them.

The Day of Grief

Jewish history sometimes seems to have been written in tears. More than most other nations, our collective story is told in terms of exiles and expulsions, persecutions and martyrdoms, inquisitions, pogroms and holocausts. Despite this, the tone of Judaism is not sad. There is more celebration than lament. Jewish teaching is expressed in stories with a happy ending. Often it is told in jokes. The Hebrew language has no real word for tragedy, and modern Hebrew had to borrow one. Judaism is a deeply optimistic faith, except on one day of the Jewish year.

On the Ninth of Av, the anniversary of the destruction of the two Temples, we fast and sit like mourners. It is the one day we give over to grief. We read that most powerful of elegies, the book of Lamentations:

> How deserted lies the city,
> Once so full of people!
> How like a widow is she,
> Who was once great among the nations!
> She who was queen among the provinces
> Has now become a slave . . .
> This is why I weep
> And my eyes overflow with tears.
> No-one is near to comfort me,
> No-one to restore my spirit.
> (Lamentations 1:1, 16)

Those words were spoken over the first destruction of Jerusalem by the Babylonians. The sense of desolation at the second destruction, by the Romans, was no less intense. There were Jews who vowed never again to eat meat or drink wine so long as Jerusalem lay in ruins. A rabbi of the second century, Shimon bar Yohai, ruled that Jews were forbidden ever to laugh until the land was rebuilt. To this day we break a glass at every Jewish wedding to remember this grief in the midst of joy.

Yet the sheer force of that anguish turned other tragedies into events Jews could live through. Many centuries ago a rabbi was asked why Jews no longer set aside new days as anniversaries of sorrow. He answered: Because there are not enough days in the year. So, gradually, all grief came to be concentrated on that one day, the Ninth of Av. It is then that we remember the medieval martyrs and the victims of the Crusades and the pogroms. It is then that we say the memorial prayer for the six million Jewish victims of the Nazis.

The Jewish laws of mourning for a lost relative are strictly defined.

There is a period of grief, but it has an end. It is followed, not by forgetting, but by consolation. As with an individual, so with a people. After the Ninth of Av come seven weeks of consolation in which we read from the closing chapters of Isaiah, the magnificent poetry of national hope.

The Jewish calendar is far more than a cycle of holy days. It is a way of structuring our emotions, leading us through different feelings at different times so that no one mood overwhelms us. Jewish life has its contradictions, but they are resolved not by ruling that one attitude is right, the other wrong, but by saying that each has its proper time. As Ecclesiastes says, there are times to work and times to rest, times to remember the past and times to hope for the future, times to grieve and times to be comforted.

The calendar of Judaism assigns moods to days so that the whole Jewish people moves through a collective rhythm of feeling. By concentrating our grief into the Ninth of Av, Judaism ensured that the tragic past would never be forgotten, but neither would it overshadow all else. For we can no more live today under the perpetual shadow of the Holocaust than the Jews of the first century could under the agony of the Temple's ruin. Lamentations is our book of tears, and the Ninth of Av is its day. Then the book is closed until next year. We rise and return to the celebration of life.

Resistance

One of the turning points in Jewish history came in the struggle against the Greeks that we celebrate in the festival of Hanukkah.

Israel had become a pawn in the struggle between the two great dynasties that followed Alexander the Great, the Ptolemies in Egypt and the Seleucids in Syria. In 175 BCE Antiochus IV came to the throne in Syria, determined to turn Israel into part of his empire, not just militarily but culturally too. In the Temple, he set up a statue of Zeus. Impure animals were offered up as sacrifices. The practice of Judaism was banned. Jews called it 'the abomination of desolation'. In Modin an old priest called Mattathias rose in revolt. His sons, most famously Judah the Maccabee, continued the struggle. Eventually they took Jerusalem and rededicated the Temple.

The revolution, though, might have died almost before it had begun. The book of Maccabees describes the moment when the rebels fled and hid in the desert. Antiochus' army pursued them. The day they found them was a Shabbat. Mattathias' supporters, all of them deeply pious Jews, refused to wage war on the day of rest. They were massacred. They died as religious heroes, but they died none the less.

Those who remained faced a fateful dilemma. Was it better to die or fight back?

> When Mattityahu and his friends heard the news they mourned greatly. But they said to one another: 'If we all do as our brothers did, and if we do not fight for our lives and teachings, we will be destroyed from the face of the earth.' That day they discussed and decided: 'If someone makes war against us on the Sabbath day, we will fight back, and let us not all die as our brothers died in their hiding place.'

That decision to resist and fight back ended in victory. Without it Israel might have remained a Greek province, its religion extinguished. There would have been no Judaism, indeed no Christianity.

Almost the same sequence of events occurred more than two thousand years later. The year was 1943, and the place, the Warsaw ghetto. There Jews were herded by the Nazis, seven to a room. More than eighty thousand died of hunger and sickness. Hundreds of thousands were taken in trains to the concentration camps. Once again the fateful question was asked: to die or fight back?

For eighteen hundred years Jews had become used to martyrdom. They had died, as they did at Auschwitz, for *kiddush ha-Shem*, 'sanctification of God's name'. But in the Warsaw ghetto a religious leader, Rabbi Isaac Nissenbaum, made a remarkable speech. 'This is a time', he said, 'for the sanctification of life, not the sanctification of martyrdom. In the past, our enemies sought Jewish souls. So Jews sacrificed their bodies and refused to give their souls. But now the enemies demand the Jew's body, so he must defend his body and preserve his life.'

It was a turning point as great as that of Mattathias. The Jews of the Warsaw ghetto rose up to defend themselves. From 19 April to 16 May, weak, few in number, poorly armed and surrounded, they held off the German army. Eventually they were defeated, but they had won a great moral victory. Since then – most notably in the State of Israel – Jewish character has been transformed. After the Holocaust, the religion of martyrdom has acquired an ethic of defence.

Jews hate wars. Perhaps no other people prays so often and so passionately for peace. But sanctifying life may mean defending life. In an unredeemed world, one may sometimes have to take up arms to save life itself. It took two extraordinary crises to provoke the Jewish people into resistance, the one in Modin, the other in the Warsaw ghetto. For there is only one thing Judaism values above peace – and that is life itself.

From the Ends of the Heavens

In almost his last words, Moses addressed the Israelites and drew a terrifying picture of the future. They had not yet crossed the Jordan or entered the land, but already he foresaw a time when the people would lose direction. They would desert the covenant. They would fight and lose wars and be scattered to the winds of dispersion. Then he looked beyond even this distant future to the far horizon of hope:

When all these blessings and curses I have set before you have come to pass, and you take them to heart in all the countries to which the Lord your God has banished you; and when you and your children return to the Lord your God and obey Him with all your heart and soul, according to everything I command you today, then the Lord your God will bring you back from captivity and bring you back in love. He will gather you from all the nations where he scattered you. Even if you have been banished to the ends of the heavens, from there the Lord your God will gather you and bring you back. (Deuteronomy 30:1–4)

That vision brought together the two great contrasting Jewish themes: *exile* and *exodus*, dispersion and ingathering. It has been the key text of the State of Israel these past four decades.

The Jews of Israel are one of the most ethnically and culturally diverse populations anywhere. In its small population of just over three million there are grandchildren of the East European pietists who came in the nineteenth century in search of the messianic age, and of the secular intellectuals who saw Israel as the rational solution to anti-semitism. There are the children of Holocaust survivors, and there are the immigrants from Britain, South Africa, the United States and South America who have come in search of a place where Jewishness shapes the public domain, not just private life.

The story of the ingathering has had a series of dramatic moments. In 1949 almost all the fifty thousand Jews of the Yemen, who had formed a community there since pre-Islamic times, was airlifted to Israel. These Jews, who had had little contact with the modern world, were not surprised when they saw the planes that were to carry them. Had the Bible not said that God carried the Israelites on eagle's wings? Here were the eagle's wings again, even if made and piloted by man.

In 1950 another ancient community, the 120,000 Jews of Iraq, was resettled in Israel in what was known, again with a biblical echo, as

Operation Ezra and Nehemiah. At the end of the 1984 Operation Moses brought to Israel most of the 25,000 Jews of Ethiopia, people who had lost contact with mainstream Judaism since antiquity. And there is the continuing trickle of Jews from the Soviet Union and the hope that one day soon there will be more.

There are white Jews and black Jews, speaking more tongues than were heard at Babel. There are some whose culture is modern, others medieval, others ancient. Each carries a family history of persecutions and deliverances, traditions and cultural borrowings, from which one could almost piece together an encyclopaedia of human civilisation over the past two thousand years. It makes for a society that is as unpredictable as a storm and as multicoloured as a rainbow. Yet each is a child of Abraham, sharing the covenant, its history and hopes.

Israel is a secular state which is religious despite itself. Many of the Jewish leaders who dreamed of the return of Zion were consciously trying to change the course of Jewish history, from a story dominated by God into one written by human beings. But it keeps writing itself in biblical terms, nowhere more so than in the modern ingathering, a story unprecedented, yet foretold by Moses: the coming together of Jews from the furthest corners of the earth.

The People of the Book

Throughout these portraits, I have been suggesting that certain biblical events and images recur repeatedly throughout Jewish history: the exiles and wanderings and national homecomings; scenes of catastrophe and rebirth; the conflicts between brothers and the reconciliations; the never-ending argument with God about the justice of history and society. It is not simply that Jews are the people of the Book. It is as if the Bible were the Book of the people, uncannily telling its story in advance.

It is well over two thousand years since the last sentences of the Hebrew Bible were written, but its themes have stayed with us, perhaps more so in the twentieth century than in any other. Search the contemporary literature, and you will find no more terrifying description of the Holocaust than Moses' visions of future catastrophe, no more searching reflections on God after Auschwitz than the book of Job, no more precise metaphor of the revival of Jewish statehood forty years ago than Ezekiel's vision of the valley of dry bones that came together and lived again. Biblical themes form the *leitmotifs* of collective Jewish experience, seemingly without end.

Why? From the vantage-point of faith, we would call such a history *providence*, the working out of an ancient covenant between God and Abraham, reaffirmed at Mount Sinai with the Israelites, and renewed again by the returning exiles in the days of Ezra. Perhaps such a momentous claim needs less of a leap of faith than it seems. For a covenant is mutual. It needs the agreement of two partners. Not only did God commit Himself to the destiny of a particular people. The Jewish people in turn committed itself to God and His word. The story of Jewish survival testifies not only to the presence of God in history but also to the decisions of generation after generation of Jews to continue the covenant. The human aspect of Jewish history is no less awe-inspiring than the mysteries of providence.

For this is a people that decided to live by a Book. George Steiner once used the phrase, 'Our homeland, the text'. By this he meant that for most of their history, Jews were dispersed through many lands, languages and cultures, united only by the past and future and way of life they found in the Bible's pages. It was their home, and they kept returning to it. Their laws, literature and philosophy were cast in the form of biblical commentaries. How then could they avoid seeing what happened to them as another kind of commentary to the Bible? Their conflicts with surrounding cultures were Jacob wrestling with the angel. Their suffering was Isaac bound on the altar. Their exile was Egypt. Their hope was another exodus.

There is a special Jewish word for this kind of commentary – *midrash*. It was practised by the rabbis, and before them by the prophets. Literally it means 'exposition' or 'investigation' of the biblical text. But what it represents is the reading of the present into the past. When Jews no longer had miracles or prophets, they still held in their hands the text of the word of God. So they searched it for an explanation of their situation. Midrash, or commentary, took the place of prophecy. Jewish history itself became a series of commentaries to words already written.

Of course, the Jewish people did not survive intact. There were persecutions, conversions, defections and assimilations. Isaiah said that a remnant would return, and only a remnant did. But somehow that remnant was the one that held most tenaciously to the biblical vision, as if the words themselves had given it strength. That, perhaps, is as near as we will come to the mystery of Jewish survival. To paraphrase a famous saying: More than the Jewish people has preserved the Book, the Book has preserved the Jewish people.

28

Jewish Economic Ethics

There have been many hypotheses as to the religious origins of the market economy. Max Weber wrote a famous study entitled *The Protestant Ethic and the Spirit of Capitalism*. Recently the distinguished scholar Michael Novak has written a volume entitled *The Catholic Ethic and the Spirit of Capitalism*. Karl Marx, in an essay written in 1844, had no doubts. Capitalism was a bad thing; therefore it was Jewish. Ironically, Marx's own family background and that of some of his followers was later turned against them, and Jews were blamed for communism as well. My concern here is not with such contentious matters. It lies with the morality, not the history, of markets; not with 'The Jewish Ethic and the Spirit of Capitalism' but with 'The Jewish Spirit and the Ethic of Capitalism'. For as Adam Smith saw, there is more to the market than its transactions. There is a spirit that drives its transactions. The author of *The Wealth of Nations* was also the author of *The Theory of the Moral Sentiments*. More than most, he understood that the open economy rested on a subtle balance between self-interest and fellow-feeling, egoism and altruism, individual and collective gain. That balance is easily disturbed, and one of the tasks Judaism set itself was to maintain it: to set enterprise in a moral frame.

As we survey the Hebrew Bible and the rabbinic literature we find less concern with the question, 'What kind of economy should we have?' than with the question, 'How can we ensure that the economy we have is an ethical enterprise?' Within a given system, how can we mitigate its hazards and injustices? How can we protect human dignity? How can we preserve fair dealing and integrity? How can we recognise the exigencies of economic endeavour and at the same time keep alive other and more spacious values? Jewish law and ethics devote great attention to what John Gray calls 'the moral foundations of market institutions', sometimes at the level of broad principle, often in minute detail. But it does not seek to determine a particular economic regime. Its values are timeless, whereas economic systems, like political ones, change over time. That is why a religious voice will always be important in economic affairs, judging the present against less relative standards than its own, sifting out the bad from the good in any particular dispensation and taking its stand on the *ought* not the *is* of human affairs.

The literature on Jewish business ethics is large and I attempt here no more than a brief survey of a few leading themes. It is, though, an important subject. Religious ethics can sometimes seem bland and ano-dyne for they evoke a world without conflict, far removed from the market-place, the industrial dispute and the competitive economy. The Judaic tradition has the virtue of being rooted firmly within these realities. Yeshayahu Leibowitz called Jewish law the prose rather than the poetry of religious life, and that is one of its strengths. Michael Novak, comparing Jewish faith with his own Catholicism, notes that:

In both its prophetic and rabbinic traditions Jewish thought has always felt comfortable with a certain well-ordered worldliness, whereas the Christian has always felt a pull toward otherworldliness. Jewish thought has had a candid orientation toward private property, commercial activity, markets, and profits, whereas Catholic thought – articulated from an early period chiefly among priests and monks – has persistently tried to direct the attention of its adherents beyond the interests and activities of this world to the next.

I cannot vouch for the contrast, but certainly the prophets and the rabbis felt that their teachings had as much to do with the market-place as with the house of prayer, for it is here that religious values are put to the test.

Work and its Ethic

The first thing to be said is that, for Judaism, work matters. If not itself a religious act, it comes close to being a condition of the religious life. 'Six days shall you labour and do all your work, but the seventh day is a Sabbath to the Lord your God.' With few exceptions, Jewish tradition understood the verb in this verse as 'shall' rather than 'may'. We serve God through work as well as through rest. By labour we become, in that striking rabbinic phrase, 'partners with God in the work of creation'.

The rabbinic attitude is well brought out in the following passage:

Rabbi Shimon ben Elazar said: Great is work because even Adam did not taste food until he had performed work, as it is said, 'The Lord God took the man and placed him in the Garden of Eden to till and preserve it' (Genesis 2:15). Only then do we read, 'The Lord God commanded the man: From every tree of the garden you may eat' (Genesis 2:16).

It is a subtle observation. A superficial reading of Genesis can convey the impression that work is not a blessing but a curse. For it was only when he was exiled from paradise that man was told that his fate would be toil: 'By the sweat of your brow you will eat your food.' Not so, says Rabbi Shimon. For in Eden itself Adam was told to till the earth. Though food lay all around him, he had to labour first.

The Jewish liturgy for Saturday night – as the day of rest ends and the time of work begins again – culminates in a hymn to the values of work and the family (Psalm 128): 'When you eat of the labour of your hands, you are happy and it shall be well with you.' On this the rabbis commented: 'You are happy' refers to this life; 'It shall be well with you' refers to life in the world to come. Work has spiritual value. How so? A Talmudic comment provides us with a clue:

When the Holy One, blessed be He, told Adam, 'The ground will be cursed because of you . . . it will bring forth thorns and thistles,' Adam wept.

He said, 'Lord of the Universe, am I and my ass to eat in the same manger?'

But when he heard the words, 'By the sweat of your brow you will eat bread,' he was consoled.

Labour elevates man, for by it he *earns* his food. What concerned the rabbis was the essential dignity of work as against unearned income. To eat without working was not a boon but an escape from the human condition. Animals found sustenance; only mankind created it. As the thirteenth-century commentator Rabbenu Bachya put it, 'The active participation of man in the creation of his own wealth is a sign of his spiritual greatness.' Jewish law invalidates gamblers from serving as witnesses since they are not members of the productive economy. They do not 'contribute to the settlement of the world'.

The mainstream of Jewish thought was set against the various temptations to see work as demeaning. These came from many directions. Some lay in the early history of rabbinic Judaism. Its protagonists, the Pharisees, were confronted with other groups such as the Sadducees and the Essenes. The Sadducees were a propertied aristocracy. The Essenes, like the Qmran sect known to us from the Dead Sea Scrolls, were an apocalyptic group living in imminent expectation of the end of the world. For the former, physical labour may have been unnecessary. For the latter it was an unspiritual compromise with the world of everyday.

There were significant voices within rabbinic Judaism itself – most famously Rabbi Shimon bar Yochai – who believed that the ideal was unceasing Torah study, and any time taken to earn a living was time diverted from the pursuit of eternal life. Against these views, and summing up the dominant consensus, Rabban Gamliel III said, 'Torah study is good together with a worldly occupation, for the exertion needed for them both causes sin to be forgotten. All Torah study that is not accompanied by work will be abandoned in the end, and leads to sin.'

The greatest of medieval rabbis, Moses Maimonides, waged a war against the institution of supporting a leisured class of rabbinic scholars through public charitable funds. 'One who makes his mind up to study Torah and not to work but to live on charity, profanes the name of God, brings the Torah into contempt, extinguishes the light of religion, brings evil upon himself, and deprives himself of life hereafter.' It was a controversial campaign, never entirely successful, for in Judaism study is the highest value, and there were always those who believed that there should be a scholarly élite relieved of the burden of having to enter the labour force. Maimonides, though, saw the dangers of such an arrangement. It compromised the independence of the scholar. 'Better', he told his disciple Joseph ibn Aknin, 'to earn a penny as a tailor, carpenter or weaver than to depend on the income of the Exilarch.' It removed the rabbi from the world in which his disciples had to live. And it turned a religious vocation into a paid profession.

The result was that Judaism never developed either an aristocratic or a cloistered ethic, dismissive of the productive economy. The great rabbis were also labourers or businessmen or professionals. They were called on to advise on communal economic policy and to adjudicate in business disputes, and they knew whereof they spoke. They knew too that 'the world which is entirely rest' is 'life in the world to come', not in the here-and-now. In the meantime, the Jewish community needed an economic as well as a spiritual base. Accordingly, the Talmud lists as one of the religious duties of a parent, to teach one's child a craft or trade through which he can earn a living. Maimonides rules that one who is wise 'first establishes himself in an occupation which supports him, afterwards he buys a home, and after that he marries'. More powerfully still, he states that the greatest charity is to provide a person in need with a job:

The highest degree of charity, exceeded by none, is that of a person who assists a poor Jew by providing him with a gift or a loan or by accepting him into a business partnership or by helping him find employment – in a word, by putting him where he can dispense with other people's aid. With reference to such help, it is said, 'You shall strengthen him, be he a stranger or a settler, he shall live with you' (Leviticus 25:35), which means strengthen him in such a manner that his falling into want is prevented.

All other forms of charity leave the recipient dependent on charity. This alone restores his dignity and independence. 'Make your Sabbath a week-day (i.e. eat less on that day)', said Rabbi Akiva, 'rather than depend on other people's charity.' 'Flay carcasses in the market-place', said Rav, 'and do not say: I am a priest and a great man and it is beneath my dignity.'

The significance of these teachings is that they do not belong to a Tolstoyian love of labour nor to an ethic of acquisitive individualism. The same rabbis who spoke of the dignity of work also taught its limitations. Judaism is as much defined by the times in which it is forbidden to work – the Sabbath and festivals – as by those in which it is permitted. Besides which, Jews are enjoined to spend time every day throughout their lives in study. Hillel taught, 'Anyone who is excessively occupied in business cannot become a scholar.' Rabbi Meir taught, 'Reduce your business activities and engage in Torah study.' If Judaism has a distinctive genius it lies in the principled pursuit of balance. Work has intrinsic value but only within a framework of other values. It is part of what it means to imitate God, but not all. There are other realities: the Sabbath world of rest, the festival world of celebration, and the house of study with its service of the mind. A Jewish life is above all a structured life in which each of these worlds has its dedicated days and hours. This, as we will see, is crucial to a Jewish economic ethic.

Wealth Creation and its Responsibilities

No less important than the value placed on work is Judaism's positive attitude to the creation of wealth. The world is God's creation; therefore it is good. Asceticism and self-denial have little place in Jewish spirituality. What is more, God has handed the world over to human stewardship. The story of man's creation begins with the command, 'Be fruitful and multiply, fill the earth and subdue it.' To be sure, we must conserve as well as create. We do not own, we merely hold in trust. But prosperity is God's blessing so long as we see it as God's blessing and do not say, 'My power and the strength of my hands have produced this wealth for me' (Deuteronomy 8:17).

God, taught Rabbi Akiva, left the world unfinished so that it could be completed by the work of man. Industry is more than mere labour. It is the arena of human creativity, 'perfecting the world under the sovereignty of God'. The late Rabbi Joseph Soloveitchik taught that the more control man develops over his environment, the more he is transformed from object to subject, and the greater his moral dignity. Above all, human creativity provides us with the resources to alleviate poverty and suffering and is therefore a religious good.

The rabbis had the sanest view of poverty I know, and they did so because most of them were poor men. They refused to rationalise it. It is not a blessed condition. It is, they said, 'a kind of death', and 'worse than fifty plagues'. They said: 'Nothing is harder to bear than poverty, for he who is crushed by poverty is like one to whom all the troubles of the world cling and upon whom all the curses of Deuteronomy have descended. If all other troubles were placed on one side and poverty on the other, poverty would outweigh them all.' They would have agreed whole-heartedly with David Hume when he wrote, 'Nothing tends so much to corrupt and enervate and debase the mind as dependency and nothing gives such noble and generous notions of probity as freedom and independency.'

They neither valued poverty nor did they see in the distribution of wealth a divinely ordained social order. I know of nothing in the literature of Judaism that speaks of submissively accepting one's 'station in life'. Rabbinic Judaism is not a religion of class and hierarchy. If anything, it is a protest against them. Admittedly, at most times there were considerable disparities between *gvirim*, the wealthy, *baalei batim*, the householders, and itinerant traders and the poor. What concerned Jews was not the construction of a society in which no one was poor. That was a utopian dream, devoutly to be wished but not imminently expected. What mattered instead was a society in which the poor had access to help when they needed it, through charity or better still job-creation, and one in which their dignity was at all times, and with the utmost sensitivity, preserved.

Hence with wealth came responsibilities. Those who had were expected to share it with those who did not. Successful businessmen (and women) were expected to set an example of philanthropy, and to take on positions of communal leadership. Wealth was sharply distinguished from consumption. Conspicuous consumption was frowned upon, and periodically banned through local 'sumptuary laws'. Judaism is not puritanical but it does not look with favour on excessive luxury. The governing principles of consumption were to be satisfied with little – 'Who is wealthy? He who rejoices in what he has' – and never to give way to envy, forbidden by the last of the Ten Commandments.

One of the great questions about Judaism, as about any concrete embodiment of social life, is how it manages the inescapable tensions between liberty, equality and fraternity. There can be little doubt that

Judaism sets a higher value on liberty than economic equality. It is the religion of a people born in slavery, longing for redemption. At its heart is the free God who seeks the worship of free human beings. It recognises private property and values economic independence. Its ideal society is one in which each person is able to sit 'underneath his own vine and fig tree'. The prophet Samuel, in his famous speech on the dangers of monarchy, warns against the intrusions of government into private life and its tendency to expropriate persons and property for the public good. Government is necessary, but the less of it and the less coercive it is, the better.

Yet Judaism undeniably values equality: the equality of human dignity as the image of God. The reason economic inequality gave the rabbis relatively little concern was that they did not see worth in terms of what a person earns and spends. The 'other worlds' mentioned above are central to Jewish life, its value structure and status attribution. The Sabbath is a day without earning and spending in which every family, even the poorest, shares in a kind of royal rest. The house of study is a democracy of the mind in which wealth carries no advantage and poverty no stigma. Precisely because access to education *could* depend on wealth, from earliest times (since the first century of the Common Era) Jewish communities have consistently built and supported Jewish schools from public funds, and subsidised education so that it is available to all. Equality, as Judaism understands it, means open access to those things which give life its value. That meant, for rabbinic law, the means of subsistence, sufficient capital to marry, religious education, and more recently health care provision. These are communal responsibilities to be met by public funds.

What binds liberty and equality together is fraternity. Not accidentally does the Hebrew Bible couch its social laws in the language of kinship: 'If one of your brothers becomes poor . . .' This is not for Jews what it was for the French Revolution, an abstract statement of 'the rights of man'. It belongs to a concrete historical sense. The history of the people of the covenant is of a community sharing a collective fate and responsibility. When Jews celebrate the festival of Passover they eat the 'bread of affliction' and remember what it is to be a slave. When they celebrate Tabernacles, they know what it is to live in a temporary home. These enactments and reminders are a more powerful education than any other of the responsibilities of wealth and its creation. However successful they might be, Jews annually tasted the salt tang of poverty and homelessness and they could not be indifferent to those for whom it was a reality, not a ritual.

Jewish experience would tend to confirm Ronald Dworkin's thesis that 'the best defense of political legitimacy . . . is to be found not in the hard terrain of contracts or duties of justice or obligations of fair play that might hold among strangers, where philosophers had hoped to find it, but in the more fertile ground of fraternity, community, and their attendant obligations'. The resolution of the conflicting principles of social order lay in the strong sense of kinship and covenant which bound the members of the community to one another, mitigating what might otherwise have been intolerably arbitrary distributions of material blessings.

The Morality of Markets

This was the moral environment in which the market was set. But the market itself had to function ethically. At one of the critical points in the Jewish calendar, on the Sabbath before the Ninth of Av, the day of mourning for the destruction of the Temple, we read in the synagogue the great first chapter of Isaiah with its insistence that without political and economic virtue, religious piety is vain:

> Seek justice, encourage the oppressed,
> Defend the cause of the fatherless,
> Plead the case of the widow . . .
> Your silver becomes dross,
> Your choice wine is diluted with water,
> Your rulers are rebels, companions of thieves;
> They all love bribes and chase after gifts.

The same message is carried through into the teachings of the rabbis. According to Rava, when a person comes to the next world for judgement, the first question he is asked is, 'Did you deal honestly in business?' In the school of Rabbi Ishmael it was taught that whoever conducts himself honestly in business is as if he fulfilled the whole of Jewish law. The Talmud suggests that one who wishes to achieve sainthood should occupy himself in study and practice of the laws dealing with commerce and finance. The perennial temptations of the market – to pursue gain at someone else's expense, to take advantage of ignorance, to treat employees with indifference – needed to be fought against. Canons of fair trading had to be established and policed. This was part of the religious life, for the relationship between man and God could not be divorced from that between man and man. God's law belongs to the market-place no less than to the synagogue.

The Hebrew Bible places great emphasis on accurate weights and measures, and the rabbis established supervisors to check on them. On the basis of the biblical command, 'When you buy or sell to your neighbour, do not cheat one another' (Leviticus 25:14) they established a threshhold for fair profit. An overcharge of more than a sixth above the market price was in most cases sufficient to invalidate the sale. It was forbidden to mislead customers by making old goods look new, or covering bad produce with a layer of good. Jewish law recognises no concept of *caveat emptor*. The onus of fair representation lies with the vendor, not the purchaser. Giving misleading advice was forbidden under the biblical rubric of not 'putting a stumbling-block before the blind'. These and a host of similar provisions legislated for fair dealing and integrity. The rabbis recognised that a perfect market would not emerge of its own accord. Not everyone had access to full information, and this gave scope for unscrupulous practices and unfair profits, against which they took a strong stand.

In general, they were in favour of markets and competition. These lowered prices and increased choice. The rabbis were fully aware that competitiveness as such was not a virtue. But they knew also that 'all labour and achievement spring from man's envy of his neighbour' (Ecclesiastes 4:4). As they themselves put it: 'Were it not for evil inclination no man would build a house, marry a wife, have children or engage in business.' Competition released energy and creativity and served the general good. Jewish law permitted protectionist policies in some cases to safeguard the local economy, especially where the outside trader did not pay taxes. There were also times when the rabbinic authorities intervened to lower prices of essential commodities. But in general they favoured the free market, nowhere more so than in their own professional sphere of Jewish education. An established teacher could not object to a rival setting up in competition. The logic of this ruling illustrates the rabbis' general approach to such matters. They said simply, 'Jealousy among scholars increases wisdom.'

They knew too that the fair workings of an economic system could not always be defined in terms of strict law and justice. There was law and there were obligations that went *lifnim mishurat hadin*, 'beyond the letter of the law'. If a transaction had been agreed but not finalised and one of the parties retracted, there was no legal recourse. None the less the offending party could be brought before a court and the following rebuke administered: 'He who demanded payment from the generation of the Flood and of the Tower of Babel will exact penalties from one who does not stand by his word.' The Talmud records a case in which a rabbi employed porters to transport a cask of wine. They broke it, and he seized their coats in compensation for the loss. They brought the case to court, and Rav ruled that the rabbi should return the coats and pay their wages. 'Is this the law?' he asked. Rav replied: 'It is what is required by the verse, "Thus shall you walk in the ways of good men and keep to the paths of the righteous" (Proverbs 2:20).' The Talmud, in a deeply reflective moment, says: Jerusalem was destroyed because its inhabitants administered the law and did not go beyond the letter of the law.

In particular, the rabbis were willing to intervene to enforce arrangements which conferred a benefit on one party without the other suffering loss. One could be forced to sell a field (at the market price) to the owner of a neighbouring field, since one does not lose, and one's neighbour gains. To deprive someone of potential benefit which causes no loss to oneself is described in the rabbinic literature as *middat Sedom*, behaviour characteristic of Sodom whose inhabitants were famed for their unneighbourliness. Jewish behaviour was expected to be governed by *middat chassidut*, generosity, and though this was normally a moral requirement only, it was occasionally made a legal one.

The underlying principles of the market were mutual benefit and mutual responsibility, and the same applied to relationships between employer and employee. Workers were expected to give full commitment in return for their pay. Moonlighting was considered to be a form of robbing your employer by depriving him of your full energy and concentration. The rabbis even stipulated that workmen could say a shortened form of grace so as not to deprive their employers of their time. But employers, in return, had a duty to be considerate. Biblical law is particularly severe against delaying wage payments and against denying agricultural workers the right to eat from the produce they are gathering. Good labour relations have deep theological undertones in a religion which begins by seeing slavery as a denial of the human condition. The marvellous passage in Marcus Sieff's autobiography in which he describes how Marks and Spencer stopped trading with a supplier who refused to improve conditions for employees is a contemporary application of this spirit.

Conclusion

I have done no more than to hint at some of the leading features of Jewish economic ethics. The subject is vast – perhaps a quarter of Jewish law is devoted to it – and much of the literature is highly detailed and case-specific. Throughout the centuries, Jewish businesspeople sought rabbinic guidance in difficult cases, as did communal leaders in framing public policies. The glory of Jewish law lies in its concreteness: the rabbis would have appreciated Mies van der Rohe's dictum that 'God is in the details'.

What the Hebrew Bible and its rabbinic interpreters understood so well is that the market cannot be sustained by market values alone. It depends on a surrounding matrix of virtue and on the institutions that sustain it: families, communities, beliefs and traditions. It needs rules of integrity and fair dealing, and a mindset that sees the market as a place not of exploitation, but of mutual gain. Without these, its workings are too arbitrary and abrasive. With them, it is the best way we know of matching one person's talents to another's desires, of encouraging freedom, creativity and dignity, and of enhancing the conditions of life for all. If the Jewish experience of economic enterprise teaches one thing it is that ethics and business are not adversaries. In the long run they need one another. It is one of the tasks of religious teaching to show that the long run must always inform the short-term, so that economic profit does not lead to moral loss.

29

Jewish Environmental Ethics

Towards the end of the 1980s, environmental concerns moved fast from obscurity to the top of the political agenda. Throughout Europe, green parties sprouted and attracted widespread support. Politicians of the right and left announced their conversion and competed to establish their ecological credentials. It bore all the signs of a passing moral fashion.

But the issues will stay with us. For as other dangers recede, we may well come to feel that the greatest threat to human civilisation is now no longer war but peace, not the pursuit of ideology but the pursuit of affluence. As capitalist and former communist states have moved from collectivism to individualism, we have begun to fear the effects of unregulated economic growth: depletion of natural resources, destruction of rain forests, industrial pollution, damaging aerosols and car exhaust emissions, and a host of other threats to the quality and long-run viability of life. We have moved from the politics of confrontation to the politics of conservation.

This raises issues on which a religious, especially a Jewish, voice should be heard, for they overturn some of our most deeply held assumptions. For centuries we have believed that science was the key that would unlock the bounties of nature. Today we are fearful that it will destroy its ecological balance. Economics was the discipline that would allow us to plan and maximise growth. But environmental questions cannot be answered by conventional economic theory. For they pose the *ethical* dilemma of how to weigh the future against the present. By what principles shall we restrain growth for the sake of generations yet unborn?

Environmental ethics touch on the most profound features of the human situation: our relationship to nature, our responsibility to posterity and the limits to our exploitation of natural resources. These issues are in the

---

The Jewish Chronicle, 9 February 1990

deepest sense religious, and they are addressed by the Torah from its opening chapters. Judaism's guidelines remain directly relevant today.

Few passages have had a deeper influence on human civilisation than the first chapter of Genesis. Through its momentous vision of creation we see the universe as the work of God. Man is its final and supreme creation, the only being made in God's image. Nature has been handed over to his dominion. He is commanded to 'fill the earth and subdue it' and 'rule' over the animals.

It was the nineteenth-century sociologist Max Weber who argued that this chapter laid the foundations of Western rationalism and ultimately of the scientific revolution. Against paganism, the Torah set forth a vision in which nature was not sacred. It rejected mythology and magic. The world was neither unfathomable nor intrinsically hostile to man. Without this background, suggested Weber, the scientific enterprise might never have got under way.

But here lies the problem. Turning Weber's theory on its head, radical ecologists have suggested that Genesis is not the answer to our present crisis but its cause. If we are given the unrestricted right to subdue the world, there is nothing to prevent the 'rape of nature'. What has led to our present danger, they argue, is precisely the biblical ethic with its enthronement of man as nature's master. Against this, they call for a new paganism which worships the earth as a living organism with its own personality and rights.

John Passmore, the Australian philosopher, has shown that this approach is doubly mistaken. Firstly, it proposes a cure worse than the disease. To turn our back on technology will not improve but substantially reduce human welfare, now and in the future. Indeed it will impair our ability to conserve nature as well as exploit it. What is needed is not less science but a more far-sighted view of its effects.

Secondly, it misreads Genesis. For immediately after reading of man's rights we are given, in the second chapter, a statement of man's responsibilities. Adam was placed in the garden, we are told, 'to serve it and guard it'. Man is not only the *master* but also the *guardian* of nature. This is perhaps the best short definition of the ecological imperative as Judaism understands it.

A guardian is entrusted with property that does not belong to him. His task is to take charge of it and eventually return it to its owner intact. So it is with nature. The world is not ours. 'The earth is the Lord's and the fullness thereof', a fact of which we remind ourselves every time we make a blessing over the things we enjoy. It has been handed into our safekeeping only on condition that we maintain it undespoiled.

Rabbi Samson Raphael Hirsch expresses this in a striking way in his commentary to the Torah. When God is about to create humanity, He says, 'Let us create man in our own image.' Who is the 'us'? According to Hirsch it is the rest of creation. Before making mankind, with its potential for disrupting nature, God invited nature itself to give its assent. The implied condition was that man would use nature only in the service of God, its maker. Our mandate is therefore moral rather than technical. It comes with responsibilities. To exploit nature rapaciously for our own ends is *ultra vires*. It breaks the condition on which man was made.

There is, of course, no more powerful metaphor for this than the passage which immediately follows the story of creation. God sets limits to the enjoyment of nature. There is a tree from which man may not eat. Man ignores the restriction, eats from the fruit of the tree, and as a result suffers exile from Eden. Nature turns against him: 'Cursed shall be the ground because of you; by toil shall you eat of it all the days of your life; thorns and thistles it shall sprout for you.' Today we are right to read this as an ecological parable. Once we lose the idea of limits and focus instead on short-term enjoyment, we set in motion long-term disharmonies which have devastating effects on the human situation. Man must not abuse nature for he is part of nature: 'Dust you are and to dust you will return.'

Genesis sets forth a view of nature which is not man-centred but God-centred. To be sure, humanity with its unique capacity for moral choice is the focus of its concerns. But Maimonides warns us against an anthropocentric view of reality. 'The universe does not exist for man's sake, but each being exists for its own sake and not because of some other thing' (*Guide of the Perplexed*, 3:13). The climax of the book of Job, as God speaks to Job from the whirlwind, is a magnificent poem on this theme: the hubris of believing that man can subject the universe to his comprehension and control. Not only can he not tame Leviathan. Even the most harnessed of animals, the donkey, has an existence independent of man:

> Who let the wild donkey go free?
> Who untied his ropes?
> I gave him the wasteland as his home,
> The salt flats as his habitation.
> He laughs at the commotion in the town;
> He does not hear a driver's shout. (Job 39:5–7)

Passmore concludes that there *is* a strong Western tradition that man is free to deal with nature as he pleases. But we are wrong to trace it to Genesis, which though it grants man rights over the earth, at the same time 'insists that the world was good before man was created, and that it exists to glorify God rather than to serve man.' Instead, 'it is only as a result of Greek influence that Christian theology was led to think of nature as nothing but a system of resources, man's relationships with which are in no respect subject to moral censure.'

છે

Judaism has seldom been content with broad statements of principle. To be effective they must be translated into the life of society. The Torah does this in two ways: through education and direct legislation.

Each age adds its own commentary to the Torah. In the light of contemporary knowledge we can now see the three great commandments of *periodic rest* – Shabbat, the sabbatical year and the jubilee year – as powerful forms of environmental education. On Shabbat we are commanded to renounce our manipulation of the world. It is a day that sets a limit to our intervention in nature and the pursuit of economic growth. The earth is not ours but God's. For six days it is handed over to our management. On the seventh day we symbolically abdicate that power. We may perform no 'work', which is to say, an act designed to alter the state of something for human purposes. Nor may we allow our animals to work. It is a day in which we respect the integrity of nature and set limits to human striving. No secular equivalent remotely rivals Shabbat as a day of 'green' consciousness.

What Shabbat does for man and the animals, the sabbatical and jubilee years do for the land. We owe the earth its periodic rest. Indeed, the Torah stipulates that if the people of Israel do not respect this, they will suffer exile: 'Then shall the land make up for its sabbatical years throughout the time that it is desolate and you are in the land of your enemies; then shall the land rest and make up for its sabbath years' (Leviticus 26:34). Behind this are two interwoven propositions. One is environmental. As Maimonides pointed out in his explanation of the sabbatical year, land which is overexploited eventually loses its fertility. *Yishuv ha'aretz*, the settlement of the land, means conserving its resources and not pursuing short-term gain at the cost of long-term desolation. The second is theological. There is no absolute ownership of the land. 'The land', says God, 'is Mine; you are but strangers resident with Me' (Leviticus 25:23). No statement more succinctly defines the conditional nature of human stewardship. Even the promised land is never an owned land. We are guests on earth.

There are other commandments, too, which restrain our interference with nature. The Torah groups together three prohibitions: against crossbreeding livestock, planting a field with mixed seeds and wearing a garment of mixed wool and linen. It calls these rules *chukkim* or 'statutes'. Nahmanides, and later Samson Raphael Hirsch, gave this word a novel interpretation.

They understood *chukkim* to mean laws which respected the integrity of nature. To mix different species, argued Nahmanides, was an affront to the Creator and an assault on the creation. Each species has its own internal laws of development and reproduction, and these must not be tampered with. 'One who combines two different species thereby changes and defies the work of creation, as if he believes that the Holy One, blessed be He, has not completely perfected the world and he now wishes to improve it by adding new kinds of creatures.' Nahmanides saw the law against sending the mother bird away when taking its fledglings (Deuteronomy 22:6–7) as motivated by the same concern. Acts like these threatened the continuity of species. Though the Torah permits us to use some (but not all) animals for food, we must not cull them to extinction. Later authorities were particularly strong in their condemnation of hunting: killing animals *not* for the sake of food. This was wanton and destructive cruelty and had no place in Jewish life.

No one attached more far-reaching significance to biblical 'statutes' about animals and nature than Samson Raphael Hirsch. For him, *chukkim* were laws which embodied the principle that 'the same regard which you show to man you must also demonstrate to every lower creature, to the earth which bears and sustains all, and to the world of plants and animals.' The reason these commandments are difficult to understand is that we approach them from the wrong perspective: from the direction of man and his needs. If we could put ourselves in the place of animals and plant life, we would find it as easy to comprehend the 'statutes' as to understand the Torah's laws of social justice. 'They ask you to regard all living things as God's property. Destroy none; abuse none; waste nothing; employ all things wisely ... Look upon all creatures as servants in the household of creation.'

Hirsch was what today would be called a 'deep' ecologist. He believed that there is such a thing as 'justice' toward nature and that the world cannot be subordinated to the interests of man. It was a view shared by the great mystic, Rabbi Abraham Kook, who held that animals have rights and that one should not needlessly even pick a flower. 'All of creation,' he said, 'sings a song'.

These are extreme rather than representative views. For the most part, Jewish thinkers did not attach rights to nature or to animals. Indeed, as Maimonides argued (and in this he was later echoed by Hume and Kant) the idea itself is incoherent. Rights belong to the world of relationships and reciprocities inhabited by moral beings. It is one thing to say we have a duty to respect nature, another to say that nature has rights. None the less, the rich texture of biblical law is woven out of a fine balance between our mandate to use nature for human benefit and our duty to conserve it. Species should not be tampered with nor exploited to extinction. Neither the land nor animals should be worked to exhaustion. Above all, in its periodic sabbaticals of rest, biblical society enacted regular reminders of an ideal – once realised in Eden, to be recaptured at the messianic end of days – of man in harmony with nature 'not hurting or destroying in all My holy mountain'. We are not there yet, but we must not lose sight of it. That is Judaism's way of treating the inevitable conflict between the ideal and the real.

ی

Jewish law, however, required a more precise environmental ethic, one that applied to an urban as well as rural environment, and one that dealt with what we might today call a consumer society. The Talmud finds the basis for such legislation in the biblical laws of war:

> When in your war against a city you have to besiege it a long time in order to capture it, you must not destroy its trees, wielding the axe against them. You may eat of them, but you must not cut them down. Are trees of the field human to withdraw before you into the besieged city? Only trees that you know do not yield food may be destroyed... (Deuteronomy 20:19–20)

In context, this is prohibition against a 'scorched earth' policy in war. However, the rabbis understood it not as a limited provision but as an *example* of a more general imperative. They extended it to peace as well as war, to indirect as well as direct destruction, and to other objects as well as trees. It became the basis of a universal rule against pointless destruction (*bal taschit*). In Jewish law one may not needlessly waste anything of potential human benefit.

This is a remarkable constraint on human ownership. Normally, to own something is to be able to dispose of it as one wishes. Jewish law denies absolute property in this sense. You may not break plates, tear clothes or set fire to furniture in a spirit of vandalism even if they belong to you, you do so on your own property, and no one else is harmed. Vandalism is a betrayal of the condition on which things are given over to the stewardship of man.

To be sure, conservation is not an absolute value in Jewish law. Halakhah permits the destruction of natural resources in the course of constructive projects that will ultimately enhance human welfare. But the onus of proof is on the developer. And there remains a deep-seated reverence for trees in Judaism, expressed in modern times by the afforestation of Israel and the celebration of Tu Bishvat, the 'New Year' for trees. No Jew should be indifferent to the destruction of rain-forests.

The Talmud tells the story of one of the saints of early rabbinic times, Honi the Circle-Drawer:

One day Honi was journeying on the road and saw a man planting a carob tree. He asked him, 'How long does it take for a carob tree to bear fruit?' The man replied, 'Seventy years.' Honi asked, 'Are you certain that you will live another seventy years?' The man answered, 'I found carob trees in the world. As my forefathers planted them for me, so I too plant these for my children.'

That is a leading motif of Jewish law. We are guardians of the world for the sake of future generations. Trees are a symbol of the long-term nature of the human enterprise. In the book of Psalms, the wicked grow like grass, the righteous slowly like cedars. Our decisions – economic, political and military – must be taken on the basis of calculation of distant consequences (the Israelites, for example, are warned against too rapid a conquest 'lest the land become desolate and the beasts of the field multiply against thee'). The world we inherit is due to the efforts of those who came before us. The world we leave our children is dependent on what we do. Conservation is part of what Burke called the 'partnership . . . between those who are living, those who are dead, and those who are to be born.'

Beyond conservation, the rabbis extended the Torah's rule that waste should be disposed of far from human habitation. They banned garbage disposal that interfered with crops or amenities, pollution of the water supply and activities that would foul the air or create intolerable noise in residential areas. The biblical provision for open space around the levitical cities is one of the earliest examples of town planning.

So Judaism contains detailed precedents of environmental legislation as well as commands that educate us in respect for and restraint toward nature as God's creation. Admittedly environmental ethics has not yet received the same intense halakhic treatment as has medical ethics. Probably that is because medical decisions are taken by individuals while environmental decisions are usually taken by governments. An individual turns to Jewish law for guidance. Governments rarely do. But it is not because Judaism regards ecological issues lightly. To the contrary: *tikkun ha-olam*, 'perfection of the world', is one of the mandates of Judaism. Maimonides repeatedly insists that we cannot pursue spiritual ideals without first ensuring our physical survival. That has always needed long-term planning and the decision to limit consumption in the present for the sake of the viability of the future.

Judaism categorically rejects two attitudes to the environment. One, associated with the Stoic tradition, is that we have no moral duties towards nature. The other, drawn from some Eastern religions, is that nature is holy and to interfere with it is sacrilegious. The first allows technology to run rampant while the second turns its back on it altogether. Neither extreme, we believe, does justice to the challenge of human civilisation.

God, said Isaiah, did not create the world to be desolate: He formed it to be inhabited. He gave man the intelligence to control nature. Therein lies his dignity. But He charged him with the duty of preserving nature. Therein lies his responsibility.

The rabbis put it simply. They said: When God made the first man, He took him to see all the trees of the garden of Eden. He said to him: 'See how beautiful are My works. All that I have created I have made for you. But be careful that you do not ruin My world, for if you do there is no one else to put right what you have destroyed.' That is as lucid a way as any of stating one of the great imperatives of our time.

30

The Jewish Attitude to Handicap

Recently I spent a weekend with the Jewish community in Leeds. Among the institutions I visited was a project run by the Leeds Jewish Welfare Board for people with severe mental handicaps: a sheltered housing complex and a day care centre. I spent some time with the individuals there, and I was moved by the care and compassion that the project's carers devote on a daily basis to these adults, some of whom have a mental age of three or four.

I was also moved by the residents of the home. Most of them can hardly speak, in some cases not at all. One took several minutes to explain to me in a halting way what he was working on. I understood from the project workers that he had spent two years making a little rug. It was a simple thing, but it had given him a feeling of pride and fulfilment that shone from his eyes. His sense of achievement was no less than if he had been a great artist.

There was one woman to whom it had been explained that a rabbi was coming to visit. She understood, and although she could not speak, she wanted to let me know that she was pleased I had come. The only way she could do this was by holding out her hand and having me hold it, which I did. Then something further happened. She wanted to tell me that she was *very* pleased that I had come. She made various gestures, tried to articulate a word but was unable to do so, and in the end she gave up. Instead she gave me an enormous kiss! That does not often happen to Chief Rabbis. This was a powerful moment of what Martin Buber would have described as an I-Thou encounter. Two human beings met, and disability and the absence of language fell away. Somehow we touched spiritually, and it made a deep impact on me. We must never forget the mandate given to us to care, and above all to recognise – even

Lecture at Finchley Synagogue, 20 May 1992

in those individuals who are most severely handicapped – the spark of humanity that transcends all disability.

I feel reticent in speaking about handicap. I have not suffered the problem in my family. I have, though, had the opportunity of speaking to many who have. From them I have gained a sense of some of the tensions involved in caring for those with severe disabilities. This includes psychological problems which are sometimes no less acute than the practical ones: the anger, perplexity, shock, trauma and sometimes even a sense of guilt that having a handicapped child creates. There are the stresses which naturally emerge when one member of the family is so demanding of attention and so restrictive of the activities of others. And there is the social issue of being integrated into a Jewish community which does not always know how to relate to individuals with a handicap.

I am acutely aware of these problems. So my aim in this chapter is, first, to signal my support. As a community, we must care for the carers. Secondly, I wish to bring to public attention some of the problems of which many of us know all too little. There are needs for which the Jewish community must find provision. Our rabbis must become conscious of the special pastoral problems in families with a handicapped child or member. Thirdly, I want to examine what a Jewish attitude to handicap might be.

The History of Awareness

Turning to our classic sources for guidance, we find a surprising lack of explicit teaching in the Bible and the rabbinic literature about handicap. Even in the rabbinic responsa, there is little direct reference until recently.

It is important to understand why. The answer is simple and in some ways heartening. We believe that God reveals Himself in Torah, in the form of commands that do not change over time. God also reveals himself in history, and history is change over time. One of the great propositions set out in the first chapter of Genesis is that history evolves according to a Divine plan, namely the first command given to humanity, 'Be fruitful and multiply, fill the earth and subdue it.'

In the last of these phrases, 'and subdue it', we receive our mandate to be masters of our environment. Rabbi Joseph Soloveitchik, in *The Lonely Man of Faith*, says that the more we are active and not passive, the more we can shape our circumstances rather than be shaped by them, the more dignified is our existence. As a result of developments over time – in knowledge, control, medical technology, education and our range of resources and facilities – we are able to address problems in ways that previous generations were simply unable to do.

It is not only handicap that early sources do not discuss. In *The Invention of Childhood*, the French writer Philip Ariès suggests that it was only in the seventeenth and eighteenth centuries that *children* were seen as a distinctive group and not just as miniature adults. Our understanding of the needs of the elderly has undergone a similar development. It was only in the nineteenth century that Jewish communities established special homes for the elderly. *Ziknah*, old age, is certainly discussed in the classic Judaic sources, along with the special attention and respect it deserves. But for many centuries the care of the elderly belonged within the domain of the family. Only in modern times was special provision seen as a *communal* responsibility.

Handicap is not unique in being a peculiarly modern focus of attention. None the less it does mean that we must search less for explicit statements than for implicit hints in the Torah as to what our general attitude should be.

Against the Survival of the Fittest

There is no clearer starting point than the proposition with which the Torah itself starts. This was one of Judaism's greatest moral revolutions, the fundamental statement about human existence, 'Let Us make man in Our image, after Our likeness.' In creating mankind, God made something in His own image. That image is inherent in every human being, whatever his or her physical form and mental ability. It is hard to understand how radical this idea was until we examine attitudes in other cultures to disability and handicap, flowing as they do from different perceptions of the relationship between God and the world.

One attitude to be found in the pagan world, in Greece and Rome, and which today still finds echoes in social Darwinism, is that God is to be identified with nature. In nature there is a struggle between the weak and the strong in which the strong survive. Because this is natural, it is normative. Thus the weak, the disabled and the handicapped have no special claim to our attention. They are naturally fated to be excluded and to suffer. The ancient Spartans actually killed handicapped children, and the Romans left them in exposed places to die. Traces of this view still remain. The contemporary Australian philosopher, Peter Singer, argues that if a handicapped child will cause – and will itself experience – more pain than happiness, then we should consider letting it die. Judaism utterly rejects this perspective. Instead it insists that *every* person carries within him the Divine image, and is thus the subject of an obligation of care and compassion.

One way of understanding the revolutionary character of biblical ethics is this. Until comparatively recently, handicap was conceived in much broader terms than it is now. There was social handicap as well as physical handicap. If you were born to the wrong class or the wrong race you were as effectively disadvantaged as if you were born with a crippled body or an arrested mind. Thus, what the Torah says about handicap in this broader sense is worthy of our attention, even when it does not refer specifically to a physical condition.

In the Torah, God singles out for love, attention and choice, people who in the social categories of their day would have been seen as handicapped. The dominant law in patriarchal times was primogeniture. Generally it was the firstborn who was privileged to receive the family inheritance. Yet God always chooses the younger. He chooses Isaac instead of Ishmael, Jacob instead of Esau.

Another norm of the ancient world was tribalism. You were primarily concerned with the members of your own tribe and not with those of another tribe. The outsider had no standing in society. Yet the man God chose to lead the Jewish people, Moses, was an outsider, raised as an Egyptian, looking, speaking and sounding like an Egyptian. Indeed, the man who above all others in Jewish history was chosen to be the spokesman for God – out of whose mouth God's words were to be heard – was a man with a speech defect, a stammerer, 'slow of speech and tongue'.

No nations were more distrusted by Israel than Ammon and Moab. Their members 'may not enter the congregation of the Lord'. But it was from Moab that Ruth and ultimately King David came, and thus from Moab that the Messiah will ultimately trace his descent.

By contrast, the people of Sodom, for whom the natural order was to care only for the members of their own tribe, and the Amalekites who believed that might is right and that therefore it was legitimate to attack those who were 'straggling and weak' are for the Torah the embodiments of evil. For the Bible, morality is not to be found in nature, and is often contrary to nature. God gives power to the powerless and strength to those with special needs. Those whom nature has in some way disadvantaged call for our care.

Coming to Terms with Handicap

This is not always easy. The Talmud, with great candour, tells us of the difficulty some of the sages had in overcoming their instinctive feelings towards the physically or mentally disabled.

It relates, for example, that Rabbi Shimon ben Elazar was once on a journey when he saw an individual who was deformed. He asked the man, 'Are all the people in your town as deformed as you are?' The man replied, 'If you do not like the pot, go and complain to the potter (i.e. to God who made me this way).' When they arrived at Rabbi Shimon ben Elazar's town, his disciples came to greet him. The man who had been insulted said to them, 'Is this the person you call a great man? May there not be many more like him in Israel.' When the disciples discovered what their rabbi had said, they agreed that he had done wrong, but added, 'Forgive him because he is a great scholar.' The man did so on condition that Rabbi Shimon agreed not to speak likewise in future. The fact that the Talmud records such episodes, critical of the sages, is eloquent of the need to wrestle with prejudice and the difficulty we have in coming to terms with handicap.

The Torah teaches us to have special sensitivity to those who are disabled, and to treat them as we would anyone else. The *locus classicus* is Leviticus 19:14, 'Do not curse the deaf or put a stumbling-block in front of the blind, but fear your God: I am the Lord.' These are two very different commands. The prohibition against putting a stumbling-block before the blind is readily understandable. It warns us against taking advantage of the disabled to cause them harm. The moral offence here is self-evident. But the other command, 'Do not curse the deaf', is far more far-reaching. On the face of it, cursing the deaf harms no one because the person you are insulting cannot hear what you are saying. None the less it is morally wrong. If we treat disrespectfully those who are deaf or disabled, even if they are unaware of it, we diminish their humanity and thereby *our* humanity.

It follows that there is an ethical duty to treat the handicapped with respect. A *cheresh* (deaf mute) or a *shoteh* (mentally handicapped) may be regarded in Jewish law as lacking the necessary competence to be held responsible for their actions and deemed to be free of religious obligations. But we are not free of obligations towards them. They too are part of the community of concern. Their dignity makes legitimate claims upon us.

This idea was so strong that the rabbis deliberately and consistently refrained from using words signifying handicap, preferring instead to use euphemisms such as *sagi nahor*, 'clear sighted', instead of *suma*, 'blind'. This etiquette of circumlocution, so striking a feature of rabbinic language, flows from the imperative not to offend someone by referring to a condition that may cause embarrassment or shame.

Blindness was a severe disability in the time of the Talmud. Several sages of the Mishnaic era took the view that a blind person, like a deaf mute or one who is mentally retarded, is exempt from the commandments. Nonetheless, Rabbi Eliezer ben Yaakov would seat a blind person in the seat of honour at his table to show the respect in which he must be held. Rabbi Hoshaya specifically did not invite a blind teacher to come to a meal with other guests in case people were disrespectful to him. In the twentieth century, Rabbi Avraham Karelitz (known as the *Chazon Ish*) would stand in the presence of anyone disabled on the grounds that they were pure souls who were exempt from the commandments. The Almighty, he used to say, found in their souls a purity that did not need the perfection and arduous discipline of the commands.

Some types of physical blemish rendered a priest unfit for service in the Temple. We might assume that this implied that someone who had such a disability was less than perfect, and thus debarred from high religious office. But Maimonides, in *The Guide for the Perplexed* (3:44), gives a quite different explanation. It was, he says, a concession to ill-informed sentiment. People wrongly judge an individual by his physical appearance rather than by his true form. God looks to the heart, but people judge by external appearances. Thus the Torah excluded the handicapped priest from Temple service to avoid public disrespect. Maimonides himself makes it clear that the priest with a physical disability is pleasing before God. The legislation surrounding the Temple, however, involves concessions to human prejudice.

It is important for us to take these messages to heart. Often we do not know what to do when faced by someone with a severe handicap. To avoid our own awkwardness we may shun the family with a handicapped child, or on the other hand try too hard. Through our own embarrassment, we may create embarrassment in others. Against this, the Torah suggests that we must strive to integrate the handicapped and their families into the community.

The behavioural model here is *aveilut*, mourning. When faced with grief, the natural reaction is what halakhah defines as *aninut* (the period of mourning before the burial). This is a time of trauma, in which we are emotionally isolated by distress. The whole thrust of the Jewish laws of mourning and of comforting the bereaved is to lead the mourner back from isolation to re-integration into the community.

If this applies to the bereaved, all the more so does it apply to those who are concerned with the living. We must reach out to those who have a handicapped member in their family and make them feel that they are full participants in the community. We should visit them if they are in effect house-bound on Shabbat. We should encourage our children to play with children with a handicap and to feel natural and normal in their company.

The principle of integration played a part in a sixteenth-century responsum of Rabbi Aaron Slonik. He had been asked whether a blind man may be called to the reading of the Torah. After citing the authorities who rule affirmatively on the question, he adds the following consideration: 'We must allow the blind . . . to be called to the Torah and to utter blessings, in order to include them in the acceptance of God's dominion and to give them spiritual satisfaction.' Inclusion of the handicapped within the faith community was, for him, a significant halakhic factor.

Community Responsibility

To what extent in Jewish law is care for the handicapped child a responsibility of the community, or only a responsibility of the parents? Part of the history of halakhah is that, in general, as society has become more developed and we become more capable of organising facilities and services on a community basis, obligations in Jewish law have been extended from the individual to the community.

For example, education was originally the duty of parents. But from the days of Rabbi Joshua ben Gamla, in the first century of the Common Era, when the first Jewish day school system was established, it became a communal responsibility. Charity, *tzedakah*, is conceived in the Bible as an individual responsibility. In the rabbinic literature, however, it becomes a feature of organised community life. Care of the elderly, too, was initially a family responsibility. But from the middle of the nineteenth century we find Jewish communities organising homes for the aged.

The same pattern appears in the case of handicap. In the early nineteenth century, Rabbi Moses Sofer (known as the *Chatam Sofer*) wrote in one of his responsa that care for those with handicap is not simply a responsibility of the parents but one in which, according to the halakhah, the whole community must share. The late Rabbi Moses Feinstein ruled that though a community could not be compelled to make special educational provisions for such children, charity funds should be made available wherever possible.

Judaism embodies a distinctive approach to welfare, namely that care within the family and community is the most supportive environment. Hitherto, care in Western societies has developed in a different direction: in institutions apart from the family and community. Significantly the Judaic insight is beginning to gain ground in medical and welfare policy, as we come to realise that large institutions are actually less effective for delivering care and encouraging personal growth and recovery.

The health and welfare system in the United Kingdom is moving towards Community Care. We recognise, however, that certain needs are so specialised that they cannot be provided by the family, or even in some cases by the Jewish community as a whole. There is therefore a need for special facilities which in some cases may mean – if the resources are not available within the community – that a child is removed from the kind of environment we would wish for. But it is clear that, as far as possible, we must provide resources for special needs and facilities within the Jewish community itself.

The rabbinate has a significant pastoral role to play in families with handicapped children. Rabbis must develop an understanding of the problem, and communicate it to their congregations. Each of us has to undergo the exercise of imagining what it is like to be part of a family with a child with special needs. Only when we begin to understand the stresses from within can we develop an adequate support network as a community.

There can be no hiding the pain that such families go through. There is the anger, denial and sometimes a feeling of guilt that parents can feel when they begin to realise that their child is not like other children and that it and they will have a lifetime of difficulty ahead of them. There is a sense of frustration and burden and deep unhappiness. It is natural to ask, 'Why has this happened to me?'

Anger is a difficult emotion. Maimonides rules in his *Mishneh Torah* that we should never get angry. Abraham, faced with the prospect of losing his child, said nothing and remained calm. Job, having lost his children, did get angry and cursed the day he was born. Yet, says the book of Job, he was a righteous man. There is no simple answer to the question, 'Why me?' Cathartic anger may enable us to live through stress. But destructive anger can harm the family and the child itself.

Against Despair

There is one issue which as religious Jews we must fight against, namely pretending that the problem does not exist. If we are religious Jews, faith gives us the courage to see things as they are. It is not a way of wishing they were otherwise. No one is helped by denial. As people of faith, we believe that the Almighty gives us the strength to cope with reality as it is. He does not spare us pain, but He rescues us from despair.

Equally in these circumstances, one should never feel guilty. Feelings of guilt are based on a misunderstanding of the Jewish sources. The Talmud says that 'When sufferings come upon a person, he should examine his deeds'. This seems to suggest that suffering is a sign of our having done something wrong and that we are being punished. But that is not what the Talmud means.

Rabbi Joseph Soloveitchik, in his essay *Kol Dodi Dofek*, writes that when the Talmud sets out the halakhic approach to suffering, it is not seeking to answer the question, 'Why did this happen?' but rather, '*Given* that this has happened, what then shall I do?' When it instructs us to examine our lives and undergo repentance, it does not mean that suffering is punishment. It means that suffering is a source of personal challenge and spiritual growth which we would never have experienced otherwise. The pain is not diminished by this realisation. But through it we find a way of living through pain without endless, fruitless thoughts of what might have been.

We must never allow ourselves to be paralysed by guilt. That is not the Jewish way. We should not say, 'I am to blame', but rather, 'How can I see this as something sent by God to create something that could not have happened otherwise.' The rabbis were perplexed as to why God tested Abraham by asking him to give up his child. They answered by way of a metaphor. When a potter completes his vessels, he tests them by hitting them. But he only hits those that are sound, never those that are cracked. God never sends trials to those who lack the strength to live through them.

We face here the greatest mystery of the religious life. No prophet or philosopher was ever granted the answer to the question, Why do bad things happen to good people? Instead we have faith that God gives us the strength to deal with all the sufferings that befall us. We believe, with the *Zohar* (the greatest text of Jewish mysticism), that God has a special love for souls who never tasted sin, who never reached that stage of maturity that brings with it temptation and corruption. Thus He leaves some people at the mental age of children because they are precious to Him. These are mysteries and however much we speculate they will remain so. But their light, dim though it is, is enough to deliver us from guilt, shame and denial.

There is one final Jewish insight we should recall. Against the ideas of fate and determinism that have been embraced by many other cultures, we insist that there is no such thing as a decree that cannot be changed. 'Even if the blade of a sharp sword is resting on your neck', says the Talmud, 'do not lose hope.' As Jews, therefore, we welcome the change in attitude to handicap in the United Kingdom since 1971, from placing it in the context of health to locating it within the framework of education. That marks a move from seeing handicap less as a condition that cannot be cured than as a disability that to some extent can be overcome.

Indeed this fact has halakhic implications. The great nineteenth-century scholar, Rabbi Esriel Hildesheimer, was asked whether deaf-mutes were eligible to serve as witnesses in Jewish law. After considering the various halakhic positions, Hildesheimer cited the evidence of Rabbi Joel Deutsch, head of the Institute for the Deaf-Mute in Vienna. Deutsch's view was that current pedagogic techniques made it possible for deaf-mutes to become mentally capable. Hildesheimer, taking issue with the distinguished Hungarian halakhist, Maharam Schick, argued that the disqualification of deaf-mutes as witnesses was not universal. It rested on the assumption that they were mentally incompetent. New methods of teaching meant that this no longer applied. Jewish law allowed for the possibility that scientific advance might affect legal status. Hildesheimer was an enthusiastic supporter of such special education, and gave it significant endorsement.

There is an important passage in the Talmud about a certain Rabbi Preda. He had a student with profound learning disabilities. Four hundred times he tried to teach him a simple law, but the student, unable to concentrate or focus, could not learn. So Rabbi Preda said, 'I will teach you another four hundred times.' The Talmud then relates that a voice was heard from heaven saying, 'Do you prefer that four hundred years be added to your life, or that you and your generation be privileged to have a share in the world to come?' The rabbi who continued to care for his pupil even though others would have given up in frustration became a model for Jewish behaviour.

Commenting on the passage, Rabbi Samuel Edels says that anyone who fails to take this degree of care is depriving that individual of his share in the Jewish heritage. Where possible we must be prepared to devote disproportionate resources of time and patience to children with learning disabilities even if their achievements will remain limited. Such care has unique religious merit and reward.

In a different context, the Talmud relates that King Hezekiah, one of the most righteous of kings, was visited by the prophet Isaiah when he was ill. Isaiah told him, 'You are going to die.' Hezekiah protested and asked why he had been condemned to lose his share in the world to come. Isaiah replied that it was because he had chosen not to have children. Hezekiah replied that he had been given prophetic foreknowledge that if he had a child, he would be handicapped (in this case, a moral handicap not a physical one). His son – he had foreseen – would bring Israel to the brink of moral ruin. Therefore he had decided not to have a child.

Isaiah categorically rejected Hezekiah's choice. He declared that it is not our role to question the secrets of God. All we can do is what is commanded of us – to try to have children – and we must leave to God the mysteries of existence. That is what is meant by faith, and faith brings with it immense inner strength.

Maimonides asks why bad things happen to good people. His answer is this. God gives us one good thing, life itself. Existence is the one thing which is good in itself. But because our existence takes place in a physical world, it is subject to the accidents of matter: illness, disability and mortality. It could not be otherwise. To believe in God is to cherish existence as his gift. And the existence of a child with a handicap or disability is no less the gift of God.

In whatever body and whatever disabled mind, there is a soul cast in the image of God. It was that soul which I recognised when I was kissed by the lady in Leeds. It is that soul to which we as Jews must respond.

31
Leadership and Crisis

Then the word of the Lord came to him: 'Why are you here, Elijah?' He replied, 'I am moved by zeal for the Lord, the God of Hosts, for the Israelites have forsaken Your covenant, torn down Your altars, and put Your prophets to the sword. I alone am left, and they are out to take my life.' The Lord said to him, 'Go out and stand on the mountain in the presence of the Lord, for the Lord is about to pass by.'

Then a great and powerful wind tore the mountains apart and shattered the rocks before the Lord. But the Lord was not in the wind. After the wind was an earthquake, but the Lord was not in the earthquake. After the earthquake came a fire. But the Lord was not in the fire. And after the fire – a still, small voice. (I Kings 19:9–12)

In the year 1165, an agonising question confronted Moroccan Jewry. A fanatical Muslim sect, the Almohads, had seized power and were embarked on a policy of forced conversions to Islam. The Jewish community was faced with a choice: to affirm Islamic faith or die. It was not the first nor was it the last such occasion. Throughout the Middle Ages, periods of relative tolerance alternated with phases of fierce religious persecution. Under both Christian and Islamic regimes, Jews had to make the fateful choice: conversion or death.

Some chose martyrdom. Others chose exile. But some acceded to terror and embraced another faith. Inwardly, though, they remained Jews and practised Judaism in secret. They were the *conversos*, or as the Spanish were later to call them, the *marranos*.

To other Jews, they posed a formidable moral problem. How were they to be viewed? Ostensibly, they had betrayed their community and their religious heritage. No less seriously, their example was demoralising. It weakened the resolve of Jews who had been determined to resist, come

---

This chapter, first published in Tradition and Unity *(Bellew, London, 1991), was written as a tribute to Dr Robert Runcie on his retirement as Archbishop of Canterbury.*

what may. Yet many of the *conversos* still wished to remain Jewish, secretly fulfil the commandments and when they could, attend the synagogue and pray.

One of them addressed this question to a rabbi. He had, he wrote, under coercion declared his allegiance to another religion. But he remained at heart a faithful Jew. Could he obtain merit by observing in private as many of the Torah's precepts as possible? Was there, in other words, hope left for him as a Jew?

The rabbi's written reply was unambiguous. A Jew who had embraced Islam had forfeited membership in the Jewish community. He was no longer part of the house of Israel. For such a person to fulfil the commandments was meaningless. Worse, it was a sin. The choice was stark and absolute: to be or not to be a Jew. If one chose to be a Jew, one must be prepared to suffer death rather than compromise. If one chose not to be a Jew, then one must not seek to re-enter the house one had deserted.

We can understand and even admire the firmness of the rabbi's stance. It is one model of what religious leadership must be. He sets out, without equivocation, the moral choice. He refuses to becloud the issue. There are times when heroism is, for faith, a categorical imperative. Nothing less will do. His reply, though harsh, is not without courage. But another rabbi disagreed.

The name of the first rabbi is lost to us. But that of the second is not. He was Moses Maimonides, the greatest rabbi of the Middle Ages and one of the most formidable Jewish thinkers of all time. Maimonides was no stranger to religious persecution. Born in Cordova in 1135, he had been forced to leave, along with his family, some thirteen years later when the city fell to the Almohads. Twelve years were spent in wandering. In 1160, a temporary liberalisation of Almohad rule allowed the family to settle in Morocco. Within five years he was forced to move again, settling first in the land of Israel and ultimately in Egypt.

Maimonides was incensed by the rabbi's reply to the forced convert and was moved to write a response of his own. In it, he frankly disassociates himself from the earlier ruling and castigates its author whom he describes as a 'self-styled sage who has never experienced what so many Jewish communities had to endure in the way of persecution'.

Maimonides' reply, the *Iggeret ha-Shemad* ('Epistle on Forced Conversion'), is detailed, a treatise in its own right. What is striking, given the vehemence with which it begins, is that its conclusions are hardly less demanding than those of the earlier response. One faced with religious persecution, says Maimonides, must leave and settle elsewhere.

'If he is compelled to violate even one precept it is forbidden to stay there. He must leave everything he has and travel day and night until he finds a spot where he can practise his religion.' This is preferable to martyrdom. None the less, one who chooses to go to his death rather than renounce his faith 'has done what is good and proper' for he has given his life for the sanctity of God. What is unacceptable is to stay and excuse oneself on the grounds that if one sins, one does so only under pressure. To do this is to profane God's name, 'not exactly willingly, but almost so'.

These are Maimonides' conclusions. But surrounding them and constituting the main thrust of his argument is a sustained defence of those who had done precisely what Maimonides had ruled they should not do. Above all, the letter gives *conversos* hope.

They have done wrong. But it is a forgivable wrong. They acted under coercion and the fear of death. They remain Jews. The acts they do as Jews still win favour in the eyes of God. Indeed doubly so, for when they fulfil a commandment it cannot be to win favour in the eyes of others. They know that when they act as Jews they risk discovery and death. Their secret adherence has a heroism of its own.

What was wrong in the first rabbi's ruling is his insistence that a Jew who yields to terror has forsaken his faith and is henceforth to be excluded from the community. Maimonides insists that it is not so. 'It is not right to alienate, scorn and hate people who desecrate the Sabbath. It is our duty to befriend them and encourage them to fulfil the commandments.' In a daring stroke of interpretation, he quotes the verse: 'Do not despise a thief if he steals to satisfy his hunger when he is starving' (Proverbs 6:30). The *conversos* who comes to the synagogue are hungry for Jewish prayer. They 'steal' moments of belonging. They should not be despised, but welcomed.

This Epistle is a masterly example of that most difficult of moral challenges: to combine prescription and compassion. Maimonides leaves us in no doubt as to what he believes Jews should do. But at the same time he is uncompromising in his defence of those who fail to do it. He does not endorse what they have done. But he defends who they are. He asks us to understand their situation. He gives them grounds for self-respect. He holds the doors of the community open.

One could be forgiven for thinking that so complex a moral strategy would read like a study in ambivalence and equivocation. Nothing could be further from the truth. There are few documents in Jewish literature which so blaze with religious passion as Maimonides' *Iggeret ha-Shemad*.

The argument reaches a climax as Maimonides quotes a remarkable sequence of *midrashic* passages. The common theme of these sources is the idea that a prophet must be a defender of his people before God. God chooses as His prophets those who have the power to transform justice into mercy. To be sure, the voice of Heaven speaks in the language of justice. The people have sinned and must be punished. But at the same time, God sends His prophets to speak in the people's defence. If the prophet adopts the perspective of justice and he too condemns the people, then he has betrayed his mission.

So when Moses, charged with leading the people out of Egypt, replied, 'But they will not believe me' (Exodus 4:1), ostensibly he was justified. According to rabbinic tradition, the Israelites in Egypt had sunk into depravity. The biblical narrative itself suggests that Moses' doubts were well founded. Before the exodus and after, the Israelites were a difficult people to lead. But the midrash says that God replied to Moses, 'They are believers and the children of believers, but you [Moses] will ultimately not believe.'

Isaiah, too, was justified when he called Israel a 'sinful nation, a people laden with iniquity' (Isaiah 1:4). But the rabbis interpreted the later episode in which an angel touches Isaiah's lips with a burning coal (Isaiah 6:5–7) as a punishment for the prophet's slander of his people.

Maimonides cites a series of such passages and then rises to a crescendo: If this is the sort of punishment meted out to the pillars of the universe, the greatest of the prophets, because they briefly criticised the people – even though they were guilty of the sins of which they were accused – can we envisage the punishment awaiting those who criticise the *conversos*, who under threat of death and without abandoning their faith, confessed to another religion in which they did not believe?

There is nothing equivocal about Maimonides' defence of those who yielded to pressure. Nor is there any ambivalence about his later analysis of what, in fact, is the right way to behave. He invests both with equal seriousness. There *is* a moral dilemma. There *is* a correct response. But the terms of the dilemma are such that those who choose another response are to have their integrity respected without, at the same time, having their decision endorsed.

In the course of his analysis, Maimonides turns to the biblical hero, Elijah. Elijah, we recall, risked his life by being a prophet. Under the reign of Ahab and Jezebel, Baal worship had become the official cult. God's prophets were being killed. Those who survived were in hiding. Elijah none the less risked a direct confrontation with the king which resulted in the great public challenge at Mount Carmel. He faced four hundred of Baal's representatives. Elijah was determined to settle the question of religious truth once and for all. He addressed the assembled people and told them to choose one way or another: for God or for Baal. They must no longer 'halt between two opinions'. Truth was about to be decided by a test. If it lay with Baal, fire would consume the offering prepared by his priests. If it lay with God, fire would descend to Elijah's offering.

Elijah won the confrontation. The people cried out, 'The Lord, He is God.' The priests of Baal were routed. But the story does not end there. Jezebel sends a message to him: a warrant is out for his death. Elijah escapes to Mount Horeb. There he receives a strange vision. He witnesses a whirlwind that shatters rocks, then an earthquake, then a fire. But the vision leads him to understand that God is not in these things. Then God speaks to him in a 'still, small voice', and tells him to appoint Elisha as his successor.

The episode is enigmatic. It is made all the more so by a strange feature of the text. Immediately *before* the vision, God asks, 'What are you doing here, Elijah?' and Elijah replies, 'I am moved by zeal for the Lord, the God of Hosts . . .' (1 Kings 9:9–10). Immediately *after* the vision, God asks the same question, and Elijah gives the same answer (1 Kings 19:13–14). The midrash turns the text into a dialogue:

> Elijah: *The Israelites have broken God's covenant.*
> God: Is it then *your* covenant?
> Elijah: *They have torn down Your altars.*
> God: But were they *your* altars?
> Elijah: *They have put Your prophets to the sword.*
> God: But you are alive.
> Elijah: *I alone am left.*
> God: Instead of hurling accusations against Israel, should you not have pleaded their cause?

The meaning of the midrash is clear. The zealot takes the part of God. But God expects something else from His prophets. They must pray on behalf of humanity.

The repeated question and answer is now to be understood in its tragic depth. Elijah declares himself to be zealous for God. He is shown that God is not disclosed in dramatic confrontation: not in the whirlwind or the earthquake or the fire. God now asks him again, 'What are you doing here, Elijah?' Elijah *repeats* that he is zealous for God. He has not understood that religious leadership calls for another kind of virtue, the way of the still, small voice. God now indicates that someone else must lead. Elijah must hand his mantle on to Elisha.

Once again we are struck by the moral complexity set forth by the midrash. It is clear that God was with Elijah in the confrontation on Mount Carmel. He sends His fire. He vindicates His prophet. Elijah is one of the Bible's religious heroes. He is not content to hide and save his life while Israel lapses into idolatry. Yet the *midrash* insists – and in so doing is faithful to the intimations of the text itself – that religious leadership is not so simply reducible to the either/or of good and evil. To be sure, the Israelites have been unfaithful. They have 'halted between two opinions'. But if they served idols, they did so at the bidding of their king and under fear of death. If Elijah believes he is the only person of faith left alive, he is wrong.

We are far from the days of Maimonides, further still from those of Elijah. But their conflicts are ours. They repeat themselves whenever religious leadership must be exercised at a time when faith is under threat. There is no simple equation of idolatry in the days of Ahab, forced conversion in twelfth-century Spain and secularisation today. But in each case, a religious tradition is overwhelmed by forces antithetical to it, and faith is forced into heroic postures.

At such times, there is an almost overwhelming temptation to see religious leadership as confrontational. Not only must truth be proclaimed but falsehood must be denounced. Choices must be set out as stark divisions. Not to condemn is to condone. The rabbi who condemned the *conversos* had faith in his heart, logic on his side and Elijah as his precedent.

But the *midrash* and Maimonides set before us another model. A prophet hears not one imperative but two: prescription and compassion, a love of truth and an abiding solidarity with those for whom that truth has become eclipsed. To preserve tradition and at the same time the unity of those addressed by that tradition is the difficult, necessary task of religious leadership in an unreligious age.

32

Jewishness and Judaism

'The world makes many images of Israel', wrote the historian Simon Rawidowicz, 'but Israel makes only one image of itself – that of a being constantly on the verge of ceasing to be, of disappearing.' One generation after another saw itself as the last link in the chain of Jewish history, and before it lay eclipse. Rawidowicz called the Jews the ever-dying people.

It was a truth spoken only half in jest. Ever since the beginning of European emancipation, Judaism had contemplated its own obituary, as Jews converted or assimilated or married out of the faith. The great nineteenth-century school of German-Jewish enlightenment, *Judische-Wissenschaft*, or the 'Science of Judaism', conceived of its task as the curator of a culture already embalmed. Moritz Steinschneider confessed: 'We have only one task left: to give the remains of Judaism a decent burial.' Leopold Zunz foresaw the time – he placed it early in the twentieth century – when there would be no one left who could read and understand the great texts of rabbinic literature. Even the artists of literary renewal sensed that their beginning was also an ending. The poet Yehudah Leib Gordon, one of the architects of the reborn Hebrew language, wrote, 'Who will tell me . . . that I am not the last poet of Zion and you my last readers?'

The thought of one's own demise focuses the mind admirably, and obsessive Jewish preoccupation with crisis has proved to be one of the great self-refuting prophecies of all time. What none of these thinkers foresaw was the succession of events that were to change irrevocably the terms of Jewish existence: the rise of racial anti-semitism, the massive emigration from Eastern Europe to America, the Holocaust, and the creation of the State of Israel.

And yet, as late as the 1960s, thinkers as penetrating as Arthur Koestler and Karl Popper were arguing that though everything had changed,

Talk on BBC Radio 3, 19 December 1988

nothing had changed. The thesis was best expressed by the French sociologist, Georges Friedmann, in a book published just before Israel's 1967 war. It was entitled *The End of the Jewish People?* Its argument was that Jews were now faced with a choice of two assimilations, *individual* assimilation into the countries of the Diaspora, or *collective* assimilation into a secular Israeli state. Indeed it had been a long-standing assumption of secular Zionists that outside Israel, only strong religious commitment could secure Jewish continuity, and that commitment could not be sustained for the tide of secularisation was inexorable.

They seemed to be right. A series of demographic surveys of American Jewry in the 1970s showed a rapid erosion of the traditional indicators of survival. Jews were marrying late or not at all. Those that married were increasingly likely to divorce. They were proving themselves master-practitioners of birth-control. At one stage the average Jewish family was estimated at 1.2 children, the lowest rate of any religious or ethnic grouping in America, and well below replacement level. Most alarmingly to religious leaders, Jews had lost their inhibition against marrying outside the faith. One in three was doing so, and there were few of the new generation who held strong feelings about the matter, one way or another. In 1975, a Harvard computer, afflicted with more than usual melancholy, predicted that the American Jewish community would be reduced, over the next hundred years, from six million to tens or at most hundreds of thousands. The Jewish people was dying again.

But in the last few years an almost unprecedented phenomenon has appeared among the sociologists – Jewish optimism. Charles Silberman, in his major study of the state of American Jewry, concluded that Jews had finally arrived. Professions, professorships, corporate presidencies: all the closed doors were now open. The twin perils of Jewish modernity – anti-semitism from the outside, self-hatred from within – were at an end. 'American Jews', he wrote, 'now live in a freer, more open society than that of any Diaspora community in which Jews have ever lived before.'

Jews flourish in America. But does Judaism? Does there survive a coherent sense of what it is to be a Jew, or some substantive content to Jewish life? Professor Calvin Goldscheider has argued that this is the wrong question to ask. We are mistaken if we seek to measure the strength of contemporary Jewish life against traditional criteria – in terms, that is, of religious observance. For Jewish life is undergoing a transformation. Instead we should measure it by group cohesiveness and the strength and scope of its interactions. So long as Jews mix with Jews and are recognisably different from other groups, then we can speak of Jewish identity and continuity – however undefined that identity might be.

Behind the optimism lies an ironic transformation. Jews came to America in their millions between 1880 and 1920 in a flight from a Europe in which, as Heinrich Heine put it, 'Judaism is not a religion; it's a misfortune'. They came to the melting pot with a positive desire to be melted. They secularised, Americanised and acculturated with a rare fervour. The crowded inhabitants of New York's Lower East Side Jewish ghettoes, traditional and still redolent of Eastern Europe, had scattered in two generations to all the corners of suburbia. Jews wanted to disappear.

However, so successful were the attempts to scale the heights of American opportunity that Jews found themselves together again at the top. They go to university, enter the professions, management and academic life, more than any other ethnic or religious group. They find themselves clustered together educationally, professionally, geographically and socially. In striving to integrate, they have become more like one another and less like everyone else. If tradition no longer binds Jews together, overachieving does. Twentieth-century America has proved to be one long series of variations on the Jew who went to a country club to get away from other Jews, and found it full of Jews who were trying to do the same.

Nor is this all. For the second generation of American Jews, Judaism was associated with Europe, poverty, the ghetto, and parents struggling with the language; and they cast it off like an old overcoat in the sun. For the third generation and the fourth it holds no such memories. At worst it stands for suburban rectitude; at best it has its own ethnic caché. Nor is a college education now, as it was decades ago, the great generational divide. Jews too were caught up in the ethnic revival of the 1960s and became prime examples of Hansen's Law, that the third generation spends its time trying to remember what the second generation laboured to forget. There was a renewed interest in tradition, 'roots', even ritual observance. For the first time in two hundred years, assimilation was no longer a conscious goal.

There was another factor of great consequence. Israel's isolation in the weeks preceding the Six Day War had a profound impact on Diaspora Jewry. Another Holocaust seemed to be in the making, and this brought home, as nothing else had done, the full enormity of the first. Communal organisations, which had until now been largely concerned with domestic welfare and education, were mobilised in support of Israel, and a sense of kinship seized world Jewry, eclipsing all thought of divergent destinies.

The Holocaust and Israel became and have remained the dominant themes for American Jews, despite the fact, as critics have pointed out, that having escaped the one and chosen not to live in the other, this is a curiously vicarious form of identity.

Which brings us to the contemporary paradox. The American Jewish community is one of the most secularised in history. Orthodoxy, the one strand of Jewish life that makes no substantive accommodations to changing times, represents less than ten per cent of the population. Fewer than half of America's Jews are affiliated to a synagogue. In a recent survey, in answer to the question, 'Is religion very important in your life?', sixty-one per cent of Protestants said yes, fifty-six per cent of Roman Catholics, but only twenty-five per cent of Jews. Some ninety per cent of the present generation of Jewish Americans will have gone to college, making it perhaps the most educated population in history; but it will be one of the least Jewishly educated of all time.

None the less, Silberman and Goldscheider have identified the salient fact that it is a community for the most part proud and positive about its Jewishness. What has occurred, in other words, is the very thing all nineteenth-century observers agreed was impossible: secular Jewish continuity in the Diaspora.

But is it viable? It has brought in its wake some intractable problems. Behaviour that in the past would have marked an exit from the Jewish community is now considered acceptable or at least something with which the community has to live. Those, for example, who marry outside the faith often still wish to be considered as Jews. Who, in such a case, will perform the wedding ceremony? And what of their children? Jewish law defines a Jew as one born of a Jewish mother. But if a Jewish husband, married to a non-Jewish wife, wishes to raise his children as Jews, can he do so without their having to undergo conversion? Reform Judaism in America has felt itself forced to reach an accommodation. It has *de facto* accepted that many of its rabbis will officiate at mixed marriages, and in 1983 it decided to deem as Jewish the child of a Jewish father and a non-Jewish mother, subject to 'timely and appropriate acts of identification' with the religion and its people.

This, the so-called patrilineal decision, has caused a furore, for it overturns a criterion of Jewish status that has been in force for at least two and a half thousand years. As a result of this and other Reform policies, many thousands of individuals consider themselves and are considered by their congregations to be Jewish, but are not so considered by most other Jews throughout the world. Some observers have warned of an imminent split within the Jewish world that will parallel the Jewish-Christian schism nineteen centuries ago, and the scenario cannot be complacently dismissed. It acutely illustrates the problem of reconciling Jewishness with Judaism, of giving religious legitimation to secular Jewish attitudes.

That aside, others doubt the staying power of an identity so tenuously conceived. What, after all, *is* Jewish ethnicity? Does it exist? Go to Israel, and you will see among its Jews a complete anthology of ethnic diversity: punctilious Jews from Germany, traditionalists from the Yemen, the black Jews of Ethiopia, ex-refuseniks from Russia, academics from America, a dozen different types of kaftan-wearing mystics, and so on through a living encyclopaedia of cultural and behavioural patterns. Jews do not form a single ethnic group but a great many; and most of the symbols of ethnicity – food, folksong, dress, even the Yiddish language – are not originally Jewish at all but the product of the local culture, for we are inveterate borrowers. I can remember my surprise at seeing a film of a Polish Catholic wedding and hearing the same songs that were in my childhood the very essence of Jewish music. Jewish ethnicity is often less Jewish than it seems.

Besides this, contemporary Jewish identity is secular, not *secularist*. There was, throughout the nineteenth century up until the Second World War, a dazzling array of Jewish heretics of all kinds: socialists, anarchists, Bundists, Yiddish culturalists and secular Zionists, each mapping out their revolutionary utopias. But Jews have since made their peace with the world, and today's secular identity has no ideology.

At times, all that remains is a residual sense of marginality. Frederic Raphael once said, 'I feel myself alien from everyone; that is my kind of Jewishness.' Arthur Koestler remarked that 'Self-hatred is the Jew's patriotism.' Even this is more nostalgia than reality, for whether in Israel or the Diaspora, for the first time in centuries, Jews feel that they *belong*.

So a most curious phenomenon has emerged: Jewishness without Judaism, or at least Judaism as traditionally conceived. For perhaps the first time in two hundred years, since the process of emancipation began, Jewish identity is no longer regarded as a burden but a natural fact. Jews no longer seek to escape by a conscious strategy of assimilation. At the same time, and equally without precedent, Jewish identity has little identifiable content. The secular Jews of the Diaspora are happy to be Jews, but are not quite sure what that means.

Perhaps only one nineteenth-century thinker foresaw what in fact has happened, the great cultural Zionist, Ahad ha-Am. For Ahad ha-Am, Judaism as a religion was no longer tenable in a secular age. The alternative for Jewish survival was a Jewish nation in the land of Israel. But he was convinced that not all, or even a majority, of Jews would go to live there. Israel none the less would achieve what was necessary for the Diaspora as well, namely, a complete redefinition of identity. Judaism would be rewritten with the word 'God' removed, and in its place, 'the Jewish people'. Religion would be translated into a culture. Judaism would subtly be transformed into Jewishness. It would fulfil Emil Durkheim's sociological idea of the function of a religion: not a way of serving God but an instrument of social cohesion. The central value of the new Judaism would be the Jewish people itself. It seemed at the time an improbable scenario, but it has come to be.

The question is, can it continue to be? Jewish tradition brought together religion and peoplehood in the concept of covenant. To be a Jew was to be born into a people with a shared history of suffering and hope. But it was also to be born into a way of life, a religious destiny. The problem with making peoplehood alone a self-sufficient value is that, with Jews across the world sharing neither a common language, nor land, nor culture, nor belief, peoplehood itself stands in need of explanation. In the absence of tradition, Jewish peoplehood dissolves into a variety of subcultures, brought together only at moments of crisis.

There is little doubt that in the last twenty years the covenant of peoplehood has been renewed. The Holocaust has made Jewish identity seem inescapable. The State of Israel and the openness of Western multi-ethnic societies has made it tolerable. There has been a Jewish revival. But the covenant of faith has not been renewed. And the tension between religious and secular Jews in Israel, and between Orthodoxy and Reform in America, has been rising to dangerous levels. Never has Jewish unity seemed so desirable and at the same time so hard to bring about.

So the argument today is how to read the Jewish future. The optimists point to the new ethnic affirmation. The pessimists point to the old and still continuing religious decline. The ever-dying people at least knows this: that in contemplating its future pessimism has always prevailed, and that it has never once come true.

33
On God and Auschwitz

Judaism has its silences, Elie Wiesel once said, but we do not speak about them. After the Holocaust, the *Shoah*, there was one of the great silences of Jewish history. A third of world Jewry had gone up in flames. Entire worlds – the bustling Jewish townships of Eastern Europe, the Talmudic academies, the courts of the Jewish mystics, the Yiddish-speaking masses, the urbane Jews of Germany, the Jews of Poland who had lived among their gentile neighbours for eight hundred years, the legendary synagogues and houses of study – all were erased. A guard at Auschwitz, testifying at the Nuremburg trial, explained that at the height of the genocide, when the camp was turning ten thousand Jews a day into ashes, children were thrown into the furnaces alive. When the destruction was over, a pillar of cloud marked the place where Europe's Jews had once been; and there was a silence that consumed all words.

More had died in the final solution than Jews. It was as if the image of God that is man had died also. We know in retrospect that Jews – both victims and survivors – simply could not believe what was happening.

Since the Enlightenment they had come to have faith that a new order was in the making, in which the age-old teachings of contempt for the chosen-or-rejected people were at an end, and in their place would come a rational utopia. It is hard in retrospect to imagine that sense of almost religious wonder which German Jews felt for the country of Goethe, Beethoven and Immanuel Kant. That Christian anti-Judaism might mutate into the monster of racial anti-semitism, that a Vatican might watch as the covenantal people went to its crucifixion, that chamber music might be played over the cries of burning children, that the rational utopia might be *Judenrein*: these, for the enlightened Jews of Europe, were the ultimately unthinkable thoughts. Since the early nineteenth century,

Talk on BBC Radio 3, 22 December 1988

humanity had seemed to many Jews a safer bet than God; and it was that faith that was murdered in the camps. Where was man at Auschwitz?

But where, too, was God? That He was present seemed a blasphemy; that He was absent, even more so. How could He have been there, punishing the righteous and the children for sins, their own or someone else's? But how could He *not* have been there, when, from the valley of the shadow of death, they called out to Him?

Jewish faith sees God in history. But here was a definitive, almost terminal moment, in Jewish history, and where was God's hand and His outstretched arm? It seemed as if the *Shoah* must have, and could not have, religious meaning.

Wiesel has written of that time: 'Never shall I forget those moments which murdered my God and my soul and turned my dreams to dust. Never shall I forget these things, even if I am condemned to live as long as God Himself.' But to whom could one speak of these things so much larger than man, if not to God? It was a crisis of faith without precedent in the annals of belief. If God existed, how was Auschwitz possible? But if God did not exist, how was humanity after Auschwitz credible?

There is a line of theological reasoning which argues that a single moment of innocent suffering is as inexplicable as attempted genocide. The death of one child is as much a crisis for religious belief as the *Shoah*.

That is true. But it is to miss one essential of Jewish belief. There is theology, but beyond that there is covenant, the bond between God and a singular people. Even the most terrifying curse in the Bible ends with the verse, 'Yet in spite of this, when they are in the land of their enemies, I will not reject or abhor them so as to destroy them completely, breaking my covenant with them.' The faith of Israel is peculiarly tied to the people of Israel, to its existence as God's witness. If there were no Christians, Christianity might still be true. If there were no Jews, Judaism would be false. The survival of the Jewish people is the promise on which the entire covenant rests.

Jews had faced inquisitions and pogroms before. They had even, in the book of Esther, recorded Haman's decision 'to destroy, kill and annihilate all Jews – young and old, women and children – on a single day'. But redemption had always come, or if not redemption, refuge. In the Holocaust, perhaps for the first time, Jews came face to face with the possibility of extinction. The covenant, the one Jewish certainty, was within sight of being broken. Not only the present and future, but the Jewish past too would have died.

And so, for twenty years after the *Shoah*, there was an almost total theological silence. The questions were too painful to ask. It was as if, like Lot's wife, turning back to look on the destruction would turn one to stone.

There were, in those years, a few attempts to break the silence. But they only served to show how broken the traditional categories were. The late Rabbi Joel Teitelbaum, leader of the Hassidic community of Satmar and himself a survivor of Bergen-Belsen, invoked biblical theology and declared the Holocaust a punishment for sins. The Jewish people had, according to the Talmud, taken an oath to wait patiently in exile, but secular Zionism had broken this promise by forcing the course of Jewish history, and bringing a premature ingathering to the holy land. The *Shoah* was a punishment for Zionism.

An Israeli thinker, Menachem Hartom, pursued the same logic to its opposite conclusion. Throughout its history, he argued, the Jewish people had regarded exile as punishment, as not-being-at-home. That is, until the Emancipation. Then, for the first time, Jews argued that Europe was where they belonged. Some abandoned the hope for a return to Israel, others deferred it to a metaphysical end of days. For the first time Jews ceased to be Zionists. And for this they suffered a devastating retribution. Germany, the country more than any other that Jews had worshipped, became the avenger. The *Shoah* was a punishment for anti-Zionism.

This kind of argument led everywhere and nowhere. An American Jewish theologian, Richard Rubinstein, drew the radical conclusion. If there is a God of history, he argued, we must see the *Shoah* as a punishment for sin. But there is no sin that could warrant the deaths of a million children. There can be no vindication of the ways of Providence. Therefore there is no God of history. An ancient heresy had been proved true. There is no justice and no judge.

Rubinstein became a kind of religious atheist. But ironically, only a hair's-breadth away, was a position found in classic Jewish thought. And it was now taken up by such leading Orthodox thinkers as Rabbi Joseph Soloveitchik and Eliezer Berkovits.

In the Bible there are references to *hester panim*, the hiding of the face of God. There are moments, perhaps eras, in which God withdraws from history. The rabbinic literature contained an extraordinary statement, which by a slight textual emendation, turned the phrase 'Who is like you, God, among the mighty?' into 'Who is like you among the silent?' God, as it were, holds Himself back in self-imposed restraint, allowing men freedom, including the freedom to do evil. God was neither present nor absent at Auschwitz: He was hidden. The line of thought was barely comforting, for it argued an exile of God from the human domain that was little short of complete eclipse.

But it was in 1967, in the weeks surrounding Israel's Six Day War, that an extraordinary transformation took place in Jewish sensibilities. It seemed, in the anxious days before the war, as if a second holocaust was in the making. And the memory of the first, so suppressed for two decades, broke through with terrible force, in the form of an imperative: Never again.

Israel's sudden victory released a flood of messianic emotion. For some it seemed as if God had finally re-entered history after His long exile. And when the mood subsided a deeper sense began to form – that the State of Israel was a powerful affirmation of life, a determination never again to suffer the role of victim. Virtues which had long been at the heart of Judaism in exile – martyrdom, passivity, trust – had been overthrown. They now seemed, in retrospect, to be unwitting accomplices to genocide. A quite new Holocaust theology began to emerge.

Its most articulate theoretician was Emile Fackenheim, who argued that the Holocaust was not to be understood, but responded to. His boldest move was to claim that the *Shoah* had created a new commandment – and he meant the word in its religious sense. Jews are forbidden to hand Hitler a posthumous victory. Because Hitler made it a crime simply to exist as a Jew, simply to exist as a Jew became an act of defiance against the force of evil. Choosing to have children after the *Shoah* was itself a monumental act of faith. The old dichotomy between religious and secular had now lost its meaning. For even the most secular Jew who chose to remain Jewish in the face of a possible future holocaust was making a religious act of commitment. Jewish survival became *a*, perhaps even *the*, religious imperative.

Fackenheim spoke to a new Jewish consciousness. There was a sense, shared by many, that secular activity had been charged with religious meaning. Israel's victory, her determination to survive, the intense involvement of Jews everywhere in her fate, all combined to place Jewish peoplehood and survival at the centre of the religious drama. God may have hidden His face. But the Jewish people had disclosed a new one of its own. God may have withdrawn from history. Israel, at least, had re-entered it.

The American theologian, Irving Greenberg spoke of a new era in which the covenant had been voluntarily renewed, but in which man, not God, had become the senior partner. Never before had survival *per se* carried such religious weight.

But there was to be a further twist in the dialectic. In the twenty years since Fackenheim's commandment to survive, it has become clear that not all sectors of the Jewish world have heeded its call. In the Diaspora, Jewish birth-rates fell to below replacement levels. The momentum of assimilation has accelerated. Frustrating Hitler has proved to be no base for Jewish survival.

One group of Jews, though, has obeyed Fackenheim's command to the letter. They have had children in great numbers. They have rebuilt their lost worlds. They have proved themselves the virtuosi of survival. The irony is that they are a group who would deny the entire basis of Fackenheim's thought. They are the ultra-religious, for whom piety, not peoplehood, is the dominant value, and to whom secular survival is not Jewish survival at all.

This was the one group whose responses to the Holocaust lay unconsidered, and only slowly has the written testimony come to light. It makes remarkable reading. For we now know that there were Jews in the concentration camps who lived in the nightmare kingdom as if it were just another day, patiently confronting the never-before-imagined questions and finding answers.

May a father purchase his son's escape from the ovens, knowing that the quotas will be met and another child will die in his place? May a Jew in the Kovno ghetto recite the morning benediction, 'Blessed are you, O Lord, Who has not made me a slave'? May one pronounce the blessing over martyrdom over a death from which there is no escape? What blessing does one make before being turned to ashes? The rabbis searched the sources and gave their rulings, and some of their writings have survived.

Over one who uninterruptedly studies God's word, said the rabbis, even the angel of death can win no victory. How true this was of the pious Jews of Auschwitz and Treblinka and Bergen-Belsen, discovering as they did that in the face of ultimate evil, the word of God was not silent. It had an awe-inspiring resonance. God did not die at Auschwitz, they said. He wept tears for His people as they blessed His name at the gates of death. Their bodies were given as burnt offerings and their lives as a sanctification of God's name. 'The fire which destroys our bodies', said Rabbi Elchanan Wasserman before he was killed, 'is the fire which will restore the Jewish people.' And so it was. The Jews of faith, who were able to sanctify death *in* the Holocaust, turned out to be the most determined to sanctify life *after* the Holocaust.

So, once the silence was broken, Jewish responses to the *Shoah* have been many and conflicting. But one above all deserves mention, all the more remarkable for having been written fifteen hundred years before the event.

The Talmud contains an enigmatic passage, which says that when the Israelites stood at Mount Sinai they were reluctant to accept the covenant. They did so only because God threatened to let the mountain fall on their heads. For centuries they kept the faith only because they were coerced. When, then, did they finally accept it voluntarily? The Talmud answers: in the days of Ahasuerus, when Haman threatened to kill all Jews.

Only now, in retrospect, does the meaning of the passage become clear. The threat of genocide created a new dimension of covenant: the covenant of a shared fate. Every Jew, after Auschwitz, knows that in some sense he is a survivor, an accidental remnant, and he shares that knowledge with every member of his people. As the covenant of faith seemed to be breaking, the covenant of fate has risen to take its place.

And the stubborn people has shown its obstinacy again. Faced with destruction, it has chosen survival. *Lo amut ki echyeh*, says the Psalm: 'I will not die, but I will live.' And in this response there is a kind of courage which rises beyond theology's reach.

One writer about the *Shoah* records that he met a rabbi who had been through the camps and who, miraculously, seemed unscarred. He could still laugh. 'How', he asked him, 'could you see what you saw and still have faith? Did you have no questions?' The rabbi replied, 'Of course I had questions. But I said to myself, if you ever ask those questions, they are such good questions that God will send you a personal invitation to heaven to give you the answers. And I preferred to be here on earth with the questions than up in heaven with the answers.'

As with the rabbi, so with the Jewish people. Without answers, it has reaffirmed its covenant with history. The people Israel lives and still bears witness to the living God.